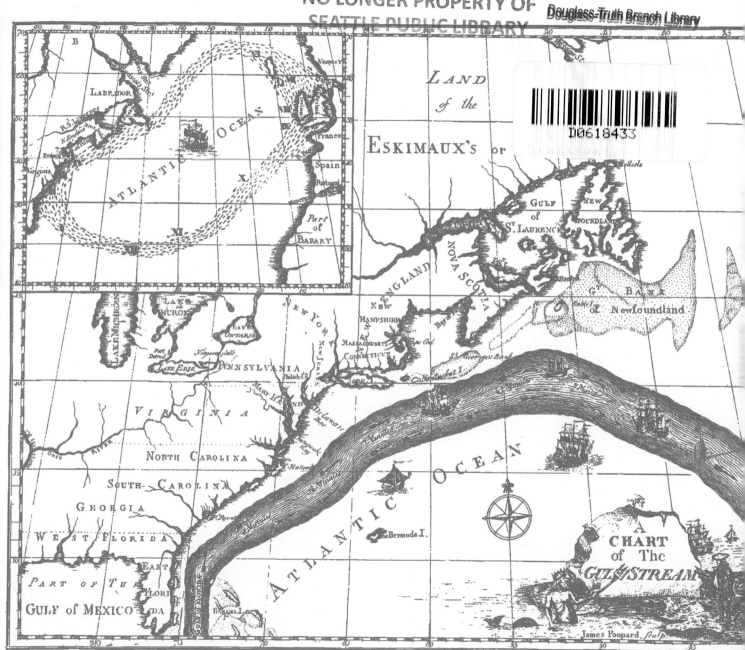

A CHART of The GULF STREAM

James Poupard Sculp.

INVENTORS, MAKERS, BARRIER BREAKERS

Tumblehome Learning, Inc.
201 Newbury St, Suite 201
Boston, MA 02116
http://www.tumblehomelearning.com

Library of Congress Control Number: 2018944765
ISBN 978-1-943431-42-7

Noyce, Pendred
Inventors, Makers, Barrier Breakers / Pendred Noyce - 1st ed

Design: Yu-Yi Ling

Printed in the United States of America

10 9 8 7 6 5 4 3 2 1

Inventors, Makers, Barrier Breakers

PENDRED NOYCE

To my father, Robert Noyce,

and all the other dreamers and tinkerers out there.

With thanks for the support of the Gordon and Betty Moore Foundation.

INTRODUCTION

When I was eleven years old, my parents invited the Borovoys to dinner. Roger Borovoy was the patent attorney at Fairchild Semiconductor, where my father worked at the time. His wife, Brenda, was lively, lovely, and a heroine in my eyes because she was always taking classes and learning new things. They brought their daughter, Amy, who was two years old at the time and quite precocious.*

As the adults sipped their cocktails, which people did in those days, Roger asked Amy, "What did Bob Noyce invent?"

My ears perked up. My father had invented something?

Amy jumped up and called out, "The integrated circuit!"

It was news to me. I had no idea what an integrated circuit was, but it sure sounded important.

I decided to write this book to introduce young people like you to inventors like my father—people who loved to play, to make new things, and to figure out how to make the world better. My father never stopped tinkering, whether with an oscilloscope and electronic components in the basement or with the sprinkler system in the garden. He believed in people and thought they could do great things. Somehow he inspired others to believe in themselves. He always let his children know that he'd be behind them no matter what dream they followed.

This is a book about people following their dreams and making their ideas come to life. The dreamers in this book include founding fathers, women, slaves, immigrants, and people of all races. All of them faced setbacks; all of them made mistakes. But they learned from their mistakes and pressed on. My hope is that you, the reader, can see something of yourself in them, and that they will help you recognize the inventor, maker, and barrier breaker inside you.

~ Pendred Noyce, February 4, 2018

*Amy Borovoy is now a cultural anthropologist and associate professor of East Asian studies at Princeton University.

AUTHOR'S NOTE

As a historical work about diverse people, this book sometimes refers to racial or ethnic groups in ways that today may seem offensive or dated. For example, in this book the words *Negro* and *colored* appear in photos, quotations, and names of organizations and institutions, or in places where the terms are both historically accurate and the way that the inventors, makers, and barrier breakers of this book would have described themselves at the time. The author has included these words to enhance the historical context of the book.

CONTENTS

"Energy and persistence conquer all things."

— Benjamin Franklin

1. Lightning Tamer

Benjamin Franklin
(1706–1790)

The first great American inventor was a cheerful, self-educated man. He loved England but became a committed revolutionary. A tradesman who rose to wealth and fame through his own effort, he embodied the new American man. Blessed with an outgoing, amiable personality, he made a study of how to win friends and gain influence. He had little use for authority. Instead, he had faith in the good sense of the common "middling" man. He believed that the best way to serve God was by doing good for his fellow human creatures.

As one of our senior founding fathers, Benjamin Franklin participated in writing the Declaration of Independence, the Articles of Confederation, and the Constitution. In the years prior to the American Revolution, he was a diplomat who represented the unhappy colonies to England. During the Revolutionary War, he spoke for the newly independent colonies to France. He achieved excellence as a writer and statesman, but it is his achievements as a scientist and inventor that are the focus of this chapter.

Writing the Declaration of Independence

Benjamin Franklin

Benjamin Franklin was born in Boston, Massachusetts, on January 17, 1706. He was the thirteenth child and tenth son in the family. His father, Josiah, was a tradesman, a "tallow chandler" who made both soap and candles. Envisioning a future in the ministry for Ben, his father sent him to study at the Boston Latin School when he was just eight. Young Ben quickly rose to the top of his class and then skipped a grade. Still, after only a year, Josiah took Ben out of Boston Latin and sent him down the street to a more modest private teacher. Ben later speculated that his cheeky ways made him seem too rebellious to make a good minister.

THE FIRST LATIN SCHOOL, ON NORTH SIDE OF SCHOOL STREET, 1635.

First Latin School, 1635

At age ten, Ben left school to work in his father's business. He never mastered mathematics. Instead, he read all the books he could get his hands on. Throughout his teens, he also worked on his writing style. He read famous essays, took notes, and a few days later restated the author's ideas in his own words. Then he compared his style to the original.

Ben's life wasn't all work. He explored the streets and wharves of Boston, tripping over cobbles and piles of rope and smelling the fresh fish curing in the salt air. He learned to swim and taught other boys to do the same. At the age of twelve, he came up with his first invention: a pair of oval wooden paddles with thumb holes. The paddles made his stroke more powerful. He also experimented with letting a kite pull him across a pond as he floated on his back "without the least fatigue and with the greatest pleasure imaginable."

Franklin's swim paddle

Working in the tallow shop was a lot less pleasant. The first step in making candles or soap was boiling animal fat. It was hot, smelly work. The stink of rendered fat clung to Ben's clothes for days. He rebelled and talked of going to sea. To prevent this, Ben's father walked him around Boston, as Franklin later wrote in his autobiography, to *see joiners, bricklayers, turners, braziers, etc., at their work, that he might observe my inclination, and endeavor to fix it on some trade or other on land. It has ever since been a pleasure to me to see good workmen handle their tools; and it has been useful to me, having learnt so much by it as to be able to do little jobs myself in my house when a workman could not readily be got, and to construct little machines for my experiments ...*

Tallow chandlers produced candles from suet or fat

At age twelve, Ben signed on as apprentice to his brother James, a printer. Ben learned to prepare paper, make ink, and set type. But he wanted more than manual work. He submitted anonymous articles to the paper, slipping them under the door at night. Usually, he posed as a fictional country widow named Silence Dogood. His fresh, satirical words won wide praise.

James's newspaper, the *New England Courant*, was independent and outspoken. Sometimes the authorities responded angrily. When they threw James in jail for several weeks, young Ben published the paper on his own.

The *New England Courant*, founded in Boston on August 7, 1721

James was a harsh master. By the age of seventeen, Ben had had enough. He quietly sold most of his books and used the proceeds to sail to New York. From there, he made his way to Philadelphia, Pennsylvania, where he found work with an older, ill-tempered printer named Samuel Keimer. But Ben wanted to see more of the world, so he left Keimer after a year and shipped out to England. For the next two years, he worked as a journeyman printer in London, perfecting his trade.

While in England, Benjamin Franklin read widely and conversed with learned men. During this time, he also resolved to shape his own character. He laid out a self-help program to chart and build the virtues of temperance, frugality, sincerity, and industry.

Temperance meant not drinking to excess, frugality meant not spending too much, and industry meant working hard.

On his return to Philadelphia, Franklin tried his hand at shop-keeping for a while and then worked again for Keimer. Finally, the young man saved up enough money to set up his own printing shop. At age twenty-two, he started printing a newspaper, *The Mercury*. He wrote many of the articles himself. He also created an almanac, a kind of yearly magazine, called *Poor Richard's Almanac*. The almanac was wildly popular and profitable.

Franklin's arrival in Philadelphia

Always gregarious, Franklin also surrounded himself with friends. Because he loved lively conversation, he started a club called the Junto. The members were upwardly mobile young tradesmen like him. They helped one another make business connections, but they also shared books and discussed scientific and political topics. Their reading and debates helped them educate themselves to be the responsible, middle-class citizens the new country was going to need.

Deborah Franklin

At age twenty-four, Ben Franklin entered into a common-law marriage with twenty-two-year-old Deborah Read. He had first courted her when he was seventeen, a runaway apprentice on the streets of Philadelphia. The couple took in Franklin's son William (from another relationship) and had two children of their own. Their son, Francis, died of smallpox at age four, breaking Ben's heart; their daughter, Sally, grew up to have seven children of her own. Though they treated each other with affection and wrote to each other often, Franklin and his wife spent long periods apart. Deborah refused to travel by sea, choosing instead to take care of Franklin's businesses whenever he was away.

Franklin's printing shop prospered. His reputation as a thinker, writer, and practical man also grew. At twenty-four, he was made clerk of the colony's assembly. The next year, he was appointed Pennsylvania's postmaster general, which made it easier to distribute his newspaper. With friends, he created a subscription public library and the colonies' first volunteer fire department. He loved writing out detailed rules for each new organization he created.

Later, he began to bemoan the fact that Pennsylvania had no academies like Boston's to deliver advanced education to promising young boys. He recruited a group of trustees to create the Publick Academy of Philadelphia. Only the fifth college in the colonies, the academy had a unique approach. Instead of grooming young men to be clergymen, it offered a curriculum that included practical skills, preparing boys to be community and business leaders. Franklin's Publick Academy went on to become the University of Pennsylvania.

At that time, silver coins were in short supply, making it hard to finance new businesses in Pennsylvania. Franklin started a campaign in favor of using paper money in the colony. Once his writings had convinced the Assembly, they gave him the job of printing the new money. His good idea also turned out to benefit him financially.

Franklin's next flurry of zeal for planning came during the French and Indian War. The peace-loving Quaker leadership of the Pennsylvania colony dragged its feet about providing for defense. Not Benjamin Franklin. He organized a militia, and the men of one regiment elected him their colonel.

Through all these efforts, Franklin and others like him became the inventors and makers of a new kind of social order. These unlikely men, born into the working class and often lacking formal education, created a self-reliant, smoothly working society. They didn't need aristocrats telling them what to do: they could govern themselves.

A **magic square** is a grid arrangement of numbers from one to a square number such as nine or sixteen, with each number appearing just once. The numbers in each row and column, as well as those in the two diagonals, must all add up to the same sum.

16	3	2	13
5	10	11	8
9	6	7	12
4	15	14	1

A 4x4
magic square

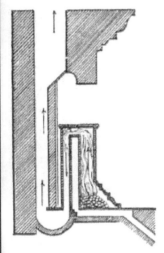

Franklin Stove
cross-sectional
diagram

At age forty-two, already wealthy, Franklin retired from the daily work of printing. He turned the printing shop over to a partner with the terms that half the profits for the next eighteen years would come to Franklin. Henceforth, he said, he would devote more time to science.

Franklin's scientific studies were moved by curiosity rather than the hope of riches. Even in his days as secretary to the assembly, as he sat in long meetings and got bored by long debates, he amused himself by creating magic squares. He freely admitted they had no practical use. On the other hand, he was eager to offer practical suggestions where he could. To see how different-colored fabrics absorb heat, he laid squares of cloth out on the snow and measured the rate of melting. Snow under dark squares melted faster, indicating that dark squares absorbed more heat. Franklin concluded that people should wear dark clothes to keep warm during cold months.

Franklin's interest in heat led in 1744 to his first truly useful invention. Buildings at the time were heated by fireplaces. But fireplaces were troublesome: most of the warm air escaped up the chimney, while smoke poured out into the room. Franklin designed a stove to place inside the fireplace. Wood burned inside the stove and heated a dark plate on top. The hot, smoky air inside the stove then flowed past a separate chamber of the stove that filled with cool air from the basement. The warm, smoky air heated the clean air from the basement, which then flowed out to heat the room. Meanwhile the smoky air escaped up the chimney.

Pennsylvania's governor was such a fan of the new stove that he offered Franklin a lucrative patent. Franklin turned it down. He wrote in his autobiography, "As we enjoy great advantages from the invention of others, we should be glad of an opportunity to serve others by any invention of ours, and this we should do freely and generously." Franklin never did seek to patent any of his inventions. Inventing was fun, he had enough money, and he was doing what he wanted—that was enough.

A couple of years later, on a visit to Boston, Benjamin Franklin got a chance to see some electrical demonstrations performed, rather clumsily, by a Scotsman named Dr. Spence. Franklin supplied himself with a glass tube and began experimenting. No doubt he constructed a Leyden jar for storing electrical charge. He began to wonder about the nature of the charge; he suggested that electricity was a single fluid, with charge either positive or negative. (Before, it had been theorized that there were two types of static electricity, one found in glass and another in amber.) Franklin even taught an unemployed neighbor to go from town to town doing electrical demonstrations for money.

At some point, Franklin began to think about whether lightning might be a discharge of static electricity like what he could see in his demonstrations. A cloud, he thought, could separate an electrical charge just as the glass of the Leyden jar did. Then a giant spark might leap across the space between cloud and some high point. Noticing that a spark leaps more readily toward a pointed metal object, he proposed an experiment to find out if the charge in a thundercloud was the same as that created by rubbing glass with cloth. His first suggestion was to build a high platform and let a man stand there holding up a metal spike. However, he didn't try this himself.

When Franklin sent his ideas to the Royal Society, the scientists in London didn't react. But two French scientists gave his experiment a try, and to their amazement it worked. Before news of the success reached Philadelphia, Franklin, in secret, tried a variation of his own. With his son William, he flew a silk kite in a gathering thunderstorm. From the top of the kite projected a foot-long, pointed metal rod. Franklin stood in a shed, holding onto a

A **Leyden jar** is a device that stores static electricity by creating a voltage difference between sheets of metal foil plastered to the inside and outside of a jar. When the two sides of the jar are connected by a wire, the charge is released in a jolt of electricity.

Franklin's "dissectible" Leyden jar, 1876

Drawing electricity from the sky

Lightning rod after
being struck by lightning

dry silk handkerchief—an insulator—tied to the other end of the kite's string. Fastened between string and handkerchief hung a key. As a storm approached, Franklin saw strands of the string shiver and stand up. With trepidation, he brought his knuckles, wrapped in the handkerchief, close to the key. Sparks leaped across the gap. This was not a matter of lightning striking the kite, which might well have been deadly. Franklin was drawing electrical charge from the sky before it built up to the point of a discharge of lightning. When electrical charge traveled down the wet string (a conductor) from the cloud, Franklin directed it from the key into a Leyden jar.

Franklin had succeeded. His jar was charged with "electric fire" identical to that produced by rubbing a glass rod with silk. With his captured lightning, Franklin could do all the experiments he did with electricity. This momentous discovery won Franklin honorary degrees from Harvard and Yale as well as fame across Europe. Immediately, he pursued a practical application. What if he placed a pointed rod reaching up from the highest point of a roof and attached it by wire to the ground? Benjamin Franklin had described his ideas in a letter to his friend, the botanist Peter Collinson, dated July 29, 1750: "The electrical fire would, I think, be drawn out of a cloud silently, before it could come near enough to strike ..."

Franklin had invented the lightning rod. As the device caught on in America and then Europe, deaths and destruction from lightning strikes fell abruptly. Here, truly, was an invention that served others.

Throughout this period of scientific creativity, Benjamin Franklin continued his career of public service and diplomacy. Before the American Revolution, he spent twelve years in London. There he represented the interests first of Pennsylvania and then of other colonies. At the same time, he continued his scientific investigations. In a playful spirit, he created a musical instrument he called the armonica. He had seen people run a moistened finger around the edge of a wineglass to make it ring out a single tone. Why not make an instrument based on glass?

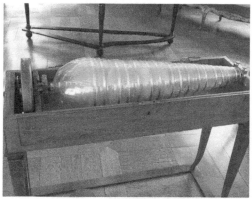

Franklin arranged thirty-seven crystal bowls of increasing size on a single spindle. By pumping a foot treadle, he turned the spindle. As the bowls turned, he touched wet fingers to the different bowls, creating an ethereal, haunting music. Franklin wrote of his invention in a letter to the Italian physicist Giambattista Beccaria on July 13, 1762, "...its tones are... sweet beyond those of any other... the instrument, being once well tuned, never again wants tuning." More than a hundred composers, including Mozart and Beethoven, wrote pieces for the armonica, and Marie Antoinette, Queen of France, took lessons on it. Today, you can see armonicas at the Museum of Fine Arts, Boston, and at the Franklin Institute in Philadelphia.

Glass armonica

In London, Franklin's diplomatic efforts helped convince the British Parliament to lift the Stamp Act. Unfortunately, it was replaced with the still more onerous Townshend Acts. When Franklin became convinced that a break with England could not be avoided, he sailed for home, making scientific observations of ocean currents along the way. Back in Philadelphia, he helped Thomas Jefferson write the Declaration of Independence.

During the Revolutionary War (1775–1783), though Franklin was in his seventies and suffering from gout, the Continental

The Townshend Acts, passed in 1767, imposed import taxes on glass, lead, paint, paper, and tea coming into the colonies—taxation without representation, according to many Americans. One response was the Boston Tea Party, where colonists dressed as Native Americans dumped English tea into the Boston Harbor.

Congress sent him as an ambassador to France. His charge was to obtain military and financial help for the American colonies in their fight against England. Franklin's great scientific fame helped him in his mission. People flocked to be near him. Women flirted with him. Artists painted his portrait. Spies gathered around. Franklin enjoyed it all hugely, and he successfully negotiated to get arms shipments, loans, and finally an outright alliance with France. Without this alliance, the American colonies might not have won the war with Britain.

When the war was over, Franklin returned to the new America. He contributed to the Articles of Confederation and served three one-year terms as president of the Council of Pennsylvania. In 1787, he served as Pennsylvania's delegate to the Constitutional Convention. At age eighty-one, he was the convention's oldest delegate.

And he kept inventing. He had been wearing spectacles since the late 1750s, but as he aged, he realized that he needed two pairs: one for distant objects and one for print. In 1785, he explained in a letter to his friend George Whatley how he had built "double spectacles" by having half circles of two pairs of eyeglasses reassembled into one. Franklin wrote, "… as I wear my spectacles constantly, I have only to move my eyes up or down, as I want to see distinctly for or near." Others may have invented bifocals earlier, but Franklin invented them independently, and he certainly helped popularize them.

Franklin died in Philadelphia on April 17, 1790, at the age of eighty-four. The Constitution was well on its way to ratification by all the states, and Franklin could be confident that his beloved American republic would thrive. In his will, Franklin left a thousand pounds each to the cities of Philadelphia and Boston. He directed that the bequest be allowed to gather interest for 200 years before any of it was spent. The bequest was pure Franklin, at once an experiment, a demonstration of a scientific concept (the power of compound interest), and a public statement of his faith in the future of his nation. Over two centuries, the funds grew to millions of dollars. The Philadelphia money paid for scholarships, and the Boston fund set up a trade school that became the Franklin Institute of Boston.

Optimistic, patriotic, endlessly eager to learn, Benjamin Franklin provides the model for all the inventors in this book. He was always looking around for a way to make objects, institutions, and government better. In the course of a long life at a time of great opportunity and challenge, he helped to invent not just the lightning rod or the armonica, but the American nation itself.

"An act of Congress authorising the issuing patents for new discoveries has given a spring to invention beyond my conception."

— Thomas Jefferson, June 27, 1790

Thomas Jefferson
(1743–1826)

T homas Jefferson, our third president, would have loved to be a full-time scientist. On March 2, 1809, at the age of sixty-five, he wrote to his friend Pierre-Samuel du Pont de Nemours, "Nature intended me for the tranquil pursuits of science, by rendering them my supreme delight. But the enormities of the times in which I have lived, have forced me to ... commit myself on the boisterous ocean of political passions."

On that "boisterous ocean," Jefferson made huge contributions—he wrote the Declaration of Independence and served as ambassador, secretary of state, and president for the new nation. He also founded the University of Virginia. His years of public service framed and provided context for his scientific pursuits.

Jefferson was born in the colony of Virginia on April 13, 1743. In 1776, as a member of the Continental Congress, the thirty-three-year-old Jefferson drafted the Declaration of Independence. Immediately afterward, he served in the Virginia legislature. From

Presenting the Declaration of Independence.
Jefferson (tallest standing) and
Franklin (to the right of Jefferson)

1779 to 1781, during the Revolutionary War, he was Virginia's governor.

Virginia's first lady was Martha Wayles, Jefferson's third cousin, whom he had married in 1772. Together they had six children; only two daughters survived to adulthood. Then, in 1782, not long after Jefferson completed his governorship, Martha died. She asked Jefferson never to marry again, and he did not.

Jefferson spent the two years after Martha's death in a kind of retreat, writing and farming. Then, in 1784, he was sent to France as trade minister for the Congress of the Confederation, which was the new nation's ruling body before the Constitution was written. When Ben Franklin retired as ambassador to France, Jefferson took on that position too. He brought along with him to France one of his wife's slaves who was also her half-sister, Sally Hemings. At the time of her voyage to France, Hemings was only fourteen years old. Most historians believe Jefferson began a long-term relationship with Hemings while in France or shortly after their return. Jefferson most likely fathered all of Sally Hemings's six children, and he eventually freed the four who survived to adulthood.

Eston Hemings, son of
Jefferson and Sally Hemings

In 1790, George Washington made Thomas Jefferson the country's first secretary of state. After Washington's terms ended, Jefferson became vice president to John Adams. In 1801, at age fifty-eight, he succeeded Adams as our third president. During Jefferson's presidency, he made the Louisiana Purchase and sent Lewis and Clark on their great journey of exploration.

Throughout his political life, Jefferson tinkered with mechanical gadgets and inventions, and mused about the role of science and invention in the young republic. He kept up with scientific theories and advances through his reading and his correspondence with scientists. His personal library of 6,000 books included 800 on science. He wondered about mastodon bones and meteorites: How could rocks fall from the sky? Science made him skeptical of religious dogma. How could the earth suddenly stop turning—as reported in the story of Joshua—Jefferson wondered, without everybody suddenly falling over because of inertia? Eager to measure and describe the natural world, Jefferson ordered thermometers from Europe and tried to perfect a barometer of his own.

He loved to think up gadgets that would make life and work more convenient. Clever with a pen, he could draw and explain his ideas. That was important, because although he had a fine set of tools, Jefferson didn't put together his inventions himself. Jefferson, like some property owners in the South, owned slaves. He depended on them to provide the physical labor needed to run his plantation. These slaves, some of them expert in carpentry and cabinet-making, also put together his inventions. Early in his career, Jefferson devised a three-legged folding campstool. Next came a revolving chair with an arm rack for holding books and documents. It is said that he sat in this swivel chair while writing the Declaration of Independence.

At the time, most educated Europeans thought of Americans as rough-cut backwoods hicks (apart from the eminent Benjamin Franklin, of course). In 1782, a French nobleman who had commanded the French forces at Yorktown wrote of his surprise, on visiting Jefferson at Monticello, to find in the ex-governor "an

Comte de Buffon

American, who, without ever having quitted his own country, is Musician, Draftsman, Surveyor, Astronomer, Natural Philosopher, Jurist and Statesman."

In 1761, the Comte de Buffon, a famous French naturalist, had written that the Americas were a bleak and dismal place where both people and animals were small and sparse compared with those of Europe. Jefferson couldn't bear to let such nonsense stand unchallenged. In the early 1780s, he responded with a book, *Notes on the State of Virginia*. The book was published in Paris in 1785 and London in 1787. In it, he described the biology, geology, climate, economy, manners and governance of his native land. The extensive detail and elegant writing of *Notes* made studying the American continent a legitimate thing to do.

Wealthy, educated, and patriotic, Thomas Jefferson wanted not only to celebrate the natural history of his country but also to create a new architecture worthy of a new nation. As a result,

Monticello reflected

he began designing and building his villa at Monticello at the age of twenty-six. However, most of his mechanical innovations and improvements waited until many years later, after he had served as ambassador to France and then as America's first secretary of state. He brought ideas home with him from France and began rebuilding Monticello in 1796. For example, he designed a dumbwaiter to bring wine straight from the cellar to his guests in the dining room. He may also have been the first person to introduce French fries and macaroni to America.

Jefferson liked doors. He had a revolving door built between his dining room and pantry. Next he designed a set of mechanized double doors. When a servant opened one side, the other side swung open automatically. He built a more efficient clothes closet with a turning rack, and he built a map case into a wall. The maps rolled out so he could examine them, and then rolled back for convenient storage. He built a revolving reading stand that allowed him to have five books open for reading at once.

In the entrance hall of Monticello, Jefferson created a museum of fossils and Native American artifacts. He constructed a huge clock that faced both inside and outside and measured hours, minutes, and days of the week. The clock's counterweights, a series of cannonballs on a cord, were so long that Jefferson had to cut a hole for them in the floor of the room.

A great letter writer, Jefferson wanted a quick and reliable way of making copies. At first, he worked to improve a copying press created by James Watt, who is best known for inventing the steam engine. Jefferson's design, unlike Watt's, was portable. His machine pressed damp tissue paper onto a recently inked document, and then onto fresh paper. With this device, Jefferson found he could make several copies before the ink became too light to read. Another machine, which he spent twenty years improving, was what he called a polygraph. It wasn't the lie detector we know as a *polygraph* today. Instead, it was a way to draft or sign several copies of documents at once, by connecting the pen he was actually using to a series of other pens poised over other papers.

Jefferson also came up with an improved design for the moldboard of a plow. The moldboard is the blade that turns over the soil. Jefferson used calculus to determine the ideal curve to allow a moldboard to turn the soil most efficiently. His drawings showed how it could be made from wood.

Moldboard plow

Perhaps Jefferson's most original invention was his wheel cipher. Its purpose was to create an unbreakable code. At the time, Americans sent coded messages back and forth between Europe and America. Spies almost always opened the letters, and clever spies could decode them.

You may have experimented with ciphers that replace one letter with another, like writing B to mean A and Z to mean Y. Such ciphers have been used throughout history, but they are very easy to break, even when the substitution scheme is not obvious. What helps is a way to constantly change which letter stands for which other letter. Jefferson's wheel cipher set out to do just that.

Wheel cipher

His design was simple. He stacked thirty disks on a central spindle. He numbered the disks, which could turn on the spindle. Around the edge of each disk, easy to see, were inscribed the twenty-six letters of the alphabet, each time in a different order. The writer turned the disks until one line of the cylinder spelled out the desired message. Then he chose a different line—a series of letters that made no sense—and copied it out. This nonsense message is what he sent the reader. The reader had an identical wheel cipher.He stacked his disks in the correct order, which the two had agreed to ahead of time. The reader turned the disks until the nonsense message lined up. All he had to do then was to look at other lines until he found one that made sense.

Jefferson may have had his wheel cipher built as early as 1793, when he was secretary of state under Washington. But no model remains, and there is no clear evidence that he actually used the wheel cipher. In fact, his design wasn't discovered in his papers until 1922—the same year the US Navy began using a similar model, which had been reinvented during World War I.

For all his own inventiveness, Jefferson was at first very skeptical about <u>patents</u>. For centuries, in both Europe and the colonies, the government had issued "letters patent" to the inventors of new devices and methods of making things. These patents gave the inventors a monopoly to manufacture and profit from the device or product concerned. For example, the Massachusetts General Court issued its first patent in 1641. It went to Samuel Winslow, giving him a ten-year monopoly on a new process he had come up with for making salt.

But patents had often been abused. Rulers sometimes gave out monopolies to their friends and political allies, even without a true invention. Besides, Jefferson believed strongly in the free exchange of ideas. Scientific advances would pile on one another, he thought, as long as scientists communicated with open enthusiasm. Blocking other people from using new ideas seemed like the wrong approach.

Other leaders of the emerging American nation disagreed. They thought patents would motivate inventors. In fact, they wrote patents right into the Constitution. The Constitution gives Congress the specific power to authorize patents for inventions and copyright for written work. In 1790, one year after the Constitution was ratified, Congress filled out details in "An Act to promote the Progress of Useful Arts." Under the law, patent examiners could issue a fourteen-year monopoly on use of a new invention. During this time, the inventor would be the only one to profit from his work. Then he could renew the patent for another fourteen years. After that, anyone could freely use the invention.

"I am not afraid of new inventions or improvements, nor bigoted to the practices of our forefathers."

—Thomas Jefferson, Letter to Robert Fulton, March 17, 1810

U.S. Patent Office in 1880, 90 years after Jefferson first served as a patent officer.

Ironically, the act made Jefferson, in his position as the first US Secretary of State, one of a three-man board to examine patent applications. Jefferson took his duties on the patent board seriously. The outpouring of ideas he received impressed him, and he wrote to a friend that the law had "given a spring to invention beyond [his] conception."

Jefferson examined the models sent in to make sure they worked and were truly new. Over its first three years, the board granted fifty-five patents. They rejected many more. Examining all those models was time-consuming, and in 1793, Congress opened up the process. Models were no longer required, and patents were issued automatically. By 1836, close to ten thousand patents had been issued. As Jefferson wrote in a letter to Dr. Benjamin Waterhouse in 1818, "One new idea leads to another, that to a third, and so on through a course of time until someone, with whom no one of these ideas was original, combines all together, and produces what is justly called a new invention." This idea, that each new invention draws on the ideas and work of many people, remains true today.

Jefferson still believed strongly that science and technology advanced most when scientists built on one another's ideas. He also believed that the spread of science was closely tied to the spread of liberty and self-government. Perhaps he expressed these ideas best in a letter to Isaac McPherson in 1813, thirteen years before his death.

He who receives an idea from me, receives instruction himself without lessening mine; as he who lights his taper at mine, receives light without darkening me. That ideas should freely spread from one to another over the globe, for the moral and mutual instruction of man, and improvement of his condition, seems to have been peculiarly and benevolently designed by nature... Inventions then cannot, in nature, be a subject of property. Society may give us exclusive right to the profits arising from them, as an encouragement to men to pursue ideas which may produce utility ...

Over time, it became apparent that receiving a US patent had become too easy. The quality of patented ideas had fallen, and Congress once more set up a team of expert examiners. When Congress updated the patent law in 1836, the new version lasted pretty much unchanged until 1952. Still, the updated law left unanswered questions. For example, as seen in the next chapter, patent law did not offer a way to protect products invented by slaves.

Like Franklin, Jefferson represented the optimism and ambition of a young nation. There was no area of potential knowledge that intimidated him. He eagerly sought new ideas and insights and was unafraid to challenge what authorities told him if it didn't line up with his own observations. He loved to design and share practical devices, and he believed in the ingenuity of free minds.

The year Jefferson turned eighty-three was the fifty-year anniversary of the signing of the Declaration of Independence. Roger Weightman, the mayor of Washington, DC, invited the former president to attend the festivities. Jefferson, suffering from various ailments, could not attend, but he sent a letter dated June 24, 1826. (Jefferson died just over a week later, on July 4.) In the letter, Jefferson expressed his joy that his fellow citizens still approved the bold move a small band of rebels had made fifty years earlier, "[A]ll eyes are opened, or opening to the rights of man. The general spread of the light of science has already laid open to every view the palpable truth that the mass of mankind has not been born, with saddles on their backs ..." Thomas Jefferson firmly believed that the United States of America, with its free institutions, would someday lead the world in science and useful ideas.

*"He looks for the **law** by which things act."*

— Professor Hopkins, US Naval Academy, speaking of Benjamin Bradley

3. Inventors Slave and Free

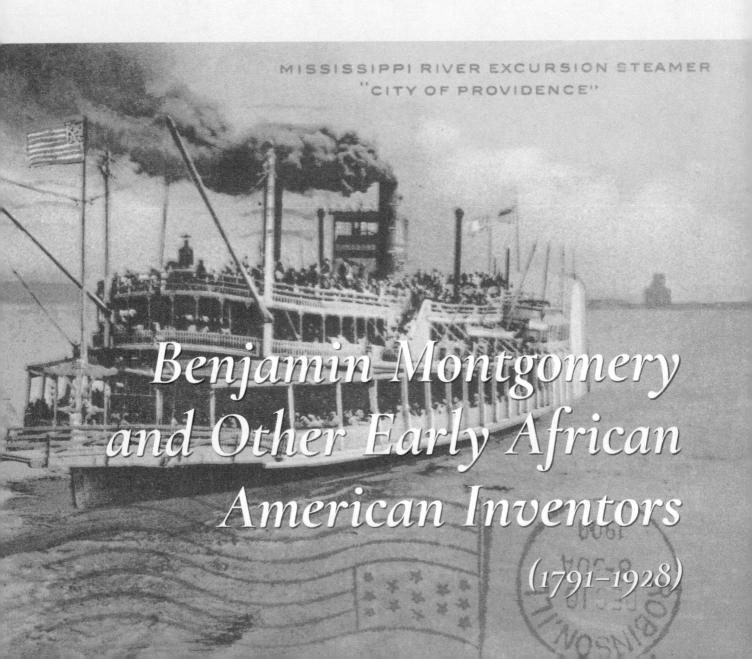

MISSISSIPPI RIVER EXCURSION STEAMER
"CITY OF PROVIDENCE"

Benjamin Montgomery and Other Early African American Inventors

(1791–1928)

"Look Out"
(Transport Steamer)
on Tennessee River

Thomas Jefferson was right: something about the young United States brought out the inventiveness in people. In 1820, 155 patents were granted for new inventions, and in 1880, there were 884. On a population basis, more patents were awarded in the United States every year than in England. Maybe it was the demands of frontier living or the feeling that the country itself was new and full of opportunity. And in spite of prejudice, barriers to education, and even slavery, some of the earliest American inventors were African American.

Thomas Jennings (1791–1856) and Dry Cleaning

Early patent applications did not always record the race of the applicant, but the first known African American to receive a patent was Thomas Jennings. Jennings was a free black American born in 1791 in New York City. As a boy, Thomas was apprenticed to a tailor. He worked hard, mastered his trade, and went on to start his own

Elizabeth Jennings
Graham, ca. 1895

clothing store and clothes-cleaning business. He married a woman named Elizabeth, who had been born to slave parents in Delaware. She worked as an indentured servant in New York until 1827.

At the age of thirty, Jennings invented a method for dry cleaning clothes, which he called "dry scouring." His system removed dirt and grease without using water. For his invention, Jennings received Patent Number 3306X from the State of New York. The document itself was lost in a fire at the US Patent Office in 1836, but Jennings had his own copy of the patent—a gilt-framed award letter that he hung over his bed.

Jennings used his early earnings to purchase the freedom of his wife and their first daughter, Matilda, born in 1824. Because both parents were now free, their next two children, Elizabeth and Thomas Jr., were born into freedom. A respected member of the community, Jennings took an active role in abolitionist causes. He helped found the Abyssinian Baptist Church, and he served as assistant secretary to the First Annual Convention of the People of Color, held in Philadelphia in 1831. But his family really drew attention in 1854, when Jennings's daughter Elizabeth, a schoolteacher and church organist, made a bold move while hurrying to church.

First horse-drawn streetcar in Manchester, NH

Running late, clasping her church hat to her head, Elizabeth leaped onto a horse-drawn streetcar that did not have a sign allowing "colored people" to board. The Irish-American conductor ordered her to leave, but Elizabeth refused. The conductor grabbed her and tried to throw her out, shouting, "You shall sweat for this!" But Elizabeth clung to a window frame and did not budge. At that point, the indignant conductor hailed a policeman who dragged Elizabeth into the street, crushing her church hat. Then he arrested her.

When he heard how his daughter had been treated, Jennings was furious. He sued the streetcar company, hiring Chester Arthur, who later became our twenty-first president, as his lawyer. Although only twenty-five at the time, Arthur won the case. The judge ruled that "colored persons if sober, well behaved, and free from disease" could not be barred from streetcars or other public transport. Still, New York State didn't officially abolish segregation on streetcars until 1873.

Chester A. Arthur

In 1955, just over a hundred years after Elizabeth Jennings won her case against the transit company, Rosa Parks refused to move to the back of the bus in Montgomery, Alabama.

The year of the verdict on Elizabeth's case, Jennings and two others founded the Legal Rights Association. The association continued to fight segregation even after Jennings's death in 1856. At his death, his copy of the patent still hung in its gilded frame above his bed.

Ned and the Cotton Scraper

Not all African American inventors were free. In 1857, a slave named Ned, who lived on a Mississippi plantation, invented a cotton scraper. The scraper was a horse-drawn device like a specialized plow. Used on one setting, it scraped soil and brush away from the sides of a growing cotton plant, allowing workers to approach and trim the plant more easily. Set differently, it pushed back a mound of weed-free soil to nourish the cotton.

Cotton in the field

Ned's owner, a man named Oscar Stuart, saw an opportunity to make some money. He applied for a patent on Ned's device. Stuart claimed he should receive the patent because the law at the time presumed that "the master is the owner of the fruits of the labor of the slave, both manual and intellectual."

Officials turned down Stuart's application. Patent Commissioner Joseph Holt ruled that neither slaves nor their owners could

In 1861, the Confederacy passed a patent law giving slave owners the rights to any of their slaves' inventions. It did them no good: of 274 patents issued before the end of the Confederacy in March 1865, none were awarded for slave inventions.

patent a slave's invention. The owner was not the inventor, and only a free human who could make a contract and own property could receive a patent.

Frustrated, Stuart decided to manufacture and sell the cotton scraper anyway. In advertising it, he quoted an endorsement from an associate, who wrote, with unintentional irony, "I am glad to know that your implement is the invention of a Negro slave—thus giving the lie to the abolition cry that slavery dwarfs the mind of the Negro. When did a free Negro ever invent anything?" Apparently, Stuart's friend had not heard of Thomas Jennings.

Regrettably, we have no further record of Ned's life or other inventions he might have made.

Benjamin Bradley (c. 1830–?), Engine Maker

Benjamin Bradley used his invention to help buy his freedom. Bradley was born a slave in Maryland around 1830; his father was probably white. From the age of eight to sixteen, he worked in a printing office, where he had access to machinery and learned to tinker. At sixteen, he used an old gun barrel, some pewter, and various bits of steel to build a model steam engine.

Around the same time, Bradley's master offered Benjamin as a laboratory assistant to a professor of science at the US Naval Academy in Annapolis, Maryland. Bradley's job was to help set up experiments for the students. This included setting up chemical reactions, arranging parabolic (curved) mirrors to concentrate heat, and making gases. Most of Benjamin's wages went to his master, but he was able to save five dollars a month toward his freedom.

Professor Hopkins found Bradley to be both intelligent and helpful. "He looks for the law by which things act," the professor wrote, contrasting Bradley's intellectual curiosity with the approach of the average student. Hopkins's children taught Benjamin to read, and on his own he learned arithmetic. Meanwhile, he kept building engines, including one "large enough to drive the first cutter of a sloop of war at six knots." He sold the engine to a midshipman, or student naval officer. Bradley put the money aside. In 1856, he built a still larger engine, this one powerful enough to propel a sloop of war at 16 knots. Still a slave, Bradley could not patent his work.

By now, Hopkins and others were urging Bradley's master to free him. His master agreed to sell him to freedom for $1,000, "although," he stated, the slave was "well worth $1,500." But there was a deadline on the offer: Bradley had to come up with the money by that October.

At that point the New York abolitionist community swung into action. One benefactor lent Bradley $500; others raised $122 as an outright gift. Somehow, he came up with all the money. His friends still worried about him. Smart as he was, Professor Hopkins wrote, Benjamin Bradley was "a mere child as to world matters." Their hope was that this mechanical genius might be able to get a job as engineer of a steamship. But whether he did or not is unknown. We have no further record of Bradley's life after he obtained his freedom.

Benjamin Montgomery (1819–1877) and the Steamboat Propeller

Benjamin Montgomery, while still a slave, designed a new kind of steamboat propeller. After the Civil War, he established a utopian community for former slaves. Born in Virginia in 1819, Benjamin was sold to a slave owner in Mississippi at the age of eighteen. By at least one account, he ran away from his new home but was quickly recaptured. At that point, his master, Joseph Emory Davis, asked Benjamin why he was discontented and agreed to make changes in his situation.

House at Davis Bend, MI

This was certainly unusual behavior for a slave owner, but Joseph Davis was an unusual man. His youngest brother, Jefferson, born when Joseph twenty-three, would later become president of the Confederacy. Joseph owned several plantations, including the Hurricane Plantation at Davis Bend in Mississippi. At this plantation, home to more than 300 slaves, Joseph planned an experiment. He would create a "community of cooperation" where his "servants" (he never called them slaves) could gain skills and largely govern themselves. Joseph provided decent housing for his slaves, along with medical and dental care.

Davis loaned Benjamin Montgomery money to open and run a general store on the plantation. It is not clear whether Montgomery could already read and write, or whether Davis encouraged him to learn. In either case, Davis soon put his "servant" in charge of negotiating with cotton buyers. Benjamin also managed all the plantation's purchasing and shipping.

Benjamin Montgomery's wife, Mary Lewis, was also literate. Montgomery paid Davis for her time so that she could stay at home with their five children. Mary taught the children to read, while she also earned extra money as a seamstress.

Mississippi steamboat J.M. White (1878)

Meanwhile, Montgomery learned other skills. He surveyed land and designed buildings. He repaired machinery and learned to navigate a steamboat. No doubt it was his experience steering a steamboat through shallow waters that led him to his invention of a new kind of propeller.

Montgomery's propeller was based on earlier designs, but it was adjustable. It could be lowered into the water at different angles, much as a motorboat engine today can be partially tipped out of the water. This adjustment allowed the propeller to work in the shallow waters of the Mississippi bayous without getting stuck in the mud. Because boats often got mudbound for weeks at a time, Montgomery's new propeller vastly shortened the delivery time of supplies the plantation needed.

Probably with the encouragement of Davis, Montgomery applied for a patent for his invention. His application was turned down because he was a slave. Later, the Davis brothers tried to patent Montgomery's invention for themselves, and they, too, were turned downed on the grounds that they were not the "true inventor."

ALABAMA,
a steam and sail-powered Confederate raider

Still, partly because of building his propeller, Montgomery became a wealthy man. Davis required his slaves to pay for labor to replace the time they took working for themselves, but beyond that amount he allowed them to keep their earnings. Montgomery's store earned a profit. Soon he built up a wholesale business and a personal library. He even experimented with a biracial school, hiring a white tutor to teach his children and the Davis children together. Montgomery's first son, Isaiah, became a personal valet and clerk to Joseph Davis. By this time, Montgomery and Davis were close. They often sat in the Davis library together after dinner, discussing philosophy.

In January 1961, Mississippi seceded from the Union to join the Confederacy. Three months later, the Civil War began. In April 1862, as the Union Army marched into Mississippi, Joseph Davis and his family fled Davis Bend. They took along some of their "servants," but they left Montgomery in charge of the plantation and its hundred or so remaining people. Montgomery tried to continue farming, but the slaves Davis had left behind began to loot his holdings. In the end, Benjamin and Isaiah Montgomery took off for the Union lines and freedom.

For a while, Benjamin Montgomery worked in Mississippi repairing Union Navy vessels. The commander of the Mississippi fleet, David Porter, called him a "brilliant mechanic" and helped the family escape to freedom in Ohio. Isaiah stayed on as the commander's cabin boy until late 1863, when he rejoined his family.

When the war ended in 1865, the US government pardoned Joseph Davis and returned his plantations. But Davis—old, weary, and impoverished—had little interest in restarting his work. Instead, he sold Hurricane and a neighboring plantation to his former slave Benjamin Montgomery for $300,000 to be paid out of future earnings. The Montgomery family returned from Ohio to take up their new role.

With 500 acres and 1,000 field hands, the Montgomerys were now the third-largest landholders in Mississippi. Benjamin jumped on the chance to try again to create a cooperative community, this time with free black tenant farmers instead of slaves. Members of the Montgomery family opened a string of stores, managed the estates, studied, and helped out in the fields. Their cotton won prizes as the best in the region—and once, at an international exhibition, was hailed as the best cotton in the world. The family lived in a fine house and kept servants to help them entertain in the old plantation style. The Montgomery daughters played the piano and attended Oberlin College in Ohio. In 1867, Benjamin Montgomery was elected justice of the peace, making him Mississippi's first elected African American official.

Isaiah Montgomery House on West Main Street, Mound Bayou

However, things took a downward turn. Floods, low prices, opposition by white farmers and years of bad crops put Montgomery behind on his payments to Davis. Then, in December 1874, Benjamin was working with a crew to pull down an old building. A wall collapsed, and Benjamin, fifty-five years old, was severely injured. He never fully recovered, and he died three years later. Soon afterward, Isaiah faced bankruptcy, and the land he and his father had struggled to farm, still not fully paid for, returned to the Davis family.

Mound Bayou Welcome Sign

Still, Isaiah Montgomery was determined to carry out his father's dream. In 1887, Isaiah and his cousin Benjamin T. Green bought 840 acres of swampy Mississippi wilderness land. Here, they proclaimed, was the new town of Mound Bayou, where free blacks could settle and be self-supporting. Families flocked in to clear the land. Soon there were businesses, three cotton mills, and a sawmill, all owned by blacks. The village grew, free and separate from surrounding white communities. Isaiah called his town the "Jewel of the Delta," and Theodore Roosevelt pointed to it as an "object lesson full of hope for the colored people." With its own school, banks, newspapers, and eventually even its own hospital, the town governed itself and remained prosperous for decades. Benjamin Montgomery's wealth, derived from his invention and his entrepreneurial spirit, had helped to create a home where hundreds of African Americans could thrive.

... And More

Many other African American inventors were born before the Civil War ended. In most cases, little is known about their lives. Here are a few of them.

Elijah McCoy (1844–1929) was born in Canada to parents who had escaped slavery on the Underground Railroad. At

Elijah McCoy

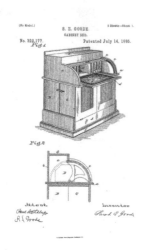

Patent for Sarah E. Goode's cabinet bed, issued July 14, 1885

age fifteen, McCoy was sent to Scotland, where he became certified as a mechanical engineer. While he was in Europe, his family moved back to the United States. Upon his return, McCoy was unable to get a position as an engineer, so he worked as fireman and oiler on the railroads. Over the course of his lifetime, he earned fifty-seven patents, many for improving lubrication systems in steam engines. The popular expression "the real McCoy," meaning "the genuine thing" became widespread when customers asked for Elijah McCoy's oil drip cup instead of a cheap copy.

Joseph Richard Winters (1816 or 1824–1916) was born in Virginia to an African American father and Shawnee mother. His grandmother was known as the "Indian doctor woman." Winters was a farmer, fisherman, hunter, and abolitionist. He wrote songs, poetry, and an autobiography that has been lost. In 1878, Winters received a patent for his invention of a new fire escape ladder. The ladder, made of metal, was mounted to a horse-drawn fire wagon.

clothes-wringer

Sarah Goode (1855–1905) was the first African American woman to be granted a patent. Some sources say she was born into slavery with the name Sarah Jacobs, while others say she was born free in Ohio. After the Civil War, Sarah moved to Chicago, where she owned a furniture store with her carpenter husband, Archibald Goode. To help her customers who lived in tiny apartments, she invented a "cabinet bed." This was a bed that could be folded into a desk with compartments for paper and writing supplies. Sarah Goode received her patent in 1885.

Ellen Eglin (1849–1890s) was born in Washington, DC, where she worked as a housekeeper and government clerk. She invented a hand-turned clothes-wringer that greatly eased the work of doing laundry. Concerned that no one would buy such a product from an African American woman, Eglin sold the rights granted by her patent to a white woman for $18.

L. H. Latimer

Lewis Howard Latimer (1848–1928) was born in Chelsea, Massachusetts, to two escaped slaves. He lied about his age so he could he join the US Navy in 1864. After an honorable discharge, he worked first as an office assistant and then as a draftsman for a patent law firm. His first invention, with Charles W. Brown, was an improved toilet system for railroad cars. Later, Latimer helped make the drawings for Alexander Graham Bell's telephone patent. In 1881, he received a patent for a better way of producing carbon filaments for lightbulbs, an improvement on Thomas Edison's design.

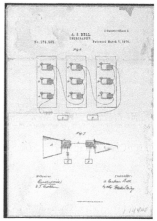

drawings for Bell's
telephone patent

Granville Woods (1856–1910), sometimes called the "Black Edison," earned more than fifty patents during his life. Granville grew up in Columbus, Ohio. After leaving school at the age of ten, he learned the trades of machinist and blacksmith. Eventually, he became a railroad engineer. Around 1880, he moved to Cincinnati, where he set up a company to manufacture electrical equipment. He sold a patent for an improved telephone transmitter, halfway between a telegraph and telephone system, to Alexander Graham Bell. The proceeds of this sale allowed Woods to devote himself to inventing.

Other inventions included an automatic railway brake and an egg incubator. One important invention was the troller. This grooved metal wheel could clamp onto an overhead wire, allowing streetcars to get electricity from a wire overhead. Woods also made improvements to the telegraph, telephone, and phonograph. But his best-known invention was a "synchronous multiplex railway telegraph." This device allowed people in a moving train to communicate by voice over telegraph wire with colleagues back in the station.

Granville Woods

Woods sold most of his inventions to manufacturing companies like Westinghouse and General Electric. He turned down an offer from Thomas Edison to make him a partner, preferring to remain independent. Despite his success, Woods often told people he was born in Australia. He thought people would respect him more as a foreigner than as an African American man.

Even for free African Americans, opportunities in the 1800s were extremely limited. Few had the chance for much education. Even for those who, like Elijah McCoy, got an advanced education outside of America, finding work to match their qualifications was difficult if not impossible. Their inventions emerged out of their work life. Those who built furniture invented better furniture; those who worked for the railways improved trains. Only a few made much money from their inventions.

"*Concentrate all your thoughts upon the work at hand. The sun's rays do not burn until brought to a focus.*"

— Alexander Graham Bell, interview with Orison Swett Marden, 1901

4. Scattered Genius

Alexander Graham Bell

(1847–1922)

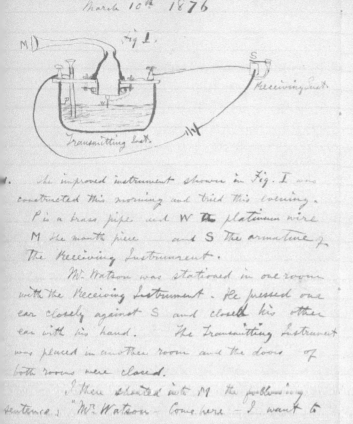

March 10th 1876

Fig. 1.

M

S

Receiving Inst.

Transmitting Inst.

The improved instrument shown in Fig. 1 was constructed this morning and tried this evening. P is a brass pipe and W the platinum wire M the mouth piece — and S the armature of the Receiving Instrument.

Mr Watson was stationed in one room with the Receiving Instrument. He pressed one ear closely against S and closed his other ear with his hand. The Transmitting Instrument was placed in another room and the doors of both rooms were closed.

I then shouted into M the following sentence: "Mr Watson — Come here — I want to see you". To my delight he came and declared that he had heard and understood what I said. I asked him to repeat the words. He answered "You said 'Mr Watson — come here I want to see you'." We then changed places and I listened at S while Mr Watson read a few passages from a book into the mouth piece M. It was certainly the case that articulate sounds proceeded from S. The effect was loud but indistinct and muffled. If I had read beforehand the passage given by Mr Watson I should have recognized every word. As it was I could not make out the sense — but an occasional word here and there was quite distinct. I made out "to" and "out" and "further"; and finally the sentence "Mr Bell Do you understand what I say? Do — you — un — der — stand — what — I — say" came quite clearly and intelligibly. No sound was audible when the armature S was removed.

S ound, hearing, and speech ruled young Alexander Graham Bell's life. The middle son of three, Alec was born on March 3, 1847, and grew up in Edinburgh, Scotland. His father, Melville, was a former actor who gave speech lessons to help people get rid of their lisps or their Scottish accents. Alec's mother, Eliza, had damaged her hearing during an illness. Alec learned to talk to his mother by standing close and speaking in a deep voice to her forehead. The vibrations traveled through her facial bones, allowing her to make out his words. Alec also learned the tactile alphabet, spelling out sentences by touching different parts of his "listener's" hands.

Young Alec himself was gifted with a remarkable ear. He had perfect pitch and played the piano with a passion. He could play by ear any piece of music he heard. He loved to entertain guests by imitating barnyard animals or by throwing his voice to make puppets recite nursery rhymes.

Notebook by Alexander Graham Bell about telephone experiment (above)

Alexander Graham Bell

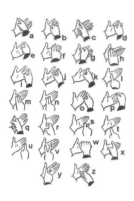

Tactile alphabet

Melville Bell expected his sons to pursue the family business of speech and phonetics. He taught his sons to recite in a proper British accent. While he coached his clients, he demanded absolute silence in the house. But his life's work was developing a new system to note down the sounds of human speech. For hours, Melville stood in front of a mirror making every sound he could think of while he observed the position of his lips, cheeks, and tongue. Then he translated his mouth's motion into the written symbols of his great invention, "Visible Speech."

The boys' mother, Eliza, taught them at home when they were young, and their father gave them tasks of his own. One time, he challenged his two oldest sons to create a machine that could imitate human speech. The boys studied the human skull in their father's study. They modeled jaws, palate, and tongue out of wood, wire, and a rubber-like material called gutta-percha. Then they fashioned a larynx and blew into the throat with a tin tube. Ultimately, they figured out how to manipulate their machine to cry out like a wailing baby, "Mama!" The two boys tested their creation on the stairs of the building where they lived. To their delight, worried tenants emerged from the doors below to comfort the crying baby.

Once Alec started secondary school, he was a careless and untidy student. He often skipped classes to go bird-watching. He collected fossils, bird's eggs, shells, and plants for his home "laboratory," and he neglected his Greek. Once, for a classmate's father who owned a mill, he invented a machine that removed the husks from grain. At home, he learned the new art of photography and dissected animals to show his friends.

In 1862, when Alec was fifteen, his parents sent him to London. There he lived for a year with his widowed grandfather, another Alexander Bell. His grandfather, also an actor turned speech teacher, taught Alec manners, how to recite Shakespeare, and how to dress like an English gentleman.

By this time, Alec wanted to earn money to further his education. He found a job teaching piano and elocution (proper pronunciation) at a boys' boarding school in Elgin, on the northeastern coast of Scotland. But after eighteen months, Alec's father called his seventeen-year-old son home. Professor Melville Bell wanted to promote Visible Speech, and he needed his sons to help. Melville trained the three boys in his methods and took them on the road. In packed theaters, with his sons offstage, he asked audience members to suggest new sounds. Then he invited one of his sons onstage to read the symbols and reproduce the sounds. The demonstrations were a huge success.

This period of triumph ended when the youngest Bell son, Edward, began to cough and waste away from tuberculosis. The family could not afford to send him to a sanatorium. Instead they moved to London for better medical care. Alec taught school in nearby Bath, and he tried to continue his own studies. He experimented with tuning forks and stretched membranes, seeking to understand how sounds made air vibrate. Often, he worked until dawn, and he began to suffer from severe headaches that plagued him all his life.

In 1867, when Alec was twenty, Edward died. Reluctantly, Alec moved home to comfort his heartbroken parents. He challenged himself to teach the family dog to talk. The little terrier learned to "say" *Ow ah oo ga ma ma* (How are you, Grandmama?). Alec mixed with scholarly colleagues of his father, took classes at the University of London, and used Visible Speech to teach deaf children at a private school in Kensington.

Only three years later, Alec's older brother, Melly, died, also of TB, at the age of twenty-five. After losing Melly, Alec's father decided to move the remaining family out of London's soot and smoke to the healthy air of Canada. Alec hated to leave. But he, too, was sick. More than six feet tall, he weighed only 130 pounds. His headaches were worse, and he coughed a lot. He later admitted, "I went to Canada to die."

The family found a house in the little town of Brantford in southern Ontario, and there Alec sat in the garden most of the summer, resting and reading. He stopped coughing and began to gain weight. Soon he was back at his experiments. Two new problems fascinated him: Could electricity carry sound? And could telegraph wires carry more than one message at a time?

By this time, the telegraph was more than twenty years old. Wires crowded overhead in cities. Each wire could carry only one message, in one direction, at any one time. Telegraph companies desperately wanted to change that. Alec Bell had the idea that perhaps a single telegraph wire could transmit several different messages at once if each used a different tone. If the receiver was tuned to a specific frequency, perhaps it would pick up only messages transmitted at that frequency. With his tuning forks and wires, Bell set out to prove his hypothesis. Meanwhile, he needed a job.

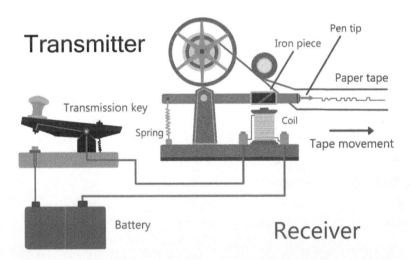

The telegraph was the first instrument for sending messages very quickly across long distances. It relies on a circuit grounded at both ends to the earth, which is a conductor. At the transmitting or sending end, there is a battery and a gap in the circuit. The person sending the message presses the telegraph key to close the circuit and send an electric signal. At the receiving end, the wire wraps around an electromagnet. The electric pulse creates a magnetic force that pulls down a lever arm, making a sound and a mark on paper. The sender closes the circuit for a shorter (dot) or longer (dash) time, making the patterns of Morse code.

The clean air of Canada and several months of rest did wonders for Alec's health—perhaps he never had tuberculosis at all. Rejuvenated, Alec moved to Boston, where he set up a private practice giving speech lessons. He also taught at the Boston School for Deaf Mutes, which continues today as the Horace Mann School for the Deaf.

A gifted and empathetic teacher, Bell never assumed that deaf children were mentally defective or naturally slow. He made faces, acted, clowned around, and got students happily imitating him. He opposed sending young children to special boarding schools where they would be separated from their speaking peers and taught primarily sign language. He wanted them to learn to speak fluently so they could have full lives in a speaking world. As Helen Keller later said of him, he fought against that "inhuman silence that separates and estranges."

After Bell gave a lecture at the Clarke Institution for Deaf Mutes in Northampton, Massachusetts, the chairman of the school's board came to see him. Gardiner Hubbard asked if Bell would teach his fifteen-year-old daughter, Mabel, who had lost her hearing after a bout of scarlet fever at age five. Mabel was bright and educated. She had spent time in Europe and could read and write both German and Italian. Although she read lips remarkably well, her speech sounded like honking and was hard to understand.

When Bell took Mabel Hubbard on as a student, he was living at the home of another young pupil, Georgie Sanders. There Bell had a laboratory where he worked all hours of the night. But now he became a frequent guest at the Hubbards' Cambridge home. One evening, Alec entertained his hosts at the piano. He showed them that by singing a pure note, he could make the strings of the piano vibrate in sympathy. This, he explained, was the principle he hoped to use to make a multichannel telegraph.

Gardiner Hubbard jumped on the idea. For years, he had been seeking a way to break into the telegraph business and shatter Western Union's monopoly. All at once, Bell had two investors—the fathers of both Mabel and Georgie—who funded him to buy equipment and hire a young assistant, an electrician Bell found named Thomas Watson.

Competition to create the multi-telegraph was intense. Thomas Edison and Elisha Gray, both hired by Western Union, were already hotly pursuing the goal. As Bell wrote to his father on November 23, 1874, "It is a neck and neck race between Mr. Gray and myself who shall complete our apparatus first. He has the advantage over me in being a practical electrician—but I have reason to believe that I am better acquainted with the phenomena of sound…. The very opposition seems to nerve me to work."

Elisha Gray

Yet Bell allowed himself to be distracted. He couldn't let go of the idea that telegraph wires could also be made to carry the human voice. Instead of opening and closing a circuit to make dots and dashes, what if he made the current flowing through the wires somehow undulate as the voice does? Impatient with Bell's flights of fancy, Gardiner Hubbard urged him to focus on the multi-telegraph, which would yield a sure profit.

The relationship between Bell and his sponsor grew more complicated when Alec found himself falling in love with the seventeen-year-old Mabel. By now, he was no longer teaching Mabel himself, but he often conversed with her at the Hubbards'. He wrote a heartfelt letter to Mabel's mother, asking permission to court the young girl. He didn't mention her deafness; he hardly noticed it.

Mabel's parents were taken aback, and they forbade him to speak of love to their daughter. But by summer, when Mabel left for Nantucket, Bell could bear his passion in silence no longer. He followed Mabel to the island and sent a letter through her cousin. In a return letter, Mabel responded that she did not love him and would not meet him in Nantucket but did not mind continuing the conversation. The truth was that Mabel considered Alec too old (he was twenty-eight), too stuffy, and too poor to be a good match. But having expressed his passion, Bell felt much better.

Meanwhile, Mabel's father was pressing him hard. Hubbard wrote, "I have been sorry to see how little interest you seem to take in telegraph matters." At this rate, Hubbard said Alec would never have enough money to marry. In fact, he demanded that Bell give up either Visible Speech or his courtship of Mabel. But Alec was stubborn. He refused to abandon his work for the deaf. He wrote to Hubbard, "If [Mabel] does not come to love me well enough to accept me *whatever my profession or business may be,* I do not want her at all."

By November 1875, Mabel Hubbard had decided she did want to marry Alexander Graham Bell after all. The couple became engaged, and Mabel's father backed off. Mabel, meanwhile, gently pressed her fiancé. Alec filed a patent application for his multi-telegraph. The patent examiner blocked it, because three other inventors had filed similar ideas. So Alec decided to try and patent his "speaking telegraph" idea. He wanted to file first in England, which would issue a patent only if no other country had done so. Alec sent an application by ship with his Canadian neighbor George Brown.

Bell and Hubbard waited for news from Britain, but it never came. Brown had lost interest and never filed the patent. Then something unusual happened. On February 14, 1876, without Bell's permission, Gardiner Hubbard filed for a US patent on his behalf for the voice-over-wire device. The same day, Bell's rival Elisha Gray filed what was called a "caveat"—a request for the exclusive right to work on an unfinished invention for one year. At first, the patent office declared "interference" between the two applications. That usually meant a long period of investigation before the patent office decided. But on February 26, Bell traveled to Washington, DC, to visit his future father-in-law's patent attorneys. Only two weeks later, with unheard-of speed, the patent office issued the patent to Alexander Graham Bell.

This haste was remarkable, because Bell had not yet built a working telephone. He returned to Boston that very day and set back to work. On March 9, he made a new sketch in his lab notebook—one that looks a great deal like a sketch in Gray's application for a caveat. And on March 10, using the new design, Bell made the famous appeal that traveled through wires to an adjoining room: "Mr. Watson, come here. I want you."

Elisha Gray had not built a working telephone. He had merely suggested a design for one. But Alexander Graham Bell was in the same position. Why, then, did he win his patent so quickly? Was it just the effect of Gardiner Hubbard's skilled attorneys? And why did the telephone Bell created seem to include an aspect of Elisha Gray's secret design? Although at the time Elisha Gray congratulated Bell on his invention, he later came to believe Bell had stolen his ideas. The matter led to years of court battles between Western Union, which employed Gray, and the new Bell Telephone Company. Bell Telephone won every time.

"I do not, however, claim even the credit of inventing it, as I do not believe a mere description of an idea that has never been reduced to practice... should be dignified with the name of invention."
—Elisha Gray, Letter to Alexander Graham Bell, March 5, 1877

Once he had a working telephone, Bell began to demonstrate it. Hubbard pressed him to attend the Philadelphia World Exhibition in May 1876. At first, Bell refused to go because he was helping his deaf students study for exams. But Mabel tricked him into going to the train station, and once there she told him that either he went to Philadelphia or their engagement was off. Alec went. He and Watson set up their device in a corner of the exhibition hall. The judges included the emperor of Brazil and the famous physicist William Thomson, the future Baron

Kelvin. Bell won gold medals for both his telephone and his multi-channel telegraph.

That summer, in Canada, Bell continued his demonstrations. Slow to write up the report he needed to submit for his gold medals, he complained to Mabel, "The real reward of labour such as mine is *success*, and medals and certificates of merit only lower it to a vulgar level." But he did file for an updated telephone patent in January 1877. By this time, the telephone looked like a box camera with a tube for speaking and listening. Businesses began to set up single telephone lines between buildings. In early July, there were 200 such lines; by the end of August, there were 1,300.

An early model wall mounted telephone, in the Champaign County Historical Museum, Champaign, IL

On July 11, 1877, Alexander Graham Bell married Mabel Hubbard. Alec was thirty and Mabel nineteen. When they married, Alec gave his wife all but ten shares of his stock in Bell Telephone. To turn over such wealth to a woman was almost unheard of, but it was a good decision. Mabel had a much better head for business than Alec ever did.

After a trip to Niagara Falls and Scotland, the newlyweds spent a year in London, England. Alec demonstrated his telephone to Queen Victoria. He tried to set up a British Bell Telephone Company, without much success. "Business is hateful to me at all times," he said. He wanted to return to teaching the deaf, and only the birth of his daughter Elsie kept him in England. "I am sick of the telephone, and have done with it altogether, excepting as a plaything to amuse my leisure moments," he told his wife.

The moment the Bells returned to Canada, Alec's old assistant Thomas Watson whisked him off to Washington, DC, to testify in one of the unending lawsuits that plagued Bell Telephone for years. As soon as he could, Alec broke away. For the next several

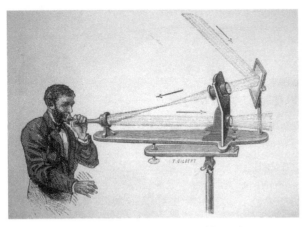

A photophone receiver and headset

Bell, his wife Mabel Gardiner Hubbard
and their daughters

years, he divided his time between teaching the deaf, which always fulfilled him, and inventing. In 1879, the family moved to Washington, DC. Using money from a French prize he had received for inventing the telephone, Bell set up the Volta laboratory. Though he had enough money from his share of Bell Telephone to work on his inventions as much as he wanted, ideas flitted through his head. He had grand, visionary notions, but he struggled to concentrate in a single-minded way on any one notion long enough to turn it into a product.

Bell envisioned a photophone that would carry a signal in a wobbling ray of light from a mirror that vibrated when a person spoke at it. He patented the idea in 1880, when he was thirty-three, but it only worked in line of sight. Not until 1977, nearly a hundred years later, were the first sounds carried by light along a fiber optic cable. Next Bell developed the spectrophone, which used sound to detect wavelengths of light beyond the visible spectrum. But the instrument had no practical use.

On July 2, 1881, when President James Garfield was shot by a madman, his doctors probed for the bullet and couldn't find it. Bell wanted to help. He invented a kind of metal detector that was meant to buzz when it hovered over the bullet. At the end of July, he was asked to come to the White House. Bell set up his apparatus in the president's sweltering sickroom, but iron springs in the sick man's mattress interfered. Alec kept working with his apparatus and tried to help the president again. But the president died on September 19. Most likely, he succumbed to an infection introduced by one of the doctors who had probed his gunshot wound with ungloved hands.

Worse, while Bell was in Washington, DC, Mabel lost a baby boy at birth. Alec never forgave himself for being absent when his wife most needed him. When he learned that infant Edward had died because he could not take an adequate breath, he worked feverishly on a new invention. His "vacuum jacket" was a metal cylinder that could be placed around the patient's torso. Air pumped into and out of the cylinder would cause the patient's chest to expand and contract. Later, this principle led to the iron lung, which saved many people from death when polio paralyzed their breathing. But Alec's invention never made it into production, and he was once again away, this time at a scientific meeting, when his second son, Robert, also died at birth in 1883.

The 1880s were difficult years for the Bells. Besides their loss of two sons there was the fact that Alec's inventions were going almost nowhere. His head brimmed with ideas, but he didn't have the team of dedicated engineers Thomas Edison had to help him develop his inventions. Moreover, Bell constantly let himself be distracted by new ideas and responsibilities. As Mabel wrote to him before they were married, "You like to fly around like a butterfly sipping honey, more or less from a flower here or another flower there." He read the encyclopedia before bed to stir his head with new ideas. Bell wondered if odors were vibrations somewhere on a spectrum between sound and heat. He tried to find out if he could transfer his thoughts to an assistant through coils of wire wrapped around their heads.

Bell and Helen Keller

Meanwhile, he continued his efforts in deaf education. He became a champion of young Helen Keller and helped her find her teacher Annie Sullivan.

Mabel standing inside Bell's tetrahedral kite frame

It was easy for Bell to converse with Keller through finger spelling—tapping his fingers on parts of her hand that represented different letters—or allowing her to place her hand over his lips as he spoke. Mostly, however, he urged deaf people to learn to lip-read and converse aloud. Only by doing so, he thought, could they fully enter hearing society. Not everyone agreed with the importance of such integration. A faction led by the famous educator Albert Gallaudet argued that deaf children could more fully participate in deaf culture and live a richer life if they learned sign language.

The loudness of a sound is often expressed in decibels. A decibel is one-tenth of a Bel, which is a "power ratio" that the Bell Telephone Company named after Alexander Graham Bell. An increase of four decibels in a sound's power means approximately doubling the sound's loudness.

Along with inventing and teaching, Bell tried to nurture science in America. He was one of the founders of *Science* magazine, which is still the premier research journal in the United States. Bell's financial support amounted to what would be over a million dollars in today's money. And in 1898, he became the second president of the National Geographic Society. It was Bell who insisted that the *National Geographic* publish illustrations and photographs to help its articles appeal to the public.

In the late 1880s, the Bells bought land and began to build an estate on the shores of Bras d'Or Lake on Cape Breton Island in Nova Scotia. The whole family relaxed there in the summers. Mabel let her little daughters, Elsie and Daisy, wear trousers for play. Alec worked on inventions or rowed a boat on the lake. He experimented with breeding sheep, and he found excuses to delay his return to Washington, DC, every fall.

Over the years, in the nation's capital but mostly in Cape Breton, Alec worked on exciting new modes of transportation. He was fascinated by the possibilities of flight. With Mabel's financial support, drawn from her management of the telephone income, Bell put together his own small research team of mechanics and scientists in 1907. They called themselves the AEA, for Aerial Experiment Association. They pledged to each build and test an aircraft within a year.

Bell focused on manned kites. He designed several kites made up of tetrahedral cells—four triangles making a pyramid, where two of the triangles were open and two were covered in maroon silk. The three other members of the association built winged airplanes, which they called aerodromes. One of the team, Glenn Curtiss, won the Scientific American Trophy for making the first official flight of one kilometer in the Western Hemisphere.

Bell was also fascinated by the idea of a hydrofoil, a boat traveling on a cushion of air. He first rode in one in France during a world tour in 1910–1911, when he was fifty-three. Back at the Bras d'Or, Bell resolved to build his own. Soon he built a boatyard to employ yacht designers and boat builders. After World War I, the Bell team's hydrofoil boat, which they called the HD-4, set a world record speed of just over seventy miles per hour.

Glenn Curtiss in his bi-plane
July 4, 1908

Bell always used "Hoy! Hoy!" as his telephone greeting. It came from the nautical term "Ahoy!" Thomas Edison introduced the greeting, "Hello." The new words blew past the nineteenth-century concern that one should not speak to another before a proper introduction.

Bell seemed content in the last twenty years of his life. Mabel had managed the family wealth well enough to finance his interests. In his winters in Washington, DC, scientific colleagues kept him up-to-date with the newest scientific ideas. In summer, he had a place where he could live and work as he chose, imagining anything and then trying to build it with young friends. Free of concerns about lawsuits or turning inventions into businesses, he could let his genius roam like a playful child.

Alexander Graham Bell died of complications of diabetes on August 2, 1922 at the age of seventy-five. He had become a naturalized citizen of the United States in 1892. Nevertheless, so great was his fame that four countries—Scotland, England, the United States, and Canada—have claimed him as one of their most exalted citizens.

"*Don't sit down and wait for the opportunities to come. You have to get up and make them for yourself!*"

— Madam C. J. Walker, speech to the National Negro Business League convention, 1914

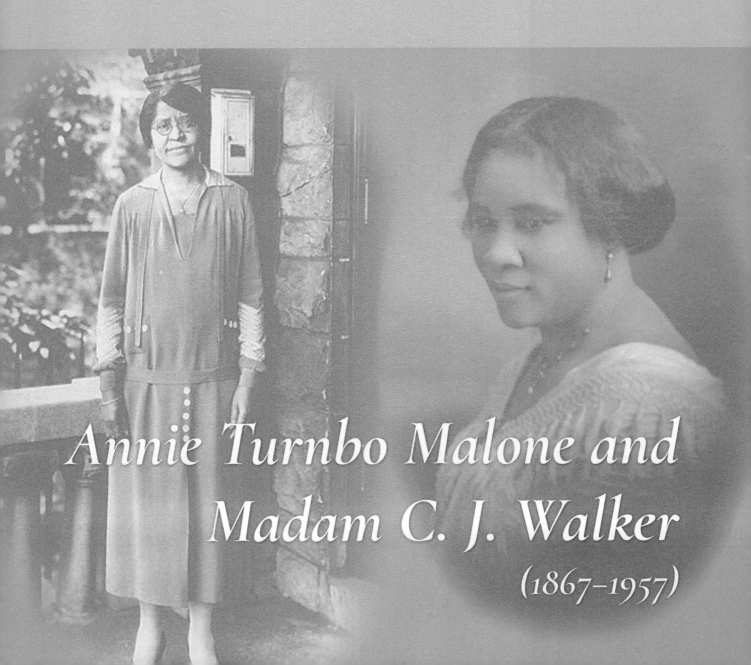

5. Hair-Care Millionaires

Annie Turnbo Malone and Madam C. J. Walker
(1867–1957)

Annie Turnbo Malone
part of an oil portrait by Victor Harvey

Who was the first self-made female millionaire in America? The two women vying for this title were both African American, both the daughters of slaves, and both pioneers in the beauty business. Both invented hair products, founded beauty schools, provided jobs to thousands of women, and gave generously to their communities. Early in their careers, one worked for the other. Later they competed. Their names were Annie Turnbo Malone and Sarah Breedlove, later known as Madam C. J. Walker.

Annie Turnbo Malone (1869–1957)

Annie Minerva Turnbo, inventor and businesswoman, was born in Metropolis, Illinois, on August 9, 1869, the tenth of eleven children. Her parents had been slaves in Kentucky. When her father ran away to join the Union Army early in the Civil War, Annie's mother fled up the Mississippi with her children to the free state of Illinois. As soon as the war ended, her husband rejoined her. Annie was born four years later.

During the Civil War, escaped slaves who joined the Union Army were referred to as "contraband," or spoils of war. The army set them to work building fortifications or doing other manual labor to support the white troops. For the first time in their lives, these men were paid wages. Later in the war, some of them joined the army as "colored troops."

Annie was still a child when both her parents died of disease. Her older sister Ada collected the young girl and brought her to live in Peoria, Illinois. Annie was clever but frail. In high school, she particularly enjoyed chemistry, but she frequently missed class because of sickness. Eventually, she dropped out of school. To help out at home, she practiced hairdressing with her sister.

At the time, many city-living African American women were changing their hairdos. They wanted to turn away from the dry, unruly, and patchy hair they associated with poverty and field-work. Fashionable hair was straight hair. To get it, women used soap, goose fat, butter, or bacon grease. To comb their hair, they used the combs shepherds used to card wool. Often, women applied a straightening mixture made of lye mixed with potatoes, which broke their hair shafts and damaged their scalps. Some even tried to iron their hair by spreading it on an ironing board.

Civil War contraband laborers repairing track

Annie Turnbo thought there must be another path to beautiful hair. She consulted her aunt, who was an herbal doctor, and experimented with various substances in her sister's house. By 1900, she had developed a hair treatment based on sage and egg rinses that she felt was safe and effective— not for straightening hair, but for making it thick, healthy, and glossy. She packaged her formula along with another she called "The Great Wonderful Hair Grower" and began selling them door to door. Soon she was driving around in a buggy making speeches about cleanliness and hygiene and giving demonstrations of her shampoo.

In 1902, at age thirty-three, Annie moved to St. Louis, Missouri. There she hired three assistants and opened a shop. That same year, she married a man named Nelson Pope.

Annie Turnbo Pope became a respected member of the community, joining the temperance movement and teaching Sunday school. To promote her hair products, she held news conferences and advertised in the black press. At the time, St. Louis was the fourth-largest city in the country. A railway hub and a center for manufacturing, the city bustled with industry. Flour,

Bird's eye view, 1904 World's Fair, St. Louis.

tobacco, beer, whiskey, paper, shoes, pet food, tobacco, paint, and bricks—all helped the city grow. African Americans from the South flocked to the city for work. Coal dust, lead dust, and grain dust choked the air.

In 1904, to celebrate the centennial of the Louisiana Purchase, St. Louis held a World's Fair. City fathers built an "Ivory City" of twelve exhibition halls that celebrated American industry and world cultures. Forty-three states and more than sixty countries exhibited. During its seven-month run, the fair attracted twenty million visitors. Annie Pope managed to get a retail booth in a section showing African American industry. There she demonstrated her hair products. Black visitors responded so enthusiastically she decided it was time to take her business national.

A St. Louis Street around 1920

At some point, the story began to circulate that Annie chose the name Poro because it was a Mende word from West Africa referring to a male secret society, but the combination of two last names appears much more likely.

Pages from the Poro College catalogue

As an African American and a woman, Annie Turnbo Pope faced obstacles to building a distribution network for her products. Black-owned drugstores or grocery stores were rare. White-owned stores catered only to white customers. To expand her territory, Annie Turnbo Pope had to build customer demand. She began to recruit and train sales associates.

One of Pope's early employees was Sarah Breedlove, a young woman who carried the products by rail to Denver to sell there. However, the two women had a disagreement, and soon Sarah, later known as Madam C. J. Walker, launched a rival business. Stunned by this move and convinced that Sarah had stolen her secret formulas, Annie realized she needed to protect her intellectual property. She copyrighted her products under the name Poro. The name combined her husband's last name, Pope, with that of her sister's husband, Roberts. She kept the company name even after divorcing Nelson Pope in 1907 after five years of marriage.

Three years after Annie's divorce, the Poro Company moved its headquarters from St. Louis to Indianapolis. There Annie bought a five-story building. When fully built out, the new headquarters had everything—a manufacturing plant, retail store, offices, meeting rooms, 800-seat auditorium, dormitory, gymnasium, roof garden, bakery, podiatry clinic, and chapel. It even had a laboratory for testing new products.

In 1914, Annie, already a millionaire, married a school principal and former Bible salesman named Aaron Eugene Malone. From then on, she called herself Annie Turnbo Malone. Impressed with her husband's sales experience, she made him president of the Poro Company. She continued to build brand awareness in the black press. Her ads emphasized that customers should demand genuine Poro products rather than imitations from other companies. To protect her business, she obtained US Design Patent No. 60,962 for an "Ornamental Design for a Sealing Tape". Products in boxes taped up with this special tape stood out as hers.

Annie continued to innovate in other ways as well. She trademarked new ointments and shampoos. In 1922, she seems to have been the first person to introduce deodorant to African American customers. However, neither Annie Turnbo Malone nor Madam C. J. Walker invented the hot comb, used to straighten hair. Both women wrestled with the temptation to market hair straighteners or skin lighteners, both popular at the time. Malone and Walker insisted that their mission was to make black women beautiful, not to make them white. Still, their hair care "systems" did include the use of warm oils and wide-toothed combs that would help loosen the curls of tightly coiled black hair.

In 1918, Malone officially opened the Poro College in her imposing building. There she provided housing as well as jobs and education for young black women. The beauty school employed two hundred people, and it taught young beauticians how to succeed—preparing them not just with beauty care skills but guidance on how to walk, talk, and dress for success.

The college, along with Madam C. J. Walker's competing one, filled an important gap. Few jobs were available to black women who left work in the cotton fields. A woman could become a domestic servant or a laundress. If she was educated, she might become a teacher. A few young women were learning to be secretaries—if their skin was light enough and their hair straight enough. But for a dark-skinned woman with an interrupted education, becoming a beautician offered a realistic chance to rise. If a woman worked hard and saved her money, she could someday open her own shop or even several shops. As Malone wrote when she advertised for agents: "You can have a profitable occupation right in your own home and build for yourself a permanent income by serving your neighbors, friends, acquaintances, and others."

"Dignity, grace, beauty, industry, thrift, efficiency, godliness—that these ideals be held aloft for the glorification of the women and girls of my Race, Poro College is constructed."
— Annie T. Malone, *"Poro in Pictures": With a Short History of Its Development,* 1926

The Apotheosis shows what has been done thru constant application and sacrifice. Three heroic figures of beautiful Negro womanhood personify Liberty, Music and Art. The presence of the Lyre on the side of Fine Arts and of Books on the side of Liberal Arts shows that in Literature and Music, the Race has made its most wonderful progress.

Page from the Poro College catalogue

In fact, in the years between 1910 and 1920, the majority of barbershops and beauty salons in the United States were owned and run by African Americans. Three times as many black women as non-immigrant white women worked as hairdressers and manicurists nationwide. As for Poro College, Malone claimed that over the years that it ran, it created jobs for almost 75,000 women in North and South America, Africa and the Philippines.

The Poro Company thrived. By 1920, the company reportedly held as much as $14 million in assets, equivalent to almost $180 million today. In 1924, Malone paid an income tax of nearly $40,000, the highest in Missouri that year. She and her husband lived modestly and gave generously to the community. The *St. Louis Argus* claimed that their donation of $25,000 to help build the St. Louis Colored YWCA was the largest to that date by any African Americans for any social cause. "Mrs. Malone said that she did not regard the money as belonging to herself and [her] husband but as belonging to God," reported the paper.

Perhaps because of the early loss of her own parents, Malone's favorite charity was the St. Louis Colored Orphan's Home. She served as its board president for twenty-four years, providing $10,000 for a new building in 1919 and then helping it move into a new facility in 1922.

During the 1920s, Malone funded every historically black college in the US to allow two students to attend full time. Among the colleges were Cheyney University, Lincoln University, Wilberforce University, Morehouse College, the Tuskegee Institute, and others. Howard University received $25,000.

By the late 1920s, the Malones' marriage was in trouble. Husband and wife clashed over control of the company. In 1927, Aaron filed for divorce. He claimed that Poro's success was due to his contacts, and he wanted half the company. Black leaders and politicians, all male, sided with him. On the other hand, Poro workers and church leaders supported Annie. So did the influential Mary

In 1946, the orphanage changed its name to the Annie Malone Children and Family Service Center. It is still active today. Among other services, it provides a crisis center, parenting education, and a therapeutic school for troubled children.

McLeod Bethune, president of the National Association of Colored Women. In the end, Annie agreed to pay Aaron a settlement of $200,000, and he left the company to her.

After the divorce, as Malone entered her sixties, she decided to try a new city. She relocated the company to Chicago, where she bought an entire city block. For a while, Poro continued to do well, but soon new lawsuits piled up. In 1937, a former employee sued, claiming credit for the company's success. To settle the lawsuit, Malone had to sell her St. Louis property. Her financial troubles continued into the 1930s. The Depression didn't help. By 1943, Malone owed the government almost $100,000 in unpaid real estate and luxury taxes. Still, the company soldiered on. In the mid-1950s, thirty-two branches of the Poro school continued to deliver classes around the country.

Malone fought hard, but she was growing older. At the age of eighty-seven, she lost her business to creditors. Soon after, she suffered a stroke and died on May 10, 1957. Childless, she left about $100,000 to her nieces and nephews.

Although she is not as well-known as her still more successful former employee, Annie Turnbo Malone was probably the first self-made female millionaire in America. Her accomplishments proved that an African American woman could invent a desirable product, market it, become a leader in her community, hold her own in a world of men, and build an international business.

Madam C. J. Walker (1867–1919)

Sarah Breedlove was born on a Louisiana cotton plantation on December 23, 1867, two years before Annie Turnbo Malone. Her parents, Owen and Minerva, were recently freed slaves, probably squatting on land taken by the Union

Birthplace of Sarah Breedlove in Delta, Louisiana

Annie Turnbo Malone	Year	Madam C. J. Walker
	1867	Born Sarah Breedlove in Louisiana
Born Annie Minerva Turnbo in Metropolis, Illinois	1869	
Orphaned. Joins sister in Peoria, Illinois	?	Orphaned, joins sister in Louisiana, then Mississippi
	1881	Runs away and marries at fourteen
	1885	Birth of daughter Lelia
	1889	Husband dies; moves with daughter Lelia to St. Louis
	1890-1900?	Suffers hair ailments and baldness; works as laundress
Begins selling her hair products	1900	
Marries Nelson Pope, moves to St. Louis and opens a shop	1902	
Hires Sarah Breedlove	1904	Moves to Denver
	1905?	Starts rival business
	1906	Marries C. J. Walker
Divorces Nelson Pope	1907	
Moves Poro headquarters to Indianapolis, Indiana	1913	Starts Lelia College in Pittsburgh
Marries Aaron Malone	1914	Charles and Sarah divorce. Travels to South America.
Opens Poro College	1918	Moves business to Indianapolis, Indiana
	1919	Dies of kidney failure
Pays highest income tax in Missouri	1924	
Aaron and Annie divorce	1927	
Moves to Chicago	1930	
Loses company; stroke and death	1957	

Army from their former owner. The plantation also housed a refugee camp and the graves of 3,200 Union soldiers who had died of typhoid, dysentery, or malaria while occupying nearby Vicksburg, Mississippi.

Sarah began life working in the cotton fields, catching crawfish in the bayous, and attending fish-fries. A friend described her as "an ordinary person, an open-faced good gal." Like her friends, she wore her hair standing out from her head in twists wrapped in string. She learned her ABCs, probably at church, but little more.

Sarah's mother died, perhaps of cholera, when she was seven, and her father died the following year. The little girl went to live in Vicksburg with her married sister Louvenia. Sarah contributed the family income by working as a washerwoman. The work was hard, and Sarah's brother-in-law treated her harshly.

At the age of fourteen, Sarah escaped the household by marrying a man named Moses McWilliams. Then, at eighteen, Sarah gave birth to a daughter whom she named Lelia. Just two years later, Moses died in an accident. Sarah and her young daughter moved to St. Louis, Missouri, where two of Sarah's brothers had set up as barbers. There Sarah found work as a laundress. She earned only $1.50 a day, but it was enough to live on. Lelia was able to attend public school, and Sarah herself attended night school to learn reading, writing, and arithmetic. She also married a man named John Davis. Unfortunately, he turned out to be a slacker, a drinker, and a womanizer. The couple often lived apart, and in later years Sarah erased him from her family story.

During the 1890s, Sarah developed a scalp ailment, perhaps severe dandruff or psoriasis, commonly known as "tetter." Whatever the cause, she lost most of her hair. The loss devastated her. Even the Bible provided little comfort. I Corinthians read, "If a woman have long hair, it is a glory to her." Sarah tried everything to reverse her baldness, both commercial products and salves she made herself. Eventually, her scalp healed and her hair grew back, thick and beautiful.

Before the Civil War, there were already forty black newspapers in the United States. By 1900, most large cities, especially in the North, had black newspapers read by the rising black middle class. Here African Americans found out about job opportunities, sports, and charity events. They could read stories by activists and writers and learn about political movements.

Walker products

In later years, Sarah claimed that she had saved her hair through prayer. In a dream, she said, a big black man came to her and gave her a secret formula for healthy hair. The formula, Sarah claimed, contained ingredients that could be found only in Africa. The true cure may have been more prosaic: better hygiene and gentler hair products bought from Annie Turnbo.

In 1904, Sarah finally separated from John Davis. She was already dating a jovial and charming boaster named Charles Joseph Walker. Walker sold subscriptions and advertising for the local black press. He loved fancy suits and always shined his shoes. Somehow, he gave Sarah confidence.

Around 1903, Sarah became one of Annie Turnbo's first sales staff, selling hair care products in St. Louis. Here, at last, was her chance to rise in the world. After the 1904 World's Fair, Sarah decided to join her sister-in-law Lucy in Denver, Colorado, to work as a Poro sales agent there. She arrived in Denver with $1.50 in her pocket. To supplement her income, she took a job as a cook. Her employer may have been a local druggist.

Sarah's great-great-granddaughter A'Lelia Bundles relays the rumor that Sarah Breedlove asked her druggist employer to analyze Annie Turnbo Malone's products so she could make her own version. Sarah herself disputed this. She claimed that no commercial product, even Malone's, ever worked for her hair as well as her own creations did. She pointed to her own experiments with shampoos and salves, which she claimed healed her hair long before she ever met Malone. Later, she came up with the story of her African dream.

Whatever the source of her formula, Sarah soon left Annie Turnbo Malone's company to sell her own products. For a while, she continued working as a cook and laundress. She mixed her hair products in an old laundry tub. Most of her ingredients are unknown, but one of them may have been coconut oil.

Besides selling hair products door to door, Sarah gave free demonstrations in a beauty salon she set up in her Denver home. Charles Walker soon journeyed from St. Louis to join her, and the thirty-eight-year-old Sarah married him in January 1906. Charles helped Sarah develop a marketing strategy based on a strong product brand, newspaper advertising, and a mail-order business. Charles also convinced Sarah to start calling herself Madam C. J. Walker, which made her sound like a leading citizen. The name helped convey dignity in an age when many white people still addressed black women by only their first names.

The Walkers embraced the power of advertising. Sarah proudly placed her own picture, with long, wavy black hair, on the covers of her products, and she advertised widely in the black press. Testimonials and before and-after pictures helped tell her story. The mail-order business took off.

By 1907, Sarah was making $300 a month from her product sales. At that point, Denver began to seem too small. Although Charles was skeptical, Sarah was convinced she could grow her business. While a Walker agent ran the mail-order business from Louisville, Kentucky, Sarah and Charles traveled for eighteen months around the South to promote her whole line of products. As their train passed through villages too small for the train to stop, they tossed advertising brochures from the windows. In each town that did have a train station, they started by contacting the local church. Then Sarah lectured and gave demonstrations of the Walker Method, using special scalp ointments, frequent shampooing, hair pomade, and a heated comb. She enrolled new Walker agents and gave them brief training in the use of her products.

With the mail-order business growing rapidly, Walker returned from her tour and set up shop in Pittsburgh, which, unlike Denver, had sixteen rail lines. There she opened a hair salon and

Madam Walker's first five products were Madam Walker's Wonderful Hair Grower, Temple Salve, Tetter Salve, Vegetable Shampoo, and Glossine. These products aimed to treat dandruff or psoriasis (tetter), prevent baldness, and cleanse the hair and scalp. Although Madam Walker promoted use of a hot comb, she did not specifically advertise use of hair straighteners. *"Let me correct the erroneous impression held by some that I claim to straighten hair,"* she told a reporter many years later. *"... I have always held myself out as a hair culturist. I grow hair."*

Madam C. J. Walker
ca. 1915

gathered endorsements from leading black citizens. She opened a small "manufactory." Around 1909, several years before Annie Turnbo Malone did the same, she established a trade school, which she called the Lelia College of Beauty and Culture.

Although she was now doing well financially, Walker still struggled for acceptance in the black business community. In 1912, while attending a convention of the National Negro Business League, she could not get Booker T. Washington to give her a speaking role. Ignoring horrified looks, Madam Walker pushed her way to the podium and spoke anyway, with pride ringing from her voice: "I am a woman who came from the cotton fields of the South. From there, I was promoted to the washtub. From there, I was promoted to the cook kitchen. And from there, I promoted myself into the business of manufacturing hair goods and preparations. I have built my own factory on my own ground." The following year, Washington put her on the program.

In 1910, at the age of forty-three, Walker moved to Indianapolis and built a factory there. "I am endeavoring to provide employment for hundreds of women of my race," she explained at the factory opening. Annie Turnbo Malone had moved to Indianapolis the year before, and though Walker approached her, there is no evidence that Malone ever reconciled with her former employee.

Walker arranged for agents, all women, to buy her beauty products at a discount and then sell them within the community, much like Tupperware and other products today. The agents also promoted Walker's vision of cleanliness and beauty in African American communities. Indoor plumbing and hot

Madame C. J. Walker driving automoblie

water were scarce. Most people bathed no more than once a week and washed their hair maybe once a month. Walker agents encouraged women to shampoo more often and use sulfur-containing ointments for scalp ailments. (Sulfur is still an important ingredient in dandruff shampoos today.) Taking control of their hygiene in this way, Walker believed, would help women rise in the workplace and society.

Sarah's daughter, A'Lelia, ca. 1926

Walker treated her agents well. She organized clubs for them with shared funeral and sickness benefits, and she recognized them not only for sales but for their good works in the community. She even encouraged them to get involved in politics. At the end of one Walker Agents convention, the women sent a telegram to President Wilson urging him to make lynching a federal crime.

But like Annie Turnbo, Madam Walker struggled with a husband who wanted to take over her business. In 1913, Sarah and Charles divorced. That year, Sarah Walker took a long voyage promoting her business in Latin America and the Caribbean. To parade her elegance and success, she had one of her three automobiles shipped to South America with her. When she returned, she moved to a townhouse in Harlem in New York City. She continued to run the hair products business, but left its day-to-day management to her forewoman in Indianapolis.

By this time quite wealthy, Walker built a mansion on the banks of the Hudson River in New York. She also devoted herself to philanthropy. She supported the National Association for the Advancement of Colored People (NAACP) and the National Conference on Lynching. She paid for scholarships and care of the elderly. She made a major donation to the Indianapolis YMCA.

Madam C. J. Walker died on May 25, 1919, at age fifty-one, of kidney failure brought on by high blood pressure. She was at the height of her success. "Wealthiest Negress Dead," announced the

Sarah's daughter Lelia became an active figure in the Harlem Renaissance. She changed her name to the more artistic-sounding A'Lelia Walker and entertained African and European royalty and the president of Liberia. Artists and writers such as Langston Hughes and Zora Neale Hurston gathered around her for art exhibitions and poetry readings.

New York Times. At the time of her death, Walker's business was valued at more than a million dollars. Her personal fortune was more than $600,000. She left one-third of it to her daughter, Lelia, and the rest to charity.

Through inventiveness and grit, Sarah Breedlove, the daughter of slaves, rose out of poverty and hardship to become one of the first female self-made millionaires in the country. Self-educated, she created her own distinctive line of hair products and methods of hair care. She embraced the power of advertising, led a large company, and innovated with both a mail-order business and a method of selling to and through a large, well-trained staff. She built company loyalty through innovative methods of educating, empowering, celebrating, and rewarding her employees. As Madam C. J. Walker, Sarah Breedlove rose to a position of respect, wealth, and generosity, opening doors to those who followed.

The Poro Company and the Walker Company were not the only two companies selling hair care and hygiene products to African American customers in the early twentieth century. But they were by far the most successful. As rivals, the two women entrepreneurs spurred each other on, not only to create new products but to find new ways of training staff, marketing a brand, and presenting themselves to the community. In doing so, they demonstrated how competition can help a new industry grow. They also proved that the American economy could deliver wealth and social position to smart and determined breakers of barriers.

Walker's Villa Lewaro in Irvington, New York, was three stories high, had thirty rooms, and cost $250,000 to build. She filled it with an $8,000 organ, statues, tapestries, and paintings.

Villa Lewaro

"The primary idea in all of my work was to help the farmer and fill the poor man's empty dinner pail."

— George Washington Carver,
January 16, 1929

6. A Feeling for Plants

George Washington Carver

(c. 1862–1943)

M oses Carver heard them again: the hooves of galloping horses beating along the sod. The year was 1862 or 1863. Carver leaped from his chair and ran out to the cabin that housed his three slaves. A fiercely independent white Missouri farmer, Moses wasn't going to let Civil War raiders steal his property. In the darkened cabin, three figures huddled: a young woman named Mary, her toddler son, Jim, and a new baby, George. Moses grabbed Jim and carried him to the house. "He tried to get me, but he couldn't," George wrote later. By the time Moses rushed back for mother and baby, the raiders had snatched them away. Moses heard the kidnappers yelling in celebration as they galloped off.

Moses knew he had to act quickly. The bushwhackers (armed gangs) from both North and South who raided isolated Missouri farms during the Civil War were a brutal bunch. Not long ago, bandits had strung Moses up from his own rafters and lit coals under his feet to make him confess where his money was hidden. He never told them.

Besides farming, Moses raised racehorses. Now he hired a neighbor to go after the stolen mother and child. He offered a racehorse for their return. The neighbor, a man named John Bentley, tracked the celebrating raiders to Arkansas, where they intended to sell the slaves for a good price. One way or another, Bentley negotiated to get the baby back—but the mother, Mary, disappeared. Her son George never found out what happened to her, but as an adult he kept her old spinning wheel in his office.

Bentley wrapped the tiny George in a coat and strapped him to the saddle. When he arrived back at the Carver farm, the baby was dehydrated and racked with whooping cough. Moses and his wife brought George and his half-brother Jim—sons of different, unknown slave fathers—into their own house. There the couple cared for them. When slavery ended at the end of the Civil War, Moses and Sarah raised the newly free youngsters as their own boys—but boys who were expected to earn their keep. Small and sickly, George suffered permanent damage to his vocal cords from his bout with whooping cough. For the rest of his life, his voice was unexpectedly high and feminine.

Moses worked George and his brother hard. They cared for the farm animals; plowed, planted, and harvested; made soap and washed clothes and dishes; and gathered honey from wild bees. George also learned to sew, knit, and play a variety of musical instruments. His "mother" Sarah taught him to write his name. He loved to wander in the woods observing birds and mushrooms. He collected rocks, admiring their tiny crystals, and he transplanted every new flower he could find into a tiny garden of his own. He later explained that he felt a connection with all of nature, and he seemed to intuit what plants needed. Neighbors brought ailing plants for him to look at, and he suggested changes in watering or light to bring them back to health. He made drawings of flowers, finger-painting his pictures with dyes he made from leaves and berries.

More than anything, George wanted to learn. He was delighted to hear of a thing called Sunday School, and after attending for a while, he talked Moses into enrolling him in the local elementary school. But other students' parents objected to having "darkies" in the classroom, so the boys were told they would have to go to the "colored school" in Neosho, eight miles away as the crow flew.

Moses wasn't going to drive his boys back and forth, so they prepared to leave home for the season. George wrapped his belongings, including a few favorite stones, in a bandanna and walked cross-country to the school. He stayed with the Watkinses, a mixed-race couple whom he called Aunt Mariah and Uncle Andy. George paid for his room and board by helping Andy in his blacksmith shop. Thus began his long school career of working at anything that offered itself in exchange for the chance to study. George grew very fond of his new surrogate parents, and all his life he kept the Bible Aunt Mariah had given him. His brother Jim, on the other hand, soon tired of school life and returned to the Carvers' farm.

George stayed for about three years in the one-room Neosha school. But once he reached thirteen, he decided to move on. Before he left for Fort Scott in Kansas, he and Uncle Andy each made a will leaving the other all his worldly possessions.

In Fort Scott, George found work by fibbing to a housewife that he was a great cook. Luckily, he learned quickly on the job. He took on another job helping a blacksmith take care of his invalid wife. Whenever he saved up enough money, he bought supplies and attended school. Once he had to drop out because a gang of white boys beat him up and stole his schoolbooks. Then, in March 1879, when he was about seventeen, a more serious incident badly frightened him. From the doorway of his employer's house, George saw a black man being lynched. The raucous crowd dragged the man by a rope around his neck, dashed his brains out on the paving stones, then hanged him anyway and burned his body. Shaken, George fled town that very night. The images and the remembered

Liatris spicata,
a prairie wildflower

smell of burning flesh lingered to haunt him all his life. In his seventies, he wrote, "As young as I was, the horror haunted me and does even now."

Once again George drifted, finding work where he could, often for only two or three weeks at a time. While most other young men either stayed on the farm or found jobs as laborers in the cities, George kept wandering. Afterward, he claimed that he hardly remembered his path in those years. Sometime in his years of drifting, he added "Washington" as his middle name. He did laundry, worked in sawmills, cleaned stables, or filled in as a field hand. He bought and learned to play an old accordion. When he could, he attended school, gradually working his way through the grades. Around 1880, another couple befriended him. He moved with them to Minneapolis, Kansas, where he attended high school, helped his new "aunt" in her laundry, acted in school theatricals, and played music. He paid his own way. At age nineteen, he visited the Carver farm to see his brother, Jim, shortly before Jim died of smallpox.

At age twenty-two, having finished high school, George tried something new to improve his prospects. He taught his white friend Chester Rarick to play organ in return for lessons in typing and stenography, or how to take notes in shorthand. At the same time, he collected letters of recommendation and applied to Highland College, a Presbyterian college he had heard of in northern Kansas. To his delight, the college accepted him. Dressed in his finest clothes, George showed up on campus and presented himself to the principal, as the heads of small colleges were called in those days. The principal looked back and forth between George and the acceptance letter and finally blurted, "But we only accept Indians here, not Negroes. You didn't tell me you were a Negro."

Devastated, penniless, George set up doing laundry in the college town. But he wanted more. Soon he became a homesteader by claiming 160 acres near a friend's holdings in western Kansas.

He built a sod house, dug a well (which never reached water), and planted fruit and forest trees, corn, and a good vegetable garden. While he waited for his own crops to grow, he hired himself out to a wealthier neighbor, George Steeley. That first winter, the temperatures dropped to 68 degrees below zero. Cows dropped dead in the barns, and so did people who stayed out too long. And when summer came, Kansas was caught in drought, so the crops hardly grew.

After two dispiriting years, George Washington Carver sold out and moved again, this time to Iowa. He found a job as head cook in a fancy hotel. Singing in the church choir, he met a wealthy white woman, Mrs. Milholland, who invited him to visit her home. She gave him singing lessons in exchange for art lessons. She also encouraged him to apply once again to college, this time to a Methodist art school named Simpson College in Indianola. Allowing himself to hope again, Carver, now in his late twenties, managed to save up enough money for his first term.

At Simpson, George Washington Carver finally found welcome. The only African American in the college, he attended art classes in airy studios surrounded by young women who liked him. He moved into an unheated shed on campus and did laundry for other students and townspeople. Soon his classmates began to leave anonymous gifts of money or theater tickets, and they even chipped in to buy him furniture. Carver beautified his shed by making it a greenhouse full of flowers. Meanwhile, he studied geometry, voice, and piano. He played on the baseball team and joined literary clubs.

Toward the end of his two-year course of study, Carver's art teacher, Etta May Budd, drew him aside. It was unlikely, she told him, that a black artist would be able to make a living. Why not pursue botany

The Homestead Act of 1862 was designed to encourage pioneers to settle the Midwest. It offered 160 acres of land to anyone who paid a small filing fee and farmed the land for five years.

Carver as artist

instead? The Iowa State College of Agriculture and Mechanic Arts in Ames had a national reputation.

George struggled with the idea of giving up his art, but his religious beliefs gave him a nudge. In agriculture, he decided, he could help his people more than in art. In 1890, he entered Iowa State College as its first black student. Once again, he was penniless, and other Iowa State students did not welcome him at first. Luckily, Professor James Wilson, later the US Secretary of Agriculture, let Carver lodge in his spare office. As usual, Carver worked at whatever offered itself, cutting wood, cleaning barns, and soon taking care of all the flower beds on campus. Through his church attendance, he began to make friends. He joined all seven of the college's literary societies and became the unofficial decorator for most student events. He gave members of the football team sideline massages. He played music, sang, and even did stand-up comedy. His friends persuaded him to enter some of his paintings in the 1893 Chicago World's Fair, and the judges picked four of them to exhibit. Carver's friends even bought him a suit so he would feel obliged to attend. He wore that same suit, always with a fresh flower in the lapel, on dressy occasions for the rest of his life.

Stink horn fungi in
Spanish Fort, AL

In 1894, Carver finally received his bachelor's degree. Immediately, he began a master's program. Specializing in mycology, the study of fungi, he gathered 20,000 fungus specimens. He accompanied his professors on lecture tours and became recognized as a fungal expert. Iowa State asked him to stay on after graduation at their "experiment station" to do government-sponsored research at a good salary. But by that time, the famous educator Booker T. Washington had resolved to lure the young botanist away. In 1896, Washington, the legendary founder of Alabama's Tuskegee Institute, urged Carver to help uplift his people by heading the agricultural department at the institute. Washington offered an annual salary of $1,000 plus room and board. When the two men met, Washington expressed his vision with such idealism and charisma that Carver had to say yes. Iowa State was sorry to see him go; his friends and professors gave him a fine microscope as a going-away gift.

George Washington Carver spent the rest of his life—forty-seven years—at the Tuskegee Institute. His tenure there was not always smooth. Built on 2,000 acres of agricultural land, the institute was more of a trade school than a college. Students often entered with only a shaky, elementary school education. They worked all over campus, constantly being reassigned from one department to another. Few of them stayed long enough to graduate. The laboratory Carver had been promised turned out to be a storeroom with one lamp as its only equipment. His pleas for laboratory supplies went unanswered. Washington loaded him with administrative duties. He asked Carver to turn a profit from the school's farms, which never happened, and expected him to carry out research and teach five different classes. Carver even served as the school's veterinarian.

Booker T. Washington

Moreover, the bulk of Carver's fellow faculty resented him, at least at first. To them, his advanced degree from a white institution and his interest in art and literature meant he was a snob. Worse, he was darker-skinned than any of them. Many of the faculty had absorbed the belief that intelligence came with added doses of white ancestry. As a result, they suspected the very black Carver to be an intellectual fraud. At an early faculty meeting, three of them tried to trip him up by presenting him with obscure plants and challenging him to identify them. Carver correctly named them all.

Despite his disappointments, Carver set to work with all his heart. Soon he had seventy-six students enrolled in his agricultural department. His students loved his gentle manner and the

The Tuskegee Institute opened its doors on July 4, 1881. At first, its founders intended it to be a training institute for "colored" teachers. But Booker T. Washington proclaimed that it should deliver vocational skills, morals, and religious principles. Academic subjects were less important. Students paid most of their tuition through work on the Institute grounds.

Sharecropper women and children

Both sharecroppers and tenant farmers worked land owned by whites. Tenant farmers owned their own equipment and paid heavy rents. They were better off than sharecroppers, who owned only their labor. Sharecroppers borrowed tools and draft animals from the owner and were generally allowed to keep only one-third of the crop they raised.

Boys picking cotton, 1935

way he treated them all as equals. In research, he set up a collaboration with the Alabama Polytechnic Institute. He identified a thousand species of fungi in the state, sixty of them brand-new. He collected native grasses for the US Department of Agriculture and medicinal plants for the Smithsonian Institution.

Carver's greatest coup was establishing a federally funded "agricultural experiment station" at Tuskegee in 1897. For a black college to win such an honor was unheard of. It came about because of Carver's reputation—and the fact that his old Iowa State mentor, James Wilson, was now US Secretary of Agriculture. Each year, the Alabama state legislature sent ten times more money to the white experiment station at Alabama Polytechnic than it did to the Tuskegee station. Still, Carver made the most of the $1,500 his station received. He launched studies of soils, fertilizers, and planting times.

Carver's work was motivated by his desire to help poor black farmers. Most African American farmers were sharecroppers or tenant farmers. All of them were trying to maximize the growth of the one cash crop they knew, cotton. But cotton growing had depleted the soil, and yields were falling. Poor farmers fell deeper and deeper into debt.

George Washington Carver was determined to show that by diversifying and rotating crops—planting different crops in different years—farmers could improve the soil and feed themselves. Carver urged them to plant sweet potatoes and legumes (beans, peas, and peanuts) to build up nitrogen in the soil. To help convince the farmers, he devised recipes and new uses for crops, especially peanuts and sweet potatoes.

On Fridays, Carver packed up a wagon and, sometimes with students in tow, drove into the countryside to talk to farmers. He taught them to make whitewash out of clay and handicrafts out of corn shucks and straw. He begged the farmers to grow their own food crops and stay out of debt to the local store. Often, he stayed with local people and spoke again at church on Sunday. In 1906, a donor named Morris K. Jesup provided him with a wagon that could carry and display products.

Motorized Jesup wagon

The Jesup Wagon became a traveling encyclopedia of knowledge useful to farming families.

Building on the trust and interest he created with his wagon trips, Carver established a Farmer's Institute back at Tuskegee. Each session began with a short lesson on raising poultry or rotating crops. Then farmers showed off their best vegetables, and committees reported on special projects such as women growing rutabagas to pay for summer school.

The Tuskegee experiment station also issued "bulletins," practical pamphlets Carver wrote to be helpful to farmers. He wrote on feeding acorns to pigs, on composting, increasing crop yields, dairying, raising poultry, preserving vegetables and 104 ways to use tomatoes. Carver wrote forty-four bulletins in all. Getting money for printing was always a struggle, but farmers as far away as South Africa read the bulletins eagerly.

Carver worked incessantly. Early in the morning, he got up to go collecting. All his life, while working or collecting, he talked to plants, stones, birds—reflections, he felt, of the

Tuskegee class in farm management, 1940

Creator. He taught classes, oversaw young men in the dormitory, served on faculty committees, and played the piano at church. He lent money to whoever needed it and wrote up to thirty letters a day, mostly to former students or colleagues. He did kitchen chemistry in his woeful laboratory and set out larger studies in the experiment station. When he had time, he painted, most often closely observed portraits of plants. Like all the Tuskegee faculty, he attended chapel every day. He even wrote a regular column, "Professor Carver's Advice," in the *Columbia University Review*.

Although he loved his students and his research, Carver found his position at Tuskegee more and more difficult. Washington ruled his college like a medieval lord or religious leader. All decisions were his, and he paid more attention to appearances—raising money from rich northerners to build more buildings—than he did to sanitation or a strong academic curriculum. For example, the school physician wrote more than once complaining about the unhealthy state of overflowing latrines, with no effect. Washington

Carver seated at center, ca. 1902

valued Carver's reputation, but wanted the always frail, kindly scientist to make money on the farm. When he didn't, Washington hired a self-promoting young man named George Bridgeforth to fix the problem—primarily to build up the school's poultry farm, which never turned a profit. Still, for years, Washington kept increasing Bridgeforth's authority and perks. George Washington Carver offered many times to resign his post, but either James Wilson or Booker T. Washington himself talked him into staying to serve the people. Besides, Tuskegee was Carver's family—the students his children, the other faculty his arguing siblings. Carver admired Booker T. Washington and wanted his approval.

During the difficult first decade of the twentieth century, as Carver reached his forties, he never openly expressed anger. By nature mild, humble, and forgiving, he renewed himself in his morning collecting trips, in playing music at church, or in his stolen hours painting. His love of color led him to a new bout of inventing. He developed paints and stains from Alabama clays. First came whitewash, then twenty-seven colored washes, then more durable paints. The Episcopal congregation in town used his paints to refurbish their church at a fifth the usual cost. But Tuskegee routinely denied Carver the equipment he needed to test, purify, and market his new products. Booker T. Washington considered Carver's paints a hobby that interfered with his real work.

Tall, thin, courteous, with a wide, pointed mustache, Carver stayed single. When he was thirty-seven, he courted a thirty-one-year-old Tuskegee English teacher named Sarah Hunt. Sarah and her sister, Adella, were outspoken supporters of woman suffrage. They loved to discuss politics, literature, and music. With them, Carver could be himself, funny or philosophical.

Hunt and Carver dated for six years, but despite their affection, they never married. Though devoted to her people, Sarah was light-skinned enough to pass for white. Segregation in the South was growing fiercer, and both teachers had witnessed how dangerous

Boll weevil
(Anthonomus grandis)

Flower of a sweet potato plant

Freshly dug sweet potato

it could be for a black man and "white" woman to be seen together. Once, a white female Yankee visitor to Tuskegee decided to ride up front next to the black driver of the wagon sent to fetch her from the station. After she dismounted at her hotel, angry white townspeople swarmed the wagon. The driver and Carver, who had ridden in back, jumped from the wagon and fled. Through that night, Carver hid in the fields, trembling. The horror of the lynching he had witnessed as a teenager came back to him. Not long after this incident, Sarah Hunt left Tuskegee for a settlement house in New Jersey.

Work and research sustained Carver. At a time when the average black farmer cultivated twenty-six acres, Carver demonstrated that just six acres, rotated among corn, cotton, fodder, and food, could grow enough to support a family. He fought the boll weevil, a beetle destroying the cotton crop. Though never fully successful, he developed a poison that had some effect as a deterrent, along with a beetle-resistant strain of cotton.

During World War I, now in his fifties, Carver learned how to extract a rubber-like substance from sweet potato, along with several kinds of glue. He figured out how to use mica, the shiny, translucent, flaky stone, in making spark plugs. But mostly, he searched for plants that were especially nutritious. He championed cowpeas (also known as black-eyed peas), sweet potatoes, soybeans, tomatoes, pecans, and peanuts. The US government asked his advice on creating sweet potato flour. He continued to build his list of uses for the lowly peanut. Missionaries in Africa hailed his recipe for peanut milk as a lifesaver for undernourished children.

In 1915, Tuskegee's founder, Booker T. Washington, died of heart failure. Despite their conflicts over the years, Carver sincerely mourned the loss of this demanding and inspiring father figure. But with the new principal, Robert R. Moton, Carver's position at Tuskegee became more pleasant. For the first time, he got a raise. Moton also eased him of some administrative duties.

By this time, Carver was widely recognized as Tuskegee's most prominent professor. In 1920, a group of peanut planters called him to Montgomery to consult. Wrestling heavy suitcases full of his samples, wearing his one patched suit, he had great difficulty getting the doorman to allow him, a "colored" man, into the convention hotel. But the white farmers were impressed with what he had to say. They called him "Doctor" and asked him to testify before Congress in Washington, DC.

In the capital, at the end of a long day of tedious hearings, the House Ways and Means Committee members smirked to see the tall, skinny, scruffy Carver struggle to set up his exhibits. But as he presented his peanut milk, flour, cakes, breakfast cereal, livestock food, instant coffee, hair pomade, and massage oil, they sat forward in their seats. Again and again, they extended his time. At the end of his testimony, the committee applauded long and loudly. In the following weeks, the Ways and Means Committee inserted a steep tariff for peanuts into the bill they were writing. American peanut farmers would be protected.

Newspapers reported widely on Carver's Congressional testimony. Soon George was in demand as a speaker everywhere. In 1921 and 1922, now sixty, he took his peanut exhibit on the road to fairs and conventions.

Even today, George Washington Carver is associated with peanuts in the popular imagination. Most people think he invented peanut butter—but in fact that product was already known. Carver's peanut products covered far more ground: axle grease, paper, shoe blacking, laundry soap, peanut "meat" loaf, peanut punch, and more.

Peanut field, Pelham

Usually, he addressed a mostly white audience. He sat in "colored only" waiting rooms, rode in the "colored only" carriage of the train, and stayed with black families. He understood how important it was for him to represent Tuskegee and, even more, to represent his race. At the same time, he claimed that it amused him to surprise his listeners. Wearing his threadbare suit and carrying his battered suitcases, he gave the impression of being poor, down-and-out, maybe a vagrant. Then he spoke with scholarly grace in his high voice, shattering people's first impressions.

Throughout the 1920s, Carver continued his research. He was especially proud of an organic, high-pH product called Mellosoil he designed to correct the acidity of the Alabama soil. As usual, he freely gave away the recipe to anyone who asked. He said, "It's not enough that you climb the mountain. You have to throw the rope over and pull someone else over the mountain."

Harvest of peanuts

During the 1920s, Carver became even more religious. He spoke at religious gatherings, seeking to inspire young people, both black and white. He became consumed by an overwhelming, unrequited love for a young YMCA leader named Jim Hardwick. Carver assured both Hardwick and himself that his love was purely spiritual, but his letters reveal that he still suffered immensely as Hardwick gradually drew away from him. But then Carver found himself caught up in another great cause—polio.

In the 1920s, George Washington Carver had begun suggesting the use of peanut oil as a skin treatment for wrinkles. Gradually, he began using it also in massages for people who came to him complaining of weakness or stiffness. By the early 1930s, some of the "patients" who arrived at Tuskegee were polio sufferers. Carver gave them a series of massage treatments before sending them home with detailed instructions and a supply of oil.

For some patients, the results appeared miraculous. A little boy who had to be carried into the room got up and walked across the floor after a month of treatments. A man who came to Carver on crutches was soon walking six to eight miles unassisted.

In the 1930s, the United States was trying to find its way through a period of panic about polio. Alabama alone had thousands of children crippled by infantile paralysis, and most of these children's parents were too poor to pay for medical treatment. As news leaked out about Dr. Carver's miraculous massages, families flowed to Tuskegee. Other doctors took notice and began writing about remarkable improvements using peanut oil massage with their own polio patients. Carver himself was careful not to make unsupported medical claims. "It has been given out that I have a cure," he said. "I have not, but it looks hopeful." He begged the administrators of the Tuskegee Hospital to set up clinical trials to investigate his treatments, but the American Medical Association withheld its approval, and the hospital declined Carver's request. In time, the furor over the peanut oil treatment subsided. Many patients improved to a point—better flexibility, smoother skin, some increase in muscle size—but there were no clear-cut cures.

During the last ten years of his life, until his death on January 5, 1943, at the age of eighty-one, George Washington Carver worked as much as his health allowed. He often traveled to lecture: as the Tuskegee Institute's most famous professor, he knew how important he was to fund-raising efforts. But travel came at a cost. Carver's lungs had always been weak. Often, after a trip, he would be bedridden for weeks or months with some combination of bronchitis and pneumonia.

In his last great project, Carver saved up money to start a museum. He wanted it to display native plants and the wide variety of products made from them—fibers, paints, building materials, cosmetics, and foods. In 1940, the Carver Museum, largely financed by the automobile industrialist Henry Ford, opened in an old laundry

"It is not the style of clothes one wears, neither the kind of automobile one drives, nor the amount of money one has in the bank account that counts. These mean nothing. It is simply service that measures success."

— George Washington Carver, "Professor Carver's Advice," newspaper column (between 1923 and 1933).

room of the Tuskegee Institute. A separate room housed Carver's artwork, including crochet, needlework, beads, and embroidery along with his paintings. Unfortunately, the art collection was almost entirely destroyed in a fire in 1947, four years after Carver's quiet death in the Tuskegee hospital.

George Washington Carver holds a unique place as an American inventor and artist. He developed hundreds of products, although none of them became commercially successful. Carver didn't care about commercial success: he gave away all the ideas he could. He used the education he had struggled so mightily to attain to improve the hard lot of his people. Through his teaching, he strived to make the grinding, unprofitable labor of poor farmers a little easier to bear. For sharecroppers who could now put more nutritious food on the table, he made a difference. With a decent, well-stocked laboratory and the five assistants, Booker T. Washington originally promised him, he could undoubtedly have achieved much more. But whatever else, George Washington Carver showed that a black man could astonish with his creativity and could navigate with dignity and wisdom among people of all races and backgrounds. Carver's example moved people, inspiring them to expect more of themselves and always to treat others with kindness and respect.

Front of the George Washington Carver Museum in Tuskegee, Alabama

"Food is the moral right of all who are born into this world."

— Norman Borlaug, Nobel lecture, December 11, 1970

7. Feeding the World

Norman Borlaug
(1914–2009)

In 1968, a book called *The Population Bomb* made a dire prediction. Because of worldwide population growth, said the authors, hundreds of millions of people were doomed to starve to death in the coming decade. The book, written by Paul and Anne Ehrlich,* became a best-seller. But it was wrong. One of the reasons the Ehrlichs' prediction never came to pass was the stubborn dedication of an Iowa farmer named Norman Borlaug.

Norman was born on his grandparents' farm in the village of Saude, Iowa, on March 25, 1914. At the age of five, he began walking a mile and a half to school to attend classes in a one-room schoolhouse. From the age of seven, he spent the rest of his time working on the farm, feeding the cows and chickens and cleaning up after them. As the oldest of four children, he had plenty to do.

When Norman finished eighth grade, his teacher, who was also his cousin, urged him to go on to Cresco High School, fourteen miles away. His grandfather also encouraged him. "Fill your head now if you want to fill your belly later on," he told his grandson. So Norman, even though he wasn't the greatest student, went to high school. He played football as a small, 145-pound guard.

---

* Anne was a co-author of the book but was not credited.

Borlaug as a
young wrestler

Sculpture of a food line during the Depression

The stock market crash of 1929 set off a worldwide financial crisis. Banks failed; people across America lost their savings and often their jobs. By 1933, one in four Americans was unemployed.

Cresco High School's wrestling coach, David Bartelma, had competed in the Olympics. He pulled Norman into the sport. Wrestling built Norman's toughness and determination. "Give the best that God gave you," Bartelma said. "If you don't do that, don't bother to compete." In his senior year, Norman placed third in the state in his weight class.

In school, Norman's vocational agriculture teacher challenged his belief that Iowa soil was the best in the world. In an experimental plot on the edge of town, Norman and his classmates planted corn in one untreated plot and in several others that they treated with varying proportions of potassium, nitrogen, and phosphorus. Some of the treated plots yielded twice as much corn as the "natural" one. Norman was impressed.

The stock market crashed while Norman was still in high school, and the Great Depression began. By the time Norman graduated in 1932, jobs were scarce. Norman had decided he wanted to go to college, but to do that he had to earn some money. He trapped mink and muskrats, cut fence posts, and hired himself out to farmers for fifty cents a day. By the end of a year, he had saved $50, enough for a year's tuition. His friend George Champlin convinced him to come along on a road trip to try out for the University of Minnesota football team.

Full of hope, Norman set off for Minnesota, but immediately he ran into two obstacles. First, he learned that he was too small for the football team. Second, he failed the university entrance exam. Instead of letting him study toward a four-year degree, the university shuttled him aside into its General College, where he could get only a two-year degree.

Humiliated by his low placement, Norman resolved to work at his studies as he had never worked before. At the same time, to support himself, he took a job at a local coffee shop, where his pay was three meals a day. There he met his future wife, Margaret Gibson, who was studying to become a teacher.

By the end of one semester, Norman had impressed his professors enough that they allowed him to transfer into the College of Agriculture for a full four-year course in forestry. But money was still terribly short. In 1935, unable to afford college tuition any longer, Margaret dropped out and got a job as a proofreader. The couple decided they would marry as soon as they saved enough money.

A CCC Poster, 1935

As a sophomore, Norman almost died of a streptococcal infection. That year, too, he found himself in downtown Minneapolis, caught in the middle of a riot for food and jobs. The desperation of the men shouting, pushing, and punching around him struck him deeply. The next summer and fall, Norman found work in a Massachusetts forest with the Civilian Conservation Corps, leading teams of unemployed men. Before getting the job, some of the men had been starving. Borlaug later said, "I saw how food changed them.... All of this left scars on me."

After his junior year, Borlaug worked in Idaho's National Forest. With a horse, three pack mules, and a mule skinner, he traveled deep into the wilderness, where he spent six-week stints alone, watching for fires. The Forest Service told him he could have a full-time job as an assistant ranger when he graduated.

With their future seemingly secure, Norman and Margaret got married. Then, just before Christmas in Norman's senior year, he learned that federal budget cuts meant his promised job no longer existed. His settled future had evaporated.

Part of President Franklin Delano Roosevelt's New Deal, the Civilian Conservation Corps (CCC) operated from 1933 to 1941. It set young, unemployed, single men to work on conservation and building projects in rural areas. CCC teams built bridges and trails, planted trees and constructed lodges. In return, the men received shelter, food, clothes, and $30 a month.

Wheat stem rust disease

At this vulnerable moment, Norman attended a lecture on rust diseases in wheat. The lecturer was Elvin Charles Stakman, head of the University of Minnesota's plant pathology department. Rust is a parasitic fungus that feeds off crops; it is hard to fight, because, like the common cold, it exists in many forms and constantly evolves. "Rust diseases are the relentless, voracious destroyers of man's food," Stakman lectured. Even worse, a rapidly growing world population meant that more people than ever were in danger of starvation. Scientific advances in agriculture were the only hope for these people. Stakman told his students that science "will make its mistakes, but it will take us further than has ever been possible to eradicate hunger and starvation from this earth."

The lecture struck home. Someday, Norman told Margaret, he'd like to study under that man. Do it, Margaret told him. They would figure out how to get by on the money she earned from proofreading. The next day, Norman went to see Stakman. At first, he got a job counting fungal spores under the microscope, but soon he was studying for a PhD in plant diseases. Before Norman even finished his thesis, Stakman helped him get a job with DuPont Chemical in Wilmington, Delaware, for what to Norman seemed like the enormous sum of $2,800 a year.

Soon after Norman Borlaug started his new job, the Japanese bombed Pearl Harbor, and the United States entered World War II. Borlaug's work was considered too valuable to the war effort for him to enlist. The DuPont team developed glue that would not dissolve in saltwater, so crates of food and supplies could be floated ashore to soldiers fighting on Pacific islands. DuPont also developed camouflage paint and chemicals to purify water. To protect troops against malaria, they manufactured large amounts of the insecticide DDT.

But even before the war ended, Borlaug was recruited to join a food project in Mexico. The project, funded by the Rockefeller Foundation in cooperation with the Mexican government, focused on improving the production of maize (corn) and wheat. Borlaug was assigned to wheat. He left his pregnant wife and their one-year-old daughter, Jeanie, at home and flew to Mexico City. With a colleague, he toured rural areas of Mexico. While traveling, he suffered from dysentery and nausea. Far more serious were the poverty and hopelessness he observed among the local farmers.

At the time, Mexico was not growing enough grain to feed itself. Rust had ruined wheat crops from 1939 to 1941. Although three-fourths of Mexicans were farmers, their status was low, and farming methods had hardly changed for centuries. Irrigation was spotty. Most farmers tilled the land with muscle power, human or animal. They harvested their crops with a hand sickle. Hardly anyone used fertilizer of any kind, so the soil had not been replenished for thousands of years. Mostly illiterate and suspicious of outsiders, the farmers resisted change.

Field of wheat in Mexico

In the midst of these difficult beginnings, Margaret telephoned to say that their second baby had been born—a son. But the little boy had spina bifida, an open spinal cord that in those days meant he couldn't survive. "This knowledge was almost impossible to bear," Borlaug wrote later. "It emptied my mind of everything else." Borlaug flew home to see his son, Scotty, one time. It must have been heartbreaking. Scotty was too fragile to come home, and there was no room to stay with a sick child. Scotty's parents had to leave him in the hospital.

Borlaug considered trying to get a job locally, so he could continue to visit his son. But Margaret told him that although Scotty had no future, he did; he should return to Mexico. So Norman made funeral arrangements and returned to Mexico. Scotty died shortly thereafter; within months, Borlaug's wife and daughter were able to join him. Four years later, the Borlaugs had a healthy son named Bill, born in Mexico City.

Crossing wheat

Norman's determination to feed the hungry kept him going. The research station he was assigned to in Chapingo, outside Mexico City, had broken-down buildings, a few hand-planted fields, and no equipment. So Borlaug went to a junkyard, where with the help of two Mexican mechanics, he salvaged parts from three machines to make one working tractor. He gathered hundreds of strains of wheat from across Mexico and the world. Among them, he identified thirty with some resistance to rust. These he crossed with the hardiest local strains he could find.

How to Cross Wheat

With tweezers, carefully remove the stamens from a tiny wheat flower. Substitute stamens from a different wheat variety. Repeat down a whole row of wheat. Each new wheat plant will mix traits from the two parent plants in a slightly different way. Separate the progeny and either let each one propagate into a new pure line, or else continue to switch in new stamens to add new traits.

Painstakingly, Borlaug checked the new hybrids for nutritional value and resistance to disease. It was slow work. Each time Borlaug decided to make a new cross, he had to wait a year for a new growing season. Frustrated by the crawling pace of his studies, he had an idea. What if he grew one crop in the highlands and another, six months later, in the lowlands, which had its own growing season?

His boss said no. "Everyone" knew seeds needed to rest before replanting. Six months would not be rest enough. Not only that, the same strain of wheat would not grow in two such different environments. In a fit of temper, Borlaug quit his job. Luckily, his old professor, Stakman, visited the project that week and convinced Borlaug's boss to give the idea a chance. Borlaug took back his resignation and accelerated his work.

With the help of his colleague Joe Rupert and a talented Mexican assistant named Ignacio Narvaez, Borlaug established two research fields 700 miles apart. One was at sea level, in the irrigated Yaqui Valley in the state of Sonora. The other was in dry, mountainous terrain near Mexico City, at 8,500 feet of elevation. Shuttling back and forth between the fields, Borlaug began to cultivate two crops a year. In Sonora, the three men slept in a rat-infested barn and used a borrowed tractor. But their rate of research progress doubled. The project made 6,000 different wheat crosses in ten years. In both sites, Borlaug began to hire local "bird boys" to chase away the birds eating the wheat. He encouraged the boys to learn all they could and continue their education. Some of the boys went on to become his most skilled technicians. One received a PhD at the University of Minnesota.

Many pure-line wheat strains have disease resistance genes to fight one kind of the dread fungal disease, rust. But rust rapidly evolves new modes of attack. What was needed, Borlaug realized, was wheat that could resist more than one form of the disease. He tackled the problem in two ways. First, he created multiline varieties. That is,

Borlaug in the field teaching a group of young trainees

he planted different strains of wheat mixed together in one field. Some individual plants would be resistant to one kind of rust; others would be resistant to another. This diversity meant no single rust infestation could wipe out a whole crop.

Second, Borlaug back-crossed varieties, crossing wheat plants resistant to one kind of rust with pollen resistant to another kind. He did this with each new generation, crowding as many disease resistance genes as he could into super-resistant varieties.

Finally, Borlaug used nitrogen-based fertilizer to make the wheat grow faster. Unfortunately, tall, thin varieties of wheat grew so fast that the heavy seed heads made the plants collapse. To solve this problem, Borlaug experimented with dwarf varieties—short, stubby wheat plants that had the strength to hold multiple heads of grain.

At one point, Borlaug's supervisors complained that he wasn't writing enough research papers. According to Ronald Phillips, Borlaug retorted, "What do you want? Paper or wheat?" Borlaug admitted later to his biographer Lennard Bickel, "I like to see action. I don't know how to deal with paperwork. Neglect of paper is my worst habit." What Borlaug loved was farming. He savored the feeling of fertile soil underfoot or running through his hands. His wheat yields were rising, but his tendency to ignore budgets and avoid writing reports almost led his boss to fire him several times.

"When wheat is ripening properly, when the wind is blowing across the field, you can hear the beards of the wheat rubbing together. They sound like the pine needles in a forest. It is a sweet, whispering music that once you hear, you never forget."

— Norman Borlaug to his biographer Lennard Bickel

The work proceeded slowly. Dwarf wheat tended to be vulnerable to disease and to yield bad-tasting flour. Borlaug crossed it with delicious bread wheat from the Midwest and with other disease-resistant wheats. The final effects were amazing. In 1956, Mexico grew enough wheat to feed itself for the first time. By 1963, less than twenty years after Borlaug began his work in Mexico, wheat yields had increased by a factor of five or six. Even with a rising population, Mexico would be able to thrive.

In his spare time, Borlaug pursued a childhood love, baseball. He wanted to bring Little League to Mexico. With his colleague John Niederhauser, he formed the first Mexican league in Mexico City, partly so he could coach his own son. The two men got local companies to sponsor boys from impoverished areas to join the league. In 1957, a Mexican team from Monterrey became the first non-US team to win the Little League World Series.

As Mexican wheat yields shot upward, other countries began to take notice. In 1960, Borlaug joined a United Nations team sent to survey wheat and barley research in fourteen countries of North Africa, the Middle East, and South Asia. He found that some countries, such as Libya and Tunisia, already had thriving research fields planted with his wheat strains. But the scientists were unwilling to act to spread the strains. They feared getting blamed if the crops failed. By the time the UN group returned to Rome to discuss their findings, Borlaug was suffering from a rare sense of helpless depression. He later wrote:

> *For several days I was gripped by mental paralysis.... Half of humanity was going to bed hungry. Their governments gave agriculture low priority. The senior scientists were so ineffectual they ignored the obvious answers before their eyes.... Then... images of Mexico's keen young students and technicians came to mind. Their enthusiasm had enlivened farmers, scientists and even politicians. All those had taken heart, and Mexico was being transformed.*

Borlaug came up with an idea: The United Nations and Rockefeller Foundation should send young scientists to study with his team in the wheat fields of Mexico for one year. There he would train them in what he called "the new aggressive approach to modern agronomy."

In 1961, the first cohort of young men arrived in Mexico from Afghanistan, Egypt, Libya, Iran, Iraq, Pakistan, Syria, Turkey, and Argentina. The very first morning, the forty-seven-year-old Borlaug led them out

Pieter Bruegel , *The Harvesters, 1565*

to the fields. For many of the new recruits, it was their first time doing manual labor. They learned planting, breeding, and research, and they became the first class of Borlaug's "wheat apostles," dedicated to feeding their home countries and the world.

In 1963, the Rockefeller Foundation sent Borlaug to speak in India. Although hunger was widespread in both India and Pakistan, the bureaucracy moved slowly, and it took two years before Borlaug could arrange to send 450 tons of his Mexican seed to South Asia. Problems dogged the program from the start. The seeds had to be driven by truck from Mexico to Los Angeles, where the Watts riots created a delay. Banks rejected payments from the Pakistani government because of a few small errors on official forms. Then, while the seed was on board ship, war broke out between India and Pakistan.

Field of wheat in Pakistan

Still, Borlaug and his team planted a half-ton wheat in Pakistan, often with the sound of explosions in the distance. Disastrously, the seed germinated at only half the usual rate—it had been fumigated too heavily in the warehouses in Mexico. Plant twice as many seeds as usual, Borlaug told his team, and triple the amount of fertilizer.

When harvest time arrived, farmers could hardly believe their eyes. Nobody in South Asia had seen such high yields before. All at once, the governments hurried to import tens of thousands of tons of Mexican seeds. Turkey joined the party, importing 21,000 tons of seed in 1967. In 1968, the US Agency for International Development began to call Norman Borlaug's innovations the "Green Revolution." At one point, Borlaug's wheat strains provided 23 percent of the world's calories. Pakistan became self-sufficient in wheat production in 1968. India took longer, until 1974, but in both countries grain production grew faster than the population.

In 1970, Norman Borlaug was back in Mexico, already working in the fields, when his wife received a 4:00 a.m. call from Oslo, Norway. Margaret drove out to the field. Norman's daughter, Jeanie, later reported that, as the sun rose, Margaret told her husband that he had been awarded the Nobel Peace Prize for his work fighting world hunger. "No, I haven't," Borlaug insisted. "Someone's pulling your leg." Eventually, Margaret convinced him.

In his Nobel acceptance speech, Borlaug argued that the prize was meant not so much to honor him as an individual but "to symbolize the vital role of agriculture and food production in a world that is hungry, both for bread and for peace." He emphasized that increases in food production would give the world a few extra decades to deal with its population problem.

Later, Borlaug lobbied the Nobel Committee to create an Agriculture Prize. When they said they couldn't, Borlaug brought the idea to his home state of Iowa. With sponsorship from the General Foods Corporation, the World Food Prize was established in 1986. Awarded each year, the brings with it an award of $250,000. It has honored pioneers and innovators from Bangladesh to Belgium, Switzerland to Sierra Leone.

As the Green Revolution spread, so did criticism from environmentalists. They objected to growing one crop on large tracts of land, to using so much fertilizer, to the need for pesticides and herbicides, to breeding new strains artificially. All of these, they argued, would ultimately damage the environment. Moreover, using high-input farming methods, such as lots of fertilizer, would replace traditional subsistence farming with big, capitalist enterprises and increase inequality.

Borlaug was more worried about starvation. As for the environment, the former forester pointed out that growing more food on less land meant that people would clear less forest. More acres could remain wild than if people clung to the old, low-yield practices. Moreover, new strains of wheat were resistant to disease and gained more growth for every pound of fertilizer applied. Borlaug agreed that population growth needed to be brought under control, but he thought some environmentalists

"Never think for a minute that we are going to build permanent peace in this world on empty stomachs and human misery. It won't happen."
— Norman Borlaug, around the time of the Nobel Prize, quoted by Ronald Phillips.

The World Food Prize Dr. Norman Borlaug Medallion

Sorghum at an
unnamed road in
Guanajuato, Mexico

were being unrealistic. In January 1997, he told the *Atlantic* monthly magazine:

They've never experienced the physical sensation of hunger. They do their lobbying from comfortable office suites.... If they lived just one month amid the misery of the developing world, as I have for fifty years, they'd be crying out for tractors and fertilizer and irrigation canals and be outraged that fashionable elitists back home were trying to deny them these things.

Opposition from environmentalists helped block Borlaug from introducing his methods to Africa. But in 1984, when famine struck Ethiopia, a Japanese philanthropist named Ryoichi Sasakawa contacted Borlaug, now seventy, to ask if he could help. Borlaug traveled to Africa intending to do research to figure out the best approach. He found hunger so severe he decided instead to start planting right away. Soon, yields of maize had tripled in some African countries, and other crops—sorghum, cassava and cowpeas—also started yielding more. Through the foundation that Sasakawa and Borlaug founded, more than 3 million small farmers in fifteen African countries learned how to increase their production by a factor of two or three.

2006 Norman
Borlaug
Congressional
Gold Medal

Norman Borlaug spent his last years of retirement splitting his time between Texas A&M University and his research station in Mexico. He died of lymphoma on September 12, 2009, at the age of ninety-five.

We don't often refer to new crop varieties or farming practices as inventions, but there is no doubt that Borlaug's innovations in agriculture changed the world. Social scientists estimate that this

Iowa farmer's patient, humble work of developing new crop varieties and new farming techniques saved hundreds of millions of lives during his lifetime. Yohei Sasakawa, son of Ryoichi Sasakawa and head of Japan's Nippon Foundation, was one of the speakers Borlaug's memorial tribute at Texas A&M, on October 6, 2009. He read a poem:

Norman,
You cultivated a dream that could empower farmers;
you planted the seeds of hope;
you watered them with enthusiasm;
you gave them sunshine;
you inspired with your passion;
you harvested confidence in the hearts of African farmers;
you never gave up.

Borlaug in the field

"Buy me some peanuts and Cracker Jack ..."

— "Take Me Out to the Ball Game,"
lyrics by Jack Norworth, 1908

8. Food, Glorious Food

(Pre-History to Modern Times)

W hether it's mud pies or fancy salads or ice cream with mix-ins, creating new food concoctions can be fun and rewarding. Such familiar favorites as hamburgers, popcorn, potato chips, chocolate chip cookies, and waffles began as someone's creative experiment. It turns out that many of our favorite food have either been invented multiple times or have seen their origins lost in the fog of history. But some products do have traceable stories.

Hamburgers

The hamburger, that most American of fast meals, is named after a city in Germany. Its invention has been attributed to at least six different cooks in the late 1800s or early 1900s, working anywhere from Hamburg, Germany, to Tulsa, Oklahoma. But the origins of ground meat go back further still. Genghis Khan's Mongol hordes packed ground meat when they went raiding in the twelfth

The average hamburger contains beef from over a thousand individual cows. They are all mixed in the processing plant.

and thirteenth century. They couldn't always take time from galloping across the steppes of Central Asia to dismount and build a fire at lunchtime. So legend tells us that the Mongols, who included a group called the Tartars, ate their ground meat raw—like the steak tartare served today in pricey restaurants.

In the eighteenth century, sailors and immigrants traveling from the port of Hamburg, Germany, to New York brought along one of their favorite foods, "Hamburg steak." It consisted of low-quality beef, shredded and flavored with bread crumbs and spices. This preparation worked its way onto American menus, but it wasn't yet a hamburger. That took adding a bun.

One claimant to the title of inventor of the hamburger is Charlie Nagreen (1870–1951) of Seymour, Wisconsin. In 1885, at the age of fifteen, Charlie was selling meatballs from a stand at the county fair. People weren't buying. All at once, Charlie realized that fairgoers wanted to wander around the concessions as they ate. So he smashed his meatballs flat and slapped them between two slices of bread. Charlie returned to the fair for the next sixty-five years, selling his hamburgers with a song:

> *Hamburgers, hamburgers, hamburgers hot,*
>
> *Onions in the middle and pickles on top,*
>
> *Make your lips go flippity flop.*

Charlie accompanied himself on the harmonica and guitar.

Another claimant to the title of hamburger inventor is Fletcher Davis (1864–1940) of Athens, Texas. Davis was a potter who also ran a lunch counter in the town's courtyard. In the late 1880s, he sold browned meat patties topped with onions and inserted between two slices of toast. Davis took his sandwiches to the 1904 St. Louis World's Fair, where he set up Uncle Dave's Hamburger Stand. But that was not the first appearance of ground beef between slices of bread. "Hamburger steak sandwiches" had shown up on menus in Reno, Nevada, Chicago, Illinois, and Los Angeles, California, in 1893 and 1894.

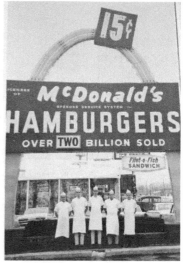

McDonald's drive-in 1967

Oscar Weber Bilby (b. 1870), from a farm near Tulsa, Oklahoma, claimed to be the first person to serve a hamburger on a true bun. On the Fourth of July, 1891, he cooked ground Angus beef patties on a hickory wood fire. Then he placed the patties between two halves of his wife Fanny's delicious homemade yeast buns. So began a yearly tradition of serving burgers on buns to more than a hundred guests under the pecan trees of Bilby's farm.

Regardless of whoever actually invented the hamburger, there was a movement during World War I to change its name. Because of negative feelings toward anything that sounded German, patriotic Americans began calling their ground-beef sandwiches "Salisbury steaks" or even "liberty burgers." After the war, the name *Salisbury steak* persisted, but only for ground beef mixed with other ingredients and usually smothered in gravy. The familiar sandwich became a hamburger again.

The hamburger got a boost in 1931, when J. Wellington Wimpy appeared in newspapers. Wimpy was a character in the comic strip *Popeye the Sailor Man* created by cartoonist Elzie Crisler Segar. Often shown with a half-eaten hamburger in hand, Wimpy was a scrounger who became famous for the line, "I'd gladly pay you Tuesday for a hamburger today." A Wimpy hamburger chain of fast food restaurants launched in Chicago in 1934. At its peak, Wimpy's had 1,500 locations in a dozen countries. But by the 1960s, Wimpy's was overtaken by McDonald's, which had sold 1 million burgers by 1963 and 20 *billion* burgers by 1974. McDonald's stopped counting hamburgers sold when it hit 99 billion in 1994.

Ketchup

Ketchup is found in 97 percent of American homes.

Early recipes for "ketchup" that appeared in England took inspiration from fish sauces found in southeast Asia. The Malays called such sauces *kecap*, pronounced "kay-chap." In the 1700s, the English versions centered on mushrooms as a main ingredient. Often, these sauces featured the tiny salt fish called anchovies. Tomato ketchup first appeared in an 1812 recipe from an Englishman named James Mease (1771–1846), who called tomatoes "love apples." His sauce contained brandy and spices, but no vinegar or sugar. Tomatoes for making Mease's ketchup had to be dried first, which took a lot of time. Storage was also a problem. Home-bottled sauce often grew mold or bacteria.

Jonas Yerkes was the first American to distribute tomato ketchup in a jar. By 1837, he was selling his product nationally. Other companies followed, and in 1876, the Heinz company began advertising its tomato ketchup with the words, "Blessed relief for Mother and the other women in the household!" Buying ketchup was a lot quicker than making it from scratch. Heinz added sugar and thickeners to what had been a thin and watery concoction.

Popcorn

Not every kind of corn kernel will pop. Kernels good for popcorn have a particularly hard outer shell, too hard to bite through. The only way to get at the grain within is to heat the kernel until steam builds up inside. The pressure rises until the kernel bursts with a satisfying *pop!*

Caramel popcorn

The first popcorn maize, or corn, grew in South America about 7,000 years ago. Migration and trading among native populations brought it to the American Southwest about 4,500 years later. The ancestors of the Pueblos used it: a thousand-year-old kernel of popped corn has been found in a cave in southwestern Utah.

Many Native Americans popped corn on flat rocks in the fire. The trick was to catch the popped kernels in mid-flight, before they fell back into the flames. The Winnebago people found another way. They pierced corn cobs with sticks and held the cobs over the fire. Most of the kernels popped right in place without flying away.

Europeans encountered popcorn as soon as they reached the Americas. Christopher Columbus reported in his diary that natives on Hispaniola wore popped corn as corsages or in headdresses. Around 1612, French explorers in the Great Lakes region reported that the Iroquois popped corn in pottery vessels filled with heated sand. On the other hand, there is no real evidence that, as sometimes claimed, the Pilgrims ate popcorn at the first Thanksgiving.

By the 1820s, popcorn kernels were sold throughout the United States. People placed the popcorn along with butter or lard in a frying pan and popped it over an open fire. Unfortunately, the butter often burned before the popcorn popped. Lard worked better, but it coated the popcorn in grease.

By the later 1800s, people began to use wire mesh boxes on long handle. Now they could pop batches of corn without losing most of the kernels, and they could shake the boxes to prevent burning. Some mesh baskets, built by blacksmiths for large batches, measured as much as eight feet across. Still, the process was slow and labor intensive, and it was hard to make sure the popcorn came out right.

In 1871, a German immigrant named Frederick William Rueckheim (1846–1937) began selling popcorn in Chicago. He used steam to heat the popcorn and then mixed it in a drum with oil and molasses—the molasses to sweeten it and the oil to keep it from sticking together. In 1896, Rueckheim registered the name Cracker Jack, a popular slang term that meant "first-rate." He added peanuts and packaged the concoction, along with a little prize, in a sealed wax bag inside a cardboard box. The double packaging was an

From the front of a Cracker Jack box

innovation that helped keep his product fresh. That same year, he trademarked the company slogan, "The More You Eat, the More You Want!" When the song "Take Me Out to the Ball Game" was released in 1908, it included the line "Buy me some peanuts and Cracker Jack." With free advertising like that, Cracker Jack quickly became a favorite snack, especially at baseball games.

Meanwhile, another innovator, Charles Cretors (1852–1934), figured out how to pop corn in large volumes. Cretors was a baker and candy maker from Ohio and later Illinois. In 1885, he began to demonstrate an improved peanut roaster on the sidewalk in front of his Chicago shop. A small steam engine roasted the peanuts in a controlled way. Cretors found that the machine could also pop kernels of corn uniformly every time. He patented his popcorn popper/ peanut roaster in 1893. That same year, he took his machine to the first Chicago World's Fair. He started off by giving the popcorn away, but soon people were lining up to buy it.

During World War II, sugar was rationed, and people ate three times as much popcorn as before the war. On the other hand, in the 1950s, as television entered the home, popcorn sales fell because fewer people were going to the movies.

Cretors began selling large, custom-made poppers to vendors all over the country. In 1900, he introduced a beautiful horse-drawn wagon called the Special. The sound of clopping hooves and the smell of buttered popcorn drew enthusiastic customers, who marveled at watching the popcorn steam and jump right before their eyes.

Next, Cretors built an electric popper. The new popper was safer and easier to use than the old steam popper. As people began going to movies in the 1920s, popcorn sellers saw an opportunity. At first, theater owners didn't want popcorn in their buildings. It was too smelly, and they didn't want popcorn kernels to be ground into their fancy carpets. Instead, the owners charged vendors who wanted to sell popcorn out on the sidewalk a dollar a day. Meanwhile, individual hawkers found their way indoors and sold Cracker Jack in the aisles. When theater owners saw how much profit they were passing up, they experimented with electric poppers inside their lobbies. During the Depression, popcorn profits helped to keep theaters open. Moviegoers grew to expect the smell and buttery taste of fresh, electrically popped popcorn. Today, concession sales account for 50 percent of a movie theater's profits.

Potato Chips

According to legend, potato chips were invented by George Crum (1822–1914), the cook at a high-class restaurant in the resort of Saratoga Springs, New York. Crum was part Native American and part African American, and his name was actually George Speck. Born in Saratoga Lake, New York, he worked as a hunter and guide in the Adirondacks. As a young man, he became a cook at an upscale Saratoga Springs restaurant called Cary Moon's Lake House. Speck's specialties included venison, duck, and other wild game.

New York State historic marker: Crum's Place

One day, a hungry and forgetful customer—legend says it was the shipping and railway millionaire Cornelius Vanderbilt—called out, "Crum, when are we going to eat?" Instead of being offended, George Speck decided he liked the name Crum. After all, he said, a crumb is bigger than a speck. He went by Crum from then on.

The potato chip incident occurred in 1853. A disgruntled customer at Moon's Lake House—again, popular custom names Vanderbilt—sent his French fries back to the restaurant kitchen, complaining that they were too thick. George Crum sliced the fries thinner, but the customer still complained. Frustrated and feeling a bit vengeful, Crum sliced the potatoes ultra-thin, doused them with salt, and fried them to a crisp. To his surprise, the customer loved them.

Cornelius Vanderbilt

The fussy customer story may be a myth. Crum never mentioned the customer in his now-lost autobiography. It might even be Crum's sister, Catherine Speck Wicks (1814–1917), who invented potato chips. Catherine worked in the kitchen, too, and her version of the story said that she accidentally dropped a thin slice of potato in hot oil. Once she fished it out and let it cool, her brother tried it and liked it so much he decided to make more.

Whoever fried the first potato chips, the snack became a hit. Moon's called them "Saratoga chips" and sold them in paper cones at 10¢ a batch. Then, in 1860, George Crum opened his own restaurant, Crum's, in Malta, New York. As at Moon's, the cuisine was fancy and the prices high. Included on the menu were the now-famous potato chips.

By the twentieth century, potato chips began to be mass-produced. Stores sold them in tins or scooped out of glass bins, usually into paper bags. Unfortunately, chips from the bottom of the tin or case were often crumbled and stale. Then an entrepreneur named Laura Clough Scudder (1881–1959) thought of a better way to package them.

Label from a Laura Scudder's potato chip bag

Scudder was born Laura Emma Clough in Philadelphia. She worked as a nurse before she married Charles Scudder and moved to Ukiah, California. While there, she studied law and became the town's first female attorney. In 1920, she and Charles moved to Monterey Park, California, where he ran a gas station and car repair business. When a falling car left Charles disabled, Laura took over running the gas station. At the same time, she decided to start manufacturing potato chips. She asked her employees to take home sheets of wax paper and iron them into bags, which could be sealed to keep the potato chips fresh. Scudder was also the first person to print a freshness date on her product. Crackling freshness was the point of her famous marketing slogan, "Laura Scudder's Potato Chips, the Noisiest Chips in the World."

Scudder's business faced difficulties during the Great Depression, but she was determined to keep her workers employed. She branched out into manufacturing peanut butter and mayonnaise, and once she turned down an offer of $9 million for the company from a buyer who would not guarantee her workers' jobs. Laura Scudder kept her workers employed, and her potato chips dominated the California market.

Scudder's television advertisements were clever and inventive. In the 1950s, one advertisement starred the real Laura Scudder as a little old lady in a rocking chair gathering noisy ingredients for her chips. A campaign in the 1960s featured the Laura Scudder's "Noise Abatement Pledge." Adorable children vowed not to run in the hallways or bounce a basketball down the stairs, "to compensate for the noise I make when eating Laura Scudders potato chips, the noisiest chips in the world." Scudder continued to run her company until her death at age seventy-seven, and it still exists today.

The average American eats more than four pounds of potato chips a year.

Chocolate Chip Cookies

For once, historians are certain about who invented the chocolate chip cookie. In 1936, Ruth Graves Wakefield (1903–1977) published the recipe in her *Tried and True* cookbook. She and her husband, Kenneth Wakefield, ran a popular restaurant called the Toll House in Whitman, Massachusetts. She developed her Toll House Chocolate Crunch Cookie to go with ice cream.

But although we know the name of the inventor and the approximate date of the first chocolate chip cookies, myths

Restored/replicated sign of the Toll House Inn, Whitman, Massachusetts

The chocolate chip cookie is the official state cookie of both Pennsylvania and Massachusetts.

have grown up around the invention. One version says that Wakefield ran out of nuts and substituted bits of a Nestlé bittersweet chocolate bar instead. A more outlandish version suggests that as Wakefield was making her usual cookies, the cookie mixer vibrated so vigorously that a chocolate bar fell off a kitchen shelf into the mixing bowl, where it was chopped into bits.

Wakefield worked purposefully and diligently to perfect her cookies. Their reputation spread, and Marjorie Husted featured them on her *Betty Crocker Cooking School of the Air* radio program. Then the Nestlé Company came knocking. For just a dollar, Wakefield sold Nestlé rights to the recipe and the Toll House name. As part of the deal, she became a paid consultant to the company and was guaranteed a free supply of chocolate for life. Nestlé still prints the Toll House cookie recipe on every bag of its chocolate morsels.

A Nestlé Toll House chocolate chip cookie sandwich

Toll House cookies grew in popularity during the Depression, and in World War II, Americans stuffed them in care packages for soldiers abroad. Chocolate chip cookies have gone on to inspire many variations, such as refrigerated cookie dough, M&M cookies, Famous Amos cookies, cookie ice cream sandwiches, Mrs. Fields cookies, chocolate chip cookie dough ice cream, and whatever version you mix up from scratch in your kitchen. Current estimates suggest that Americans eat about 70 billion chocolate chip cookies each year. That's about one cookie for each American every weekday of the year.

Waffles

Waffles have been around for centuries, but American were the first to slather them with butter and maple syrup. The ancient Greeks pressed flat cakes between two metal plates and roasted them over a fire. Church bakers in the Middle Ages pressed flour-and-water cakes into patterns that depicted scenes from the Bible or religious symbols. The first waffles to have a grid pattern of indented squares appeared in the Netherlands in the fifteenth century. One advantage of the grid pattern developed by Dutch *wafelers* was that it spread the batter over a larger baking surface, allowing for a nice, crisp *wafel*. Waffles spread across Europe as a savory snack food or a dessert with chocolate. The Dutch were probably the first to bring waffle-making to America.

In America, waffles met an existing tradition of using maple syrup in place of sugar or molasses. Native Americans in the Northeast tapped maple trees for their sap long before Europeans arrived on the continent. The importance of the maple tree shows up in the number of stories told about its sap. One legend tells how a chief went out to grab a hatchet he had thrown at a maple tree the night before. The chief set off to hunt deer, but his wife noticed liquid dripping from the gash in the tree. That night, she cooked his venison in maple sap rather than water, and soon the tribe was gashing all the maple trees they could find.

The Algonquins traditionally made a V-shaped notch in a maple tree's bark, inserted a reed, and collected the sap in a bucket made of birch bark. They concentrated the sap in one of two ways. One was to drop hot stones in the bucket until some of the water boiled away. The other way was reported by a man named James Smith who was captured by the Lenape in 1755. In wintertime, if they lacked cooking vessels, the Lenape concentrated their maple syrup by leaving maple sap out in the cold. As the sap began to freeze, they discarded the thin layer of ice. As Smith wrote in 1799, "They made the frost, in some measure, supply the place of fire, in making sugar.... I observed that after several times freezing, the water that remained in the vessel, changed its colour and became brown and very sweet."

Maple tree tap

About half of American eat waffles. About half of those usually eat frozen waffles, while the rest are split between homemade and restaurant waffles.

Maple syrup was cheaper than sugar, and it made waffles delicious. To make waffles, the cook held over an open fire a device with two hinged metal plates and a long wooden handle. Then a Dutch immigrant living in Troy, New York, devised a way to make cooking them easier. In 1869, the immigrant, whose name was Cornelius Swartwout (1838–1910), patented his new device for making waffles on the stove.

Swartwout's waffle-maker was made of cast iron. It consisted of two plates hinged together and swiveling within an iron ring. To use it, the cook lifted the stove lid out of a coal-fired stove and replaced it with the fitted waffle maker. The cook poured in the batter, and after a certain amount of time, rotated the waffle-maker in its iron ring to cook the other side.

The next step to making waffles a favorite breakfast food came in the 1930s, when the Dorsa brothers began selling fresh waffle batter to their California neighbors. Frank, Anthony, and Sam Dorsa of San Jose, California, started making fresh mayonnaise in their parents' basement in 1932. The Dorsas' mayonnaise featured "100 percent fresh eggs," and they called it Eggo Mayonnaise. Eggo Waffle Batter came next. But it was hard to send waffle batter any distance, so the brothers next created a powdered batter. All a cook had to do was to add a little milk and stir.

By the 1950s, Americans were ever more interested in quick breakfasts and frozen or instant foods. The Dorsa brothers decided they needed to mass-produce waffles for freezing. After trying

Kellogg's Eggo Thick & Fluffy Cinnamon Brown Sugar Waffles

different approaches, Frank Dorsa (1907–1996) converted a merry-go-round engine. Around the edges of the cooking carousel that resulted, he placed a passel of waffle irons. Workers at stations around the circle flipped the waffles as the carousel rotated. By 1953, Dorsa brothers' machine was turning out thousands of his "Froffles" an hour. In 1955, the company changed the name back to Eggo Waffles. Kellogg bought the brand in the 1970s and introduced the ad slogan, "L'Eggo My Eggo."

The Microwave Oven

An accident involving chocolate led engineer Percy Spencer (1894–1970) to invent the microwave oven soon after World War II. Spencer was brilliant and self-taught. Born in the small town of Howland, Maine, he lost his father soon after birth. Then his mother left him, and an aunt and uncle took him in. The family was poor; at age twelve, Percy left school to work in a factory. When the local paper mill got electricity, Percy taught himself all about the machinery. Soon he was filling in as an electrician for several different businesses.

Ad: Why Don't You Own a Raytheon Radarange

In 1912, at the age of eighteen, Spencer joined the US Navy. Inspired by tales of heroic wireless operators when the *Titanic* sank, he wanted to be a telegraph operator. To his delight, the navy sent him to radio school. After his service, Spencer worked for RCA making radio parts. In the 1920s, became employee number five at Raytheon, one of the earliest technology start-ups. There he collaborated with engineers from the Massachusetts Institute of Technology (MIT) and became an expert in designing radio tubes. During World War II, Raytheon worked with MIT to build the magnetrons used in 80 percent of British and American radar.

A magnetron is a complicated high-powered vacuum tube. It sends electrons through an electric field and a magnetic field at the same time. This makes the electrons follow a curved path. As they pass cavities in the perimeter of the magnetron, the electrons resonate like air rushing through the holes of a flute. The electrons move with so much energy that they give off microwaves. These waves can be used for radar or radio transmissions.

At Raytheon during the war, Spencer made continual improvements in the system for producing magnetrons, increasing production from 17 to 2,600 units per day. For his contributions to the war effort, he received a Distinguished Public Service Award from the US Department of Defense.

One day in 1945, Spencer paused in front of a magnetron and noticed that a chocolate bar was melting in the pocket of his lab coat. By that time, he was already an experienced inventor with 120 patents. He sensed at once that the microwaves emitted from his magnetron were heating the chocolate. He asked a colleague to bring over some unpopped popcorn, and when he put it on a plate near the magnetron, it began to pop. So microwave popcorn dates to before the microwave was invented!

Next, Spencer tried a whole egg, which he placed in a kettle with a hole in it. Then he set the magnetron next to the hole. As he waited for something to happen, a skeptical colleague leaned over to look. At that moment, the egg burst and literally left the colleague with hot egg on his face.

The first microwave ovens Percy Spencer built, each with a magnetron inside, were the size of refrigerators and weighed more than 700 pounds. In 1954, Raytheon began selling these ovens, called RadaRanges, to restaurants and ocean liners. By 1967, microwave ovens had scaled down enough in size and price that Amana, a division of Raytheon, began selling them to the home market for only $495 ($3,700 in today's money adjusted for inflation). With a microwave, Amana promised, a cook could bake a potato in just one minute. Today, 90 percent of American households have a microwave oven, and most of us use one every day to thaw or warm food, boil water, cook fish, or pop popcorn.

"Some *few* always have to set the pace and give the others courage to go on into places which have not been explored."

— Charles Drew, letter to Edwin B. Henderson, May 31, 1940

9. Blood of Life

Charles Drew
(1904–1950)

Blitz aftermath

For eight months in 1940 and 1941, German bombs fell on London, England, and nearby port cities. Civilians raced to huddle in shelters or to sleep underground in the subway tunnels. Despite the blackouts, the German bombs found their targets. Buildings collapsed; others burst into flames. During eight months of attacks, 40,000 British civilians were killed.

Across the Atlantic, the new Blood for Britain program chose a young African American surgeon named Charles Drew to lead their medical response. Dr. Drew organized blood drives and made sure the donated blood was separated, stored, and shipped according to standards he had developed. Nearly 15,000 American citizens donated blood for their British cousins. More than 5,000 liters of plasma were successfully shipped across the ocean to England, where they saved many lives.

Yet in the first sentence of Dr. Drew's doctoral thesis, published only months earlier, he had argued, "The transfusion of blood from one individual to another is still a potentially dangerous operation." It was in large part Dr. Drew's own experiments on how to keep blood from spoiling that made the Blood for Britain program work.

Charles Richard Drew was born into a middle-class African American family on June 3, 1904. His father, Richard, who had never finished high school, laid carpets for a living. Though Richard was the only non-white member of his trade union, he became its financial secretary. Charlie's mother, Nora, trained as a teacher but never taught.

Charlie and his younger siblings, Joseph, Nora, Elsie, and Eva, grew up in the Foggy Bottom neighborhood of Washington, DC. The South was still strictly segregated. Hotels, swimming pools, restaurants, and schools were usually open to one race only. Both of Charlie's parents were light-skinned, and his ancestors included English, Scots, and Irish immigrants as well as African Americans. But the family clearly identified as black.

Charles—the oldest—and siblings

Charlie's parents were devoted to their children and their church. Richard belonged to a barbershop quartet that sang in riverboats along the Potomac River. In that same river, he taught his children to swim. Both parents led Sunday Bible classes. Nora taught the children to respect their father and to value education.

The segregated black schools of Washington, DC, received less money than the white schools, but the teachers were excellent and the standards high. Charlie was a good student, though not an outstanding one. What he really cared about was sports. At age eight, he won all the medals for his age group at a local swim meet. He also liked to find ways of making money. At age twelve, he got a job selling newspapers on the street. Before long, he recruited ten other boys to work for him. He stationed his team members at street corners that factory and office workers had to pass on their way home from work. Organizing people remained one of Charlie's strengths throughout life.

At age fourteen, Charlie entered the Paul Laurence Dunbar High School, the nation's leading black academic high school. He studied Latin and Greek, got high grades in math and science, and lettered in football, track, basketball, and swimming. His classmates voted him the most popular member of the class.

Charles Richard Drew in high school (upper left)

During Charlie's senior year of high school, an influenza epidemic swept the world. Charlie's twelve-year-old sister Elsie, already ill with tuberculosis, caught the infection and died. Stunned and grieving, Charlie decided to become a doctor. "I have studied the sciences diligently since that time," he later wrote in his medical school application.

In 1922, Charlie entered Amherst College in western Massachusetts on an athletic scholarship. He was one of only 13 blacks among 600 students at the school. Six feet tall, 190 pounds, with light skin and reddish hair, he earned the nickname "Big Red." Most of his friends were black, and he addressed them by their first names, but with everybody else he was more formal, calling them "Mister" or "Professor." He became the first freshman at the college to letter in track, and he threw himself into other sports so enthusiastically that his grades suffered. A dean called him into the office to warn him, "Mr. Drew, Negro athletes are a dime a dozen." After that, Charlie sought a better balance, limiting his sports to football and track.

Even in an integrated college Charlie encountered prejudice. Traveling with the track team to Brown University, he and other black team members were barred from a restaurant and had to eat at the college dining hall. Princeton fans jeered at Charlie and a dark-skinned teammate. The Amherst Glee Club did not allow black members. Although undeniably the top athlete on the football team, Charlie was passed over for captain. Then the Scarab Club, an elite club for outstanding seniors he had qualified for, refused him membership. But this time, several white members of the club resigned in protest. Charlie remembered the racial slights he encountered, but he worked to answer them by his achievements.

During a football game in Charlie's junior year, a member of the opposing team jammed his spikes into Charlie's thigh. When the penetrating wounds became infected, Charlie spent several days in the hospital and even had to undergo surgery. Observing the work of the medical staff, Charlie became even more convinced he wanted to go to medical school.

But medical school was expensive and Charlie's parents still had three children at home, so he knew he would have to work to earn his way. After graduation, he got a job as athletic director and instructor in chemistry and biology at Baltimore's Morgan College, a black college founded in 1869. Living on a tight budget and saving his money, Charlie worked at the college for two years. He coached football and basketball with good results, and he was popular as a teacher. During the summer, he taught swimming in one of Baltimore's segregated swimming pools.

After two years, Charlie had saved enough money to apply to medical school. He planned to attend Howard University, the nation's top black university at the time. But Howard rejected him because he was two English classes short of their requirements. Instead of a place in medical school, Howard offered Drew the job of assistant football coach. Annoyed, he wrote back that if he wasn't good enough for the medical school, he surely wasn't qualified to become part of the faculty.

Now it was late to apply, and Drew had to scramble. Harvard accepted him but wanted him to wait a year for a seat to open in their next entering class. Impatient, Charlie managed to get a place for himself in the medical school class at McGill University in Montreal, Canada. Short of money, he worked as a waiter in the university dining hall. His old football coach at Amherst also helped raise money among some of his friends to help him through his first year. Still, Charlie was lonely and at times desperate. He wrote in his journal on New Year's Day in 1930, "Here I am: a stranger among strangers in a strange land, broke, busted, almost disgusted, doing my family no good.... Yet I know I must go on somehow—I must finish what I have started." At the end of that year, he received a Rosenwald Fellowship for $1,000. It meant he could continue.

There were good things about living in Canada. For the first time, Charlie found himself in a country where his race mattered little. He continued his athletic exploits, even winning the Canadian championships in hurdles, high jump, and broad jump. And despite his financial struggles, Charles Drew excelled academically at McGill. He was elected to a fraternity for top scholars, and in his fourth year he won an academic prize by besting four other top students on a special test. In the end, Charlie graduated second in his class of 137. Now he was a doctor of medicine, and he began his internship year at two hospitals in Montreal.

One night, a fire swept through the wards of a hospital where Drew was working. Several critically injured patients went into shock. Shock is a sudden loss of blood pressure, usually caused by injury. The loss of blood pressure is so severe that it leads to organ damage. The treatment for shock was blood transfusion, but finding and matching whole blood takes time. Drew had been interested in the

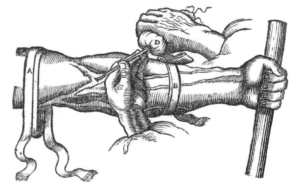

Blood transfusion, 17th century

After four years of college and four years of medical school, American doctors join a hospital-based residency program where they get further training and supervision in their chosen specialty. The first year of residency is called internship.

problem of shock before: now he wondered if he could have given his patients something quicker than whole blood.

Meanwhile, life had grown harder for Drew's family at home. It was the Depression; Drew's father was laid off from his job, and Drew had to send money home from his own small supply. Then, soon after he finished his internship, his father died of pneumonia. Charlie Drew returned home to help support his family.

The next step in a doctor's training was a residency program. Drew wanted to be a surgeon, and he applied to the prestigious Mayo Clinic in Rochester, Minnesota. Despite his excellent record, he was turned down at Mayo and everywhere else he applied. Years later, a senior surgeon explained to him that although he might do for ordinary patients, hospitals didn't want to risk upsetting their wealthy patients with a black doctor.

So Charles Drew returned to Howard University, which now knew his reputation and welcomed him. Howard hired him as a surgical resident and an assistant instructor in pathology for $150 a month. His supervisor noted on his file, "A very high type of man. Intelligent, forceful. Willing to work." Within a year, Drew advanced from assistant to full instructor. At that point, the medical school dean, who was determined to raise the prestige of the department, asked Drew to pursue a research doctorate. This would be equivalent to someone today who gets a PhD degree along with their MD. With luck, he could find this opportunity in a surgical department and keep honing his surgical skills.

In 1938, with a Rockefeller fellowship in hand, Charlie entered a graduate program under Dr. Allen O. Whipple at Columbia School of Medicine in New York City. Dr. Whipple's plan was for Charlie to stay out of sight in the laboratory, working under the supervision of Dr. John Scudder. After all, Columbia Presbyterian, although it treated many black patients, had never had a black resident physician. But with patience and charm, Charlie worked his way onto the hospital wards. No doubt, his light skin helped. Soon he was even invited to eat in the main dining room with the other residents.

Meanwhile, in the laboratory Drew studied how to store and handle blood for transfusion. Whole blood often caused bad reactions, so Drew and his supervisor John Scudder focused on separating human blood into two fractions, cells and plasma. Plasma was the pale yellow, protein-filled liquid left over when red and white cells settled out of the blood. Longer-lasting and easier to transport than whole blood, plasma was good for emergencies.

In 1939, after a year of work, Charles Drew helped Scudder set up an experimental blood bank at Columbia. Scudder later wrote of his pupil,

> *Drew was naturally great. A keen intelligence coupled with a retentive memory in a disciplined body, governed by a biological clock of untold energy; a personality altogether charming, flavored by mirth and wit, stamped him as my most brilliant pupil. His flair for organization with his attention to detail; a physician who insisted upon adequate controls in his experiments.... one of the great clinical scientists of the first half of the twentieth century.*

In the midst of his research, Drew was pursuing another goal. In the spring of 1939, he volunteered to help out at the annual clinic in Tuskegee, Alabama. On the way down, he stopped by Atlanta to visit friends at Spelman College. There he met a young home economics teacher named Lenore Robbins. For Drew, it was love at first sight. His friends invited both of them to a party, where the couple danced all evening. Three days later, stopping by again on the way home from Tuskegee, Drew asked her to marry him. Not surprisingly, she hesitated. Back in New York, Drew wrote to

Red cells carry on their surface certain markers, called antigens. There are A and B antigens; blood that carries neither kind is called type O. Transfusions between people with different blood types can lead to serious reactions with fever and destruction of the transfused blood. Plasma, while it cannot carry oxygen the way red blood cells do, is free of these risks.

Drew family

her on April 16, 1939, "I met you and for the first time mistress medicine met her match and went down almost without a fight." In five months, the couple were married. Together they had four children. They gave their first daughter the nickname Bebe, for Blood Bank.

Despite courtship and marriage, Drew's research proceeded quickly. His doctoral thesis, as thick as a telephone book, reviewed the history of blood transfusion and detailed Drew's own careful experiments with storage and transport of blood products. By the time he finished it, Drew was probably the world's expert on blood banking.

In early 1940, Drew completed his fellowship, becoming the first African American to receive the Doctor of Medical Science degree, equivalent to a PhD in medicine. He returned to Howard University with the dream of creating a premier surgical program there. No longer would people be able to think, he wrote to a former coach on May 31, 1940, that "all Negro doctors are just country practitioners, capable of sitting with the poor and sick of their race but not given to too much intellectual activity and not particularly interested in advancing medicine." He added, "This attitude I should like to change. It should be great sport."

British Red Cross testing blood for transfusion during WWII

But Drew stayed at Howard only a few months. Europe was at war, and in June 1940, scientists and officials of New York's Blood Transfusion Betterment Association (BTBA) met to discuss how the United States might support Great Britain with blood supplies. Charles Drew's work had shown that blood plasma could be safely refrigerated for at least two months. In August, the BTBA began its Blood for Britain program. The Association asked Drew to lead the effort.

Nine New York hospitals soon joined the program. Radio announcements called for volunteers to help, and 1,300 donors contributed blood each week. Drew made sure the collected plasma was sterile and safe. He standardized procedures for processing donated blood on an industrial scale. In January 1941, he submitted his final report on the Blood for Britain program. By that time, Britain was supplying its own needs for plasma.

Next, American health care workers began to wonder what they would do about the blood supply if the United States entered the war. The Red Cross stepped forward, offering to handle blood donations for the first time in its history. The organization's leadership asked Drew to stay on as medical director for three more months to start a pilot blood supply program for America. This time, instead of refrigerated plasma, the final product was dried plasma, easier to store and transport than the liquid variety. Blood was collected in industrial plants and department stores as well as hospitals, and Drew pioneered the use of mobile blood vans. As one Red Cross director wrote, "Thus was set in motion the national project for the production of the No. 1 life-saving agent of the war, ... dried plasma."

One irony of the blood collection effort was the fact that the US Army initially refused all blood donated by black volunteers. White servicemen, the army said, would not accept black blood. Drew thought this rule was stupid; blood was blood and it could save lives. After Pearl Harbor, the Army allowed blood collected from African American to be given to black soldiers only.

Segregation in the blood supply persisted until 1950, and later than that in some southern states. Drew wrote in 1942, "There is no scientific basis for the separation of the bloods of different races except on the basis of the

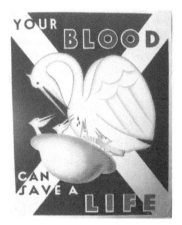

Poster
The Scottish National
Blood Transfusion
Association

Poster
American National
Red Cross

Red Cross Bloodmobile

"So much of our energy is spent in overcoming the constricting environment in which we live that little energy is left for creating new ideas or things. Whenever, however, one breaks out of this rather high-walled prison of the 'Negro problem' by virtue of some worthwhile contribution, not only is he himself allowed more freedom, but part of the wall crumbles. And so it should be the aim of every student in science to knock down at least one or two bricks of that wall by virtue of his own accomplishment."

— Charles R. Drew to Mrs. J. F. Bates, a Fort Worth, Texas, schoolteacher, January 27, 1947

individual blood types or groups." He argued quietly against the rule but continued his work. His approach had always been to use reason, education, and achievement to show that racism had no sensible foundation.

In 1943, the NAACP awarded Drew its Spingarn Medal for his work in blood plasma research. In return, Drew began to speak out more publicly against the blood segregation policy. In August 1944, he joined a demonstration against segregation in Washington, DC. But political action was a sideline. By that time, he was back at Howard University, where he focused on training black physicians to help with the war effort.

After the war ended, Drew persisted in his mission of training a generation of excellent black surgeons. He worked up to sixteen hours a day and didn't take time off for vacations. He and his wife, Lenore, rented a three-bedroom house on the Howard campus. The house had a garden with flowers, fruit trees, and a grape arbor. Drew liked gardening, cooking, playing the piano, and spending brief hours with his four children. His tastes were simple: He liked movie westerns with their uncomplicated tales of good and evil.

Charles Drew with medical residents
at Freedmen's Hospital, ca. 1945

Though he disliked administration, Drew even agreed to run the Freedmen's Hospital—the only Washington hospital that allowed African American doctors to care for patients—as medical director. But he preferred teaching. His students, he said, would be his greatest contribution to medicine. In December 1948, he sent two of his trainees to Johns Hopkins as the first Howard residents to sit for the American Board of Surgery's certification exams. As he waited to hear their results, Drew was so nervous that he took a sledgehammer down to the basement of his rented house and began to knock apart an old coal bin. Then a phone call came. His two residents had taken first and second place in the exam. Drew collapsed into a chair, his eyes full of tears.

But excellent training and performance did not open every opportunity to Drew's young surgeons. They were denied entry to medical professional societies. Although he became a member of the International College of Surgeons in 1946, Drew was never admitted to the American College of Surgeons (ACS). He gave up trying, because he considered the ACS a social club with low professional standards. The American Medical Association still excluded black southern doctors from membership one hundred years after its founding. Drew wrote a scathing letter to the *Journal of the American Medical Association* on January 13, 1947: "One hundred years of racial bigotry and fatuous pretense; one hundred years of gross disinterest in a large section of the American people ...one hundred years with no progress to report. A sorry record."

On April 1, 1950, Charles Drew drove a team of his young doctors through North Carolina to a medical conference in Tuskegee, Alabama. Lodging was hard to find in the segregated South, so the team had decided to drive through the night. One by one, the young men nodded off. Then Drew himself fell asleep at the wheel. The car drifted off the road. When the tires struck the shoulder, Drew startled awake. He overcorrected, turning the wheel so fast the car flipped. Drew was thrown half out of the car, which rolled over him, crushing his chest.

An ambulance rushed Drew to the local hospital, where the white hospital physicians, full of dread at his condition, hurried to give him a blood transfusion. It was not enough. Charles Drew died at the hospital less than two hours later on April 1, 1950. He was only forty-five years old. He left behind his wife, four children, and grief-stricken students and colleagues. Among the many people who wrote to Lenore with condolences was Eleanor Roosevelt, widow of the late president. Drew's funeral was so large, his sister recalled, that florists in Washington, DC, ran out of flowers.

Several years after his death, a rumor spread that Charles Drew had been turned away from a white hospital, or that a hospital had refused to give him blood because of his race. These rumors were untrue, but they were rooted in the sense of exclusion that segregation in all parts of their lives had brought to black citizens. Indeed, segregation, and the fact that finding a motel room was difficult for a group of black doctors, was one of the reasons Drew was driving through that long night.

Over time, the medical community came to recognize Charles Drew as the father of the blood bank. Although many people contributed to the history of blood transfusion in the United States and abroad, Drew's great contribution was to bring together what was known, add to it, and use his organizational skills to make it work at a critical time. His second great contribution lay in what he saw as his historic role—demonstrating once and for all that African American scientists and doctors could reach the very top of their profession.

All over the United States, schools and clinics are named after Charles Drew. Among them is the Charles Drew University of Medicine and Science in Los Angeles, California. Nowadays, of course, hospitals, doctors and patients welcome donated blood no matter the race of its donor.

"It was really very clear in my mind from then on what I wanted to do. How I was going to get there I wasn't so sure of."

— Gertrude Elion, interview,
March 6, 1991

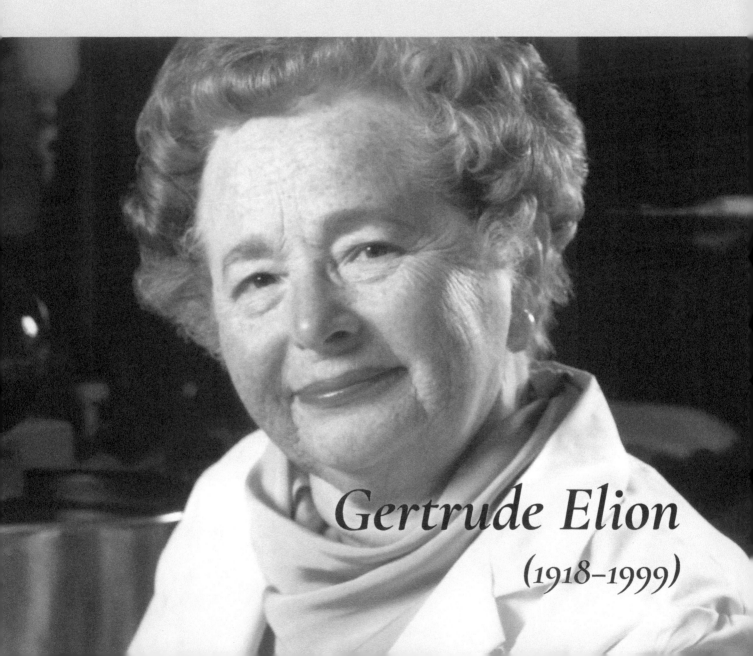

10. To Conquer Cancer

Gertrude Elion

(1918–1999)

The summer of 1933 should have been a lighthearted time for Trudy Elion. She had just graduated from high school at the age of fifteen. In September, she would be attending Hunter College, the women's college of the free City University of New York. Because she enjoyed every subject, she wasn't sure what to choose for a college major, but that would come later. For the summer, she looked forward to spending time with friends at the beach or going to concerts, and time by herself curled up with a good book at home.

But that summer, Trudy's beloved grandfather began to suffer stomach pains. A watchmaker from Russia, he had moved to the United States when Trudy was three years old. He babysat her, took her to the park, taught her Yiddish, and told her stories. When Trudy's mother grew busy with her baby brother, her grandfather spent even more time with her. He was a gentle, scholarly man, and deeply attached to his granddaughter.

Background
Gertrude Elion
oil painting by
Sir Roy Calne

Gertrude Elion

And now he was in pain and losing weight. The diagnosis was bad: stomach cancer. Trudy sat by his hospital bed, feeling helpless as he clutched his stomach and moaned. "I watched him die," she said fifty years later. She racked her brain, wondering what she could have done to save him. "I decided that nobody should suffer that much," she said. Right then and there, Gertrude Elion decided she would study chemistry so she could find a cure for cancer.

She very nearly succeeded.

Thomas Hunter Hall
Hunter College

Gertrude Elion was born in Manhattan on a cold wintery night on January 23, 1918. Her father was an immigrant from Lithuania and her mother from Russian-ruled Poland. On both sides, her ancestors included scholars and rabbis. Trudy's father worked both as a dentist and a stockbroker. When Trudy was seven years old, the family moved from the bustle of Manhattan to an outer borough—the Bronx. There she attended crowded classes in excellent public schools. She loved learning, and she learned so fast that she kept skipping grades. She described herself as "a child with insatiable thirst for knowledge." At fifteen, she entered college. Hunter College, free and all female, was a wonderful place, full of talented, eager young women. There were seventy-five chemistry majors in Trudy's graduating class. Most of them were preparing to be teachers, but Trudy kept her mind on her goal, curing cancer. She never asked if the goal was realistic, and nobody told her that women didn't become chemists.

Nobody told her, that is, until after graduation. "I hadn't been aware that there were doors closed to me until I started knocking on them," Elion later told biographer Sharon McGrayne. In 1937, armed with highest honors in chemistry, the nineteen-year-old college graduate looked forward to her next step. She wanted to attend graduate school, but she couldn't afford a PhD program without a fellowship. No one of the fifteen programs she applied to offered her money. Undaunted, she looked for a chemistry job. But once again, she found no takers. The US economy had entered the Depression; there weren't enough laboratory jobs to go around, and men were hired first. Nobody wanted to take a chance on a cute, redheaded nineteen-year-old girl, no matter how smart she was. Interviewers told her either that she'd be a distraction in the lab or that they knew she'd leave soon to marry and have a family.

Trudy had run into her first real barrier. But she was stubborn. She considered her difficulties a delay, no more. She signed up for a six-week secretarial course, but then, instead of a job as a secretary, she found a three-month job teaching biochemistry to nursing students. On the side, she volunteered without pay at a chemistry lab at Denver Chemical Company in New York. She later said that her supervisor told a different anti-Semitic joke every day, but she did her best to ignore it. "Don't be afraid of hard work," she later advised students. "Nothing worthwhile comes easily. Don't let others discourage you or tell you that you can't do it."

In those years just after college Trudy was busy for another reason. She had fallen in love with another New Yorker, a statistics student at the City College of New York named Leonard Canter. Canter considered Trudy "brilliant...a vital, fresh, spontaneous, sparkling spirit." They attended concerts and plays, went on long walks, and talked about science. Canter supported Elion's ambitious plans. The two dated for two years before Canter left for a year to study in Paris on a scholarship.

While Canter was gone, Elion's volunteer lab job became a paying one—at $20 a week. The salary was low, about a third of what an average man might earn as an assistant chemist. Still, for Elion, after three years of volunteering, the job provided hope as well as the chance to save.

Soon she had saved up enough to enroll in the graduate chemistry program at New York University; her parents helped with tuition. She also signed up for teacher-training classes and taught high school physics and chemistry as a substitute teacher. She received a master's degree in chemistry in 1941, around the same time Leonard Canter came home and completed his bachelor's degree.

When Leonard applied for a job at Macy's, he received bad news. The company doctor had diagnosed a heart condition, probably a heart murmur from a damaged heart valve. Macy's chose not to hire him. Still, Canter soon landed a job as a stockbroker. He and Elion got engaged. Then, a few months later, Leonard fell ill. Probably because of his underlying heart disease, he had contracted bacterial endocarditis, an infection of one of his heart valves. Even today, endocarditis is a dangerous illness, requiring weeks of IV antibiotics. At that time, before penicillin, the disease was fatal. Canter held on for six months before dying with Elion at his side.

Alexander Fleming discovered penicillin in 1928, and in 1938 Howard Florey figured out how to produce it. But it was only during World War II that the Americans figured out how to produce enough of it first for a few soldiers—only ten of them in 1942—and finally for civilians.

With her true love gone, work became Elion's reason for getting up in the morning. She was twenty-three years old. In later years she sometimes dated, but she never found another person she wanted to marry. "People are inclined to settle for something less than I was," she said once in an interview, speaking of marriage. Elion wasn't willing to settle.

By the time Elion was twenty-four, the armed forces were calling up American men to serve in World War II. All at once, work opportunities opened for women. Elion left her job at Denver Chemical when the A&P grocery chain hired her at a better salary to work as a food analyst. She made sure the strawberries weren't moldy and checked the acidity of pickles and the color of mayonnaise. The job was dull, but she learned about quality control.

Next she got a job at Johnson & Johnson to join the chemists who were making sulfa drugs, the first antibiotics on the market. Executives at this medical devices company wanted their scientists to work on new versions of the drugs. But within six months, the firm's leaders pulled out of drug research and assigned Elion to test the strength of surgical thread instead. It wasn't chemistry. She went back to looking for a job.

In 1944, when Elion was twenty-six, her father suggested she try a small company, Burroughs Wellcome, which had a division in nearby Westchester. When Elion phoned, she learned that the drug company had job openings, so she took the train to Westchester on a Saturday morning. This time, she was lucky. The man interviewing that day was an open-minded and visionary biochemist named George Hitchings. "I was really interviewing him," Elion told the *New York Times* years later. Indeed, instead of asking Elion lot of questions, Hitchings shared the idea he was working on—an idea so promising and yet so unlikely that, Elion said, "It was almost a pious hope that we could do this." Elion knew at once she wanted to sign up. A week later, Hitchings called with a job offer. The pay was $50 a week.

Henry Wellcome, founder of Burroughs Wellcome company (1853-1936)

In George Hitchings, Elion had found the ideal boss. He was thirty-nine years old, thirteen years her senior. Hitchings came from a family of shipbuilders and naval architects. He grew up on the West Coast, in California and Washington State. His father died when he was twelve years old, an event that gave him much the same motivation Elion had to make a difference in the world of medicine. For his high school graduation speech, he spoke about his hero, Louis Pasteur, whose scientific research had immediate practical applications that saved lives.

George Hitchings

Hitchings graduated with a degree in chemistry from the University of Washington and then received his PhD in biochemistry at Harvard Medical School in 1933. On graduation, he married and began what he later described as "a nine-year period of impermanence, both financial and intellectual." The Depression limited his job opportunities. He found a series of temporary appointments doing research on cancer, on nutrition, and on electrolytes. Finally, in 1942, he was hired as the head and sole member of a new biochemistry division at Burroughs Wellcome. He built the division slowly. His first hire was a woman named Elvira Falco, who did everything from growing bacteria to feeding the lab rats. Gertrude Elion was the second. Falco wasn't sure about Elion at first. She thought the new employee dressed too elegantly and wouldn't want to get her hands dirty with lab work. But soon Elion proved herself, and the two became fast friends. For years, they attended the opera together whenever they could.

George Hitchings wanted to move away from the trial-and-error method of finding new drugs in natural compounds. He wanted to use the knowledge beginning to emerge from the study of biochemistry. For example, it was known that for cells to multiply, they had to make nucleic acids—DNA and RNA. Cells needed to make DNA out of four building blocks called bases. Maybe Hitchings and Elion could take advantage of the fact that bacteria and tumor cells double much faster than normal human cells. This rapid doubling meant they needed to make a lot more DNA, and faster. If Elion could interfere with the building blocks of DNA, maybe she could kill off bacteria and tumors at a dose that wouldn't hurt normal cells.

When Elion began to work on DNA, she and Hitchings knew only that it was important for cell growth, not that it carried genetic information. That same year, Dr. Oswald Avery proved that DNA carried the "transforming principle" that made pneumonia bacteria deadly. As for the double helix structure of DNA, that wasn't worked out until 1952.

Hitchings assigned Elion to work on the two bases known as purines: adenine and guanine. The idea was to make a compound similar enough to one of these compounds that bacteria would try to use it to build DNA. Then, like a key getting stuck in a lock, the ill-fitting compound would gum up the works. Elion and Hitchings would be able to test the new compounds' effect on a strain of *Lactobacillus* bacteria.

Elion set to work to learn all she could about the purine bases. Although Hitchings suggested the original approach and Elion constantly consulted with him, she quickly became independent in the lab. Within two years she began to make important discoveries and publish scientific papers. She presented at scientific meetings, finding that knowledge overcame her shyness. One time, when a top scientist questioned her conclusions, she spoke right up and convinced him she was right.

Even as she was immersed in this work, Elion began to study for her PhD. Several times a week she took a late subway to Brooklyn Polytechnic Institute. She figured it would take about ten years of evening work, but after two years, the university gave her an ultimatum: become a full-time student or quit the program. Elion didn't want to leave the job where she was learning so much. She consulted Hitchings, who assured her she could succeed as a scientist without a PhD. Elion wasn't sure she believed him, but she took his advice. By this time, Hitchings's division had six or seven employees, with Elion leading her own small team.

In the year 1950, Elion made her first major breakthrough. Working separately from Falco and Hitchings, she developed a compound called diaminopurine. The Burroughs lab had been collaborating with New York's Sloan-Kettering Memorial Hospital since 1947. If a compound looked promising in bacteria, Sloan-Kettering scientists tested it on mice. Diaminopurine worked so well against mouse leukemia that Sloan-Kettering tried it on four adult leukemia patients. Two of them responded well. One woman went into remission for two years and even had a child before her leukemia returned. But in most people, the drug caused such violent vomiting that it had to be abandoned.

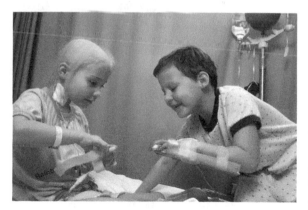

Children with leukemia receiving chemotherapy

Elion went back to the lab and kept modifying the compound. Her next candidate drug, called 6-MP, differed from a purine molecule by only one atom. The change was enough to make 6-MP effective against childhood leukemia. In 1950, children who came down with leukemia—a cancer of blood-forming cells in the bone marrow—generally died of bleeding or infection within three months.

After treatment with 6-MP, they lived six months, a year, even two years. But in the end, they always relapsed and died. It was heartbreaking.

Elion spent six years studying everything about 6-MP and how the body processed it. She learned that over time, leukemia cells become resistant to the drug. Nowadays, leukemia patients are treated with several drugs at once, and 6-MP is used in maintenance, even after signs of illness are gone. Today, with this approach, more than 80 percent of childhood leukemia patients are cured.

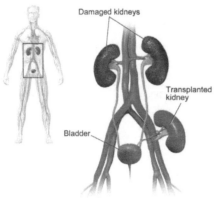

Kidney Transplant

In 1990, Joseph Murray won a Nobel Prize for his work in kidney transplantation. He could not have succeeded without Gertrude Elion's Imuran.

Tinkering with the molecules she had already made, Elion was soon designing new compounds to test. She found that small changes—a few atoms shifted around—made drugs suited to quite different diseases. For example, a drug called TG, or thioguanine, is used today in adult leukemia.

In her studies of different compounds, Elion found some that appeared to weaken the immune system. The human immune system consists of specialized blood cells that identify and attack foreign substances like viruses or tumor cells. Weakening it sounds like a bad idea—except in the case of transplanted organs. By 1958, kidney transplants were theoretically possible. A person with kidney failure could be saved by a kidney transplanted from an identical twin. But most people don't have identical twins. If anyone else donated a kidney, the patient's immune system would attack the "foreign" kidney and destroy it. What was needed was a drug to make the sick person's immune system go easy on the new kidney.

One of Elion's compounds, later called Imuran (azathioprine), turned out to be that drug. Surgeons tried it first on dogs at the Peter Bent Brigham Hospital in Boston. Elion knew many of the dogs by name. She was delighted when a collie named Lollipop lived 230 days and even successfully had puppies after a kidney transplant and treatment with Imuran. In 1961, Dr. Joseph Murray used Imuran when he transplanted a kidney between two unrelated people. It worked. For the next thirty years, Imuran was the single drug that made kidney transplants possible, saving tens of thousands of lives across the world.

By this time, Elion had refined her approach to drug discovery. She created compounds and shared them with researchers who could test them. When a drug looked promising, she learned everything she could about how the body used it and broke it down. Then she applied this knowledge to designing a new drug.

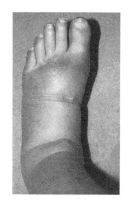

Gout in foot

One example of this approach was a new drug called allopurinol. The team she now supervised found that allopurinol slowed the breakdown of 6-MP in the body. It also reduced how much uric acid the body produced. Uric acid is a byproduct of making DNA and RNA. When too much of it piles up in the body, it can form chalky crystals in the joints or in the kidneys. In the joints, this leads to a painful form of arthritis called gout. In the kidneys, it can cause painful kidney stones and sometimes kidney failure. In 1963, doctors gave allopurinol to a night watchman crippled by gout. Within three days, he could move around again. Allopurinol is now used worldwide.

The 1950s and 1960s were tremendously productive years for the Burroughs Wellcome team. Gertrude Elion found the fact that her drugs were actually curing patients incredibly fulfilling. Work was recreation for her. She later said of research, "You sometimes feel it's almost too good to be true that someone will pay you for enjoying yourself." At the same time, she enjoyed concerts, the opera, photography, and travel. Warm, modest, and quietly confident,

Hitchings and Elion, 1948

she became good friends with the Hitchings family and with other women in the lab. Her reputation grew. In time, she authored more than 250 scientific papers.

During the early 1960s, Elion began to manage her own group of twenty, thirty, then fifty employees. Her intellectual partnership with Hitchings continued to grow. They discussed their progress, and as Elion said, "At the end of a long talk, you wouldn't really remember who said what, and whose idea it was to do the next thing. Which was great... it was very much a meeting of the minds."

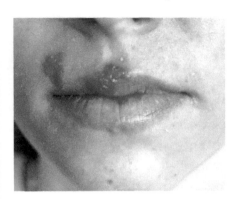

Herpes lesions on the mouth

In 1967, based on the lab's successes, George Hitchings was promoted to Burroughs Wellcome's vice president of research. Running the lab fell to Elion, now forty-nine years old. For twenty-three years she had worked under Hitchings. Now she had the chance to show what she could do on her own. She was ready. As she later said, she had "had enough already of being a junior." So, in 1968, she returned to an old idea, one Hitchings had discouraged: finding a treatment for a viral illness.

Viruses work by entering cells and inserting their own code into the cells' DNA. To destroy a virus without destroying the cells that housed it seemed almost impossible. But Elion thought it could be done. In fact, even 6-MP had shown some effect against viruses, though it was too toxic to use for that purpose. But Elion's team tweaked and tested, tested and tweaked.

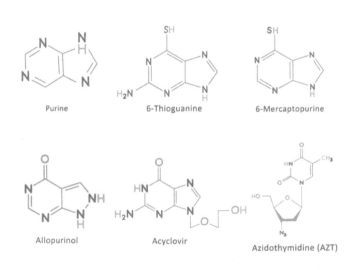

The structure of Elion's medicines resembled a purine molecule.

Finally, one young chemist had the idea of using an incomplete circle of carbon atoms in place of a normal sugar, which had six carbon atoms in a ring. This "acyclic" compound showed great efficacy in killing herpes viruses, which can cause all kinds of nasty diseases: cold sores, chickenpox, shingles (a painful rash), sexually transmitted sores, or even a deadly brain infection. The Wellcome scientists named the new drug acyclovir. They announced the news at a scientific conference in 1978. Getting it approved and into the market took another eight years, but acyclovir was making Burroughs Wellcome almost a billion dollars a year by the 1990s. This was money that could go into supporting more research.

Gertrude Elion considered the invention of acyclovir her "final jewel." Until that time, nobody had recognized that viruses, like bacteria, had many of their own unique enzymes that drugs could attack. Acyclovir opened researchers' eyes to what was possible, and many of them went to work to find new antiviral compounds.

In 1970, Burroughs Wellcome moved its headquarters from New York to Research Triangle Park in North Carolina. Leaving New York was wrenching for Elion, now fifty-two, but soon she began attending classical music concerts and college basketball games in her new hometown. As often as possible, she flew to New York to attend the opera. She traveled and took photographs in Europe, Africa, Asia, and South America.

At age sixty-five, in 1983, Gertrude Elion officially retired and became a consultant to Burroughs Wellcome. Her influence, however, was far from finished. Within a year of her retirement, the team she had trained and nurtured came up with the first specific treatment for the HIV virus, which causes AIDS. The drug, another variation of a purine base, was called azidothymidine, or AZT. With this drug and the ones that followed, AIDS shifted from a death sentence to a chronic disease that can allow a long and productive life.

In the United States, getting a new drug approved requires proving to the scientists of the Food and Drug Administration that it is both safe and effective. Such proof requires several phases of large clinical trials with hundreds of people over many years. The process usually costs hundreds of millions of dollars.

AIDS is a chronic disease that harms the immune system. It is caused by the HIV virus, which is spread through dirty needles or sexual contact. AIDS deaths in America peaked in 1995, with almost 42,000 people dying. By 2014, that number had fallen to around 6000 US deaths a year. But worldwide, a million people a year are still dying of AIDS.

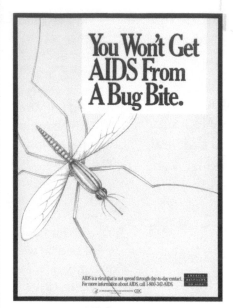

You Won't Get AIDS From A Bug Bite.

AIDS is a virus that is not spread through day-to-day contact. For more information about AIDS, call 1-800-342-AIDS. CDC

AIDS poster

At 6:30 in the morning on October 17, 1988, Elion was washing her face when the phone rang. A reporter on the other end of the line told her she had been awarded the Nobel Prize in Physiology or Medicine. At first, Elion thought the reporter was kidding, but when she heard the names of the other winners, she gradually accepted the news. She shared the prize with George Hitchings for their work developing drugs to treat leukemia, malaria, herpes, and to prevent rejection of transplanted organs, and with Sir James W. Black for his work developing a class of drugs for high blood pressure called beta blockers.

For Elion to be awarded the Nobel Prize was a breakthrough in several ways. She was a woman, she didn't have a PhD, and she had always worked in industry instead of "pure science." Moreover, some on the Nobel committee questioned whether she had just acted as Hitchings's assistant, following his directions. Others pointed out the many papers she had authored and the discovery of acyclovir when she alone ran the lab. Those who argued that she was Hitchings's equal won the day. The joint award was a tribute to the power of teamwork in innovation.

Elion brought her extended family with her to the Nobel award ceremony in Stockholm, Sweden. Her nieces and nephews had four children under five, and Elion insisted that they be given their own table at the Nobel banquet. She herself sat on the dais in an elegant blue chiffon gown, beaming and tapping her foot to the Mozart playing in the background.

After the Nobel award, Elion continued to consult and teach medical students at Duke University. She received the National Medal of Science from President George H.W. Bush and accepted a series of honorary doctoral degrees. More important than any official honor, though, were the letters of thanks she received and treasured—letters from parents of children with leukemia, adults who had survived herpes encephalitis, or people whose kidney transplants had lasted for decades.

The Nobel Prize also led to many requests for Elion to speak to students. She told an interviewer at Hunter College,

> *They want me to go and tell students that they can do it too.... And it's true.... Because there wasn't anything so exceptional about me.... I was a very hard worker, I admit. But I think if they go into something with the kind of enthusiasm that I had, and the kind of desire, really, to make it work, that they can do it. And I try to tell them how rewarding it's been, not just because of the Nobel Prize, but because of the people we've helped.*

Throughout her life, Gertrude Elion impressed people with her warmth and humility. The head of Burroughs Wellcome, by then Glaxo Wellcome, said of her, "Gertrude Elion's love of science was surpassed only by her compassion for people." When she died on February 21, 1999, at age eighty-one, Gertrude Elion had not succeeded in wiping cancer off the face of the earth, but she had struck some blows that seriously weakened it. Through persistence and dedication, she made fundamental contributions to science and saved hundreds of thousands of lives.

Hitchings and Elion, 1988

"*To me, programming is more than an important practical art. It is also a gigantic undertaking in the foundations of knowledge.*"

— Grace Hopper, quoted in *Management and the Computer of the Future* (1962) by the Sloan School of Management

11. Computer Whisperer

Grace Hopper
(1906–1992)

The US Navy's smallest admiral never went to sea. Instead, she taught computers and people to talk to one another. This great visionary of software development understood that programming should be a language everyone can learn.

Grace Murray Hopper was born in New York City on December 9, 1906. She was the oldest of three children, and she liked to organize her younger brother and sister in games of kick-the-can or cops-and-robbers. Machines fascinated her. At age seven, she took apart a whole series of alarm clocks before her mother put a stop to it. Both her parents used mathematics, her father in his work as an insurance broker and her mother just for the fun of it. Grace's grandfather, a civil engineer in New York, sometimes took her out surveying with him. "He let me hold the red and white pole," Grace said years later, in an oral history interview for the Computer Museum. "And he let me look through his gadget, and I wanted to be an engineer."

Grace Murray wanted to hurry through school. At sixteen, she applied to college. Unfortunately, she failed the Latin exam and had to go back to high school for a year. At seventeen, she entered Vassar, a leading women's college. She majored in mathematics and physics, and she earned a place as one of the smallest women on the basketball team.

After graduating with honors, Grace received a master's degree in mathematics from Yale. The following year, 1931, she began teaching mathematics at Vassar while pursuing a mathematics PhD at Yale, which would not accept female undergraduates for another forty years. Her thesis adviser was a computer pioneer named Howard Engstrom.

In 2017, Yale University renamed its controversial Calhoun College (named after a slaveholder and secessionist senator) for Grace Murray Hopper.

At age twenty-four, around the time she received her master's degree, Grace married Vincent Hopper, who was studying for his PhD in comparative literature at Columbia University. During the summers, using their wedding money, the two of them fixed up an old farmhouse in New Hampshire. They played badminton and golf with friends, and Grace hooked rugs and knitted sweaters. Except for her immersion in mathematics, Grace Hopper seemed like a typical young housewife.

Calhoun College

At Vassar, Grace Hopper taught math courses that were both popular and practical. One of the things she liked best about being on the faculty was that she was welcome to take any course on campus. She joined classes in astronomy, ethics, the history of science, geology, biology, architecture—indeed, anything she could find. Then she brought applications from these subjects back to her mathematics classes. She shook up the mathematics department with her new ideas and new courses.

On December 7, 1941, Grace and Vincent Hopper were working at a double desk in their upstairs study in New York, surrounded by books, with windows overlooking the winter-bare trees outside. All at once, the radio crackled with news of the surprise Japanese attack on Pearl Harbor. Husband and wife listened in disbelief. More than 3,500 Americans had been killed or wounded as Japanese planes bombed airports and ships of the Pacific Fleet. All at once, the Hoppers' quiet, scholarly life felt irrelevant.

Within a few days, America declared war on both Japan and Germany. Grace's husband, Vincent, and her brother Roger both left their academic careers to join the Army Air Force. "I was beginning to feel pretty isolated up there, the comfortable college professor," Hopper later recalled. Wanting to do her part, she taught a summer course to prepare mathematicians for the war effort. But she longed for a more direct role in the war. Breaking codes, she thought, would draw on her skills as a mathematician.

Grace tried to join the US Navy, but at age thirty-four and weighing only 105 pounds, she was considered both too old and too small to enlist. She kept writing to the navy to reapply. Finally, in 1943, she was accepted into the WAVES, the Women's Naval Reserve. Immediately, she shipped off to Northampton, Massachusetts, for midshipman training at Smith College. "We had to send [home] our silk stockings," she recalled. In the navy, only bunchy, uncomfortable cotton stockings were allowed.

The women's naval reserve, or WAVES (Women Accepted for Volunteer Emergency Service) was established by Congress and signed into law by President Franklin Roosevelt in July 1942. At peak strength, the WAVES had more than 86,000 members working ashore to free men up for combat roles at sea.

Grace Hopper graduated at the top of her WAVES training class. But instead of setting her to work breaking enemy codes, the navy assigned its brand-new lieutenant (junior grade) to be second in command to Lieutenant Commander Harold Aiken at Harvard's new computation lab. As a graduate student in physics, Howard Aiken had chafed at the amount of time he spent doing difficult math problems. He came up with a design for a giant automatic calculating machine. Harvard wasn't sure what to make of him, but IBM agreed to design, build, and donate the giant calculator. The machine, later called the Mark I, was delivered to Harvard in 1944.

Harwell dekatron witch 10

5 and 8 Hole paper tapes

When Hopper reported for duty on July 2, 1944, an armed guard led her to the basement of the physics building. There, her new boss looked her up and down and barked, "Where have you been?" Aiken had wanted a mathematician months ago, and he was none too pleased about getting a woman. He showed Grace the huge machine, which still had all its 750,000 moving parts exposed. Aiken ordered Hopper to learn to use it by calculating an arctangent—an inverse trig function—to a precision of twenty-three decimal places within a week. It was a task that couldn't be done by hand.

Hopper set to work. She consulted a handbook and asked advice from the two young male ensigns who had drawn straws to see who had to sit at the desk next to hers. First, she wrote out the steps the computer would have to follow. Then she translated these into a series of coded instructions from a code book. Each instruction was a short set of numbers, such as "573." But the computer could only read holes in paper tape fed into the machine. Each number of the code was represented by the position of a set of sixteenth-inch holes in one row of a three-inch wide roll of paper tape. So Hopper, the mathematician programmer, had to figure out the steps to solve the problem, translate each step into a string of numbers, and then translate that into punched holes in a paper feed. The holes caused different wheels in the machine to rotate to new settings. Clacking and whirring, with its mechanical wheels turning, the machine carried out three lines of instructions every second.

Hopper calculated the arctangent, passing her first test. Then she set out to "teach" the Mark I to calculate ballistics tables. In the war with Japan, ships were firing at enemy ships too far away even to see. How should artillery be aimed, taking into account distance, wind speed, humidity, and temperature? The Mark I could provide the answers.

Harvard Mark I Computer

Two months later, the mathematician John von Neumann showed up at Harvard with a still more difficult problem—implosion. How could a sphere be made to collapse inward evenly at great speed? None of the programmers knew that they were figuring out how to make an atomic bomb.

By this time, Howard Aiken had come to rely on his female lieutenant. "You're going to write a book!" he told her.

"I can't write a book," Hopper protested. "I've never written a book."

Harvard Mark I Computer team, 1944
Aiken in the middle of front row next to Hopper

The commander responded, "You're in the Navy now." Aiken wanted a guide to the Mark I, and in the Navy, he implied, people followed orders.

Writing about five pages a day between her other tasks, Hopper set to work. Daily, she read the pages aloud to her commander, and if he wanted changes, she made them. But when the book was finished, 561 pages long, Hopper was listed only as third author by rank.

One day, the Mark II froze up. Hopper's team opened some panels and found that a moth had short-circuited one of the connections. Hopper taped the offending moth into her lab notebook. She later wrote, *"After that, whenever anything went wrong with a computer, we said it had bugs in it."*

Hopper didn't mind not being given proper credit. She loved the navy. The strict dress code and the clear ranks, based on what a person accomplished, worked against gender bias. She was a respected member of the team, one of the boys. They often worked through the night, and when a job was done they all went out drinking together. Hopper kept up with the men. In fact, though nobody recognized the problem at first, she sometimes drank so much that she was out of commission for a day or two. Then she came back to work and proved to be as productive as ever.

After the war ended in 1945, Hopper stayed on with Aiken as a contract worker. She gave tours, planned conferences, and taught people how the Mark I worked. She wrote the manual for the Mark II. But in 1949, her contract as a research fellow ran out. Harvard wasn't that interested in Aiken's computers: the university valued pure mathematics much more. Moreover, Harvard didn't promote women. Grace Hopper was out. Not only that, during the war her marriage to Vincent had ended, as both realized they no longer had much in common. The divorce was friendly, and Hopper continued to wear her wedding ring, but that didn't change the facts. She was a woman on her own.

Hopper could have gone back to teaching, but instead she took a job at the new Eckert-Mauchly Computer Corporation (EMCC). The company was building an exciting new machine, the Universal Automatic Computer (UNIVAC). It would be entirely electronic and therefore much faster

Hopper and UNIVAC

than the mechanical Mark I and Mark II. Eager to get started, Hopper moved to Philadelphia.

ENIAC

For the first time, Hopper found herself working with a team of women programmers. One was Betty Snyder Holberton. During her first day of math class at the University of Pennsylvania, Betty Snyder's professor had asked her if she wouldn't be better off at home raising a family instead. But like Hopper, she went on to an important role in the military and the early days of computing. Holberton was one of six pioneering women programmers of another early computer, the Electronic Numerical Integrator and Computer (ENIAC), which was the UNIVAC's predecessor.

Women programmers
of ENIAC

Hopper admired her boss, John Mauchly, calling him "one of the grandest people I ever met.... He was very broadminded, very gentle, very alive, very interested, very forward looking." Unlike Aiken, who thought that computers would always be used only in the sciences, Mauchly foresaw uses for computers in business and industry.

Still, Hopper found the transition difficult. In November 1949, six months after starting work at EMCC, she was arrested for "public drunk and disorderly" on the streets of Philadelphia. The forty-three-year-old pioneer of computer science spent the night in the police station. She had changed her life for the war effort and had adapted to the regimented and hard-drinking lifestyle of the navy. Now she was part of a shaky start-up, surrounded by uncertainty. Her drinking had worsened, and she talked of suicide. The police sent her to the hospital to dry out. From there, she was released to the custody of a friend from navy days, Edmund Berkeley.

Edmund Berkeley

Berkeley wrote Hopper a long, loving, scolding letter that urged her to use her intellect to overcome her addiction. He appealed to reason: "Committing suicide cannot solve the problem you have taken into your feelings, of more financing for EMCC;

but several hours of sober, resolute intellectual effort might result in your giving some very useful suggestions to John [Mauchly]."

He concluded his letter with these words:

> *I and many other people know full well what a wonderful intellectual and emotional endowment you have. Even when you function only 70 percent of the time, you are worth to Eckert-Mauchly Computer Corporation all of the $6,500 salary they pay you. I can see in my mind's eye the marvelous things you could accomplish with the 30 percent of the rest of your time (now wasted), such as writing, teaching, living, and any of the other things at which you are so competent.*

The intervention worked. Over the next few months, Grace Hopper recovered. Her greatest contribution to computing lay ahead.

In 1950, EMCC was bought by the Remington Rand Company. The atmosphere became less fun and less friendly to women. According to Hopper's biographer Kurt Beyer, Rand had little real commitment to cutting-edge advances in computing. What Rand wanted was sales. EMCC staff were diverted to sales and customer support.

Interacting with customers who struggled with their new machines led Grace Hopper to believe that the barrier to the spread of computers was not better hardware—though that was needed—but better software. She wanted to make it easier for people to give instructions to computers. That need led her to invent the first compiler. A compiler translates a high-level computer language, one that gives commands in something approximating English, like GOTO or PRINT, into machine language—a series of numbers or holes in a tape. Hopper's idea was to free humans from the tedious work of translation. "Why not make the computer do it? That's why I sat down and wrote the first compiler....What I did was watch myself put together a program and make the computer do what I did."

In May 1952, Hopper published a paper titled "The Education of a Computer." She wrote that by using a compiler "the programmer can go back to being a mathematician." Proudly, she claimed, "UNIVAC at present has a well-grounded mathematical education fully equivalent to that of a college sophomore, and it does not forget and does not make mistakes."

After finishing the first compiler, called A0, Hopper quickly organized her team to write improved versions, A1, A2, and A3. She drew on her experiences with Aiken and Mauchly to create a close-knit, creative team. "Leadership," she said, "is a two-way street, loyalty up and loyalty down. Respect for one's superiors; care for one's crew."

In 1953, eager to share the compiler, Hopper organized a computing conference co-sponsored by the Census Bureau, which was looking for better ways to gather and store information about who lived in the United States. Hopper lectured about her A-2 compiler to about ninety programmers and technicians. Not all of them embraced Hopper's "automatic programs." User-friendly programs like hers took longer to run, and computer time was expensive. Worse, these programs threatened to take jobs from professional programmers. But by the end of the conference, most of those attending agreed to give the new compiler a try.

A-2 wasn't as easy to use as Hopper had hoped. Still, she plowed ahead. She wrote a program called FLOW-MATIC to run on business machines. Remington Rand sold it to large customers who used it to track inventory and payroll. The program was easy to alter, run, and de-bug. But Hopper thought more could be done. Instead of writing a new program for each new kind of computer, which took months and cost close to a million dollars a pop, why not create a universal business program to run on any machine? Now in her early fifties, Grace Hopper was recognized as a connector and leader in the computer industry. She knew people in business, academia, hardware, software, and the military. She knew how to organize and manage teams. No one was better suited to pulling off such a huge act of co-invention.

Computer punch card

Among the women Grace Hopper worked with were Nora Taylor, Betty Snyder Holberton, Jean Sammet, Mary Hawes, and Mildred Koss.

In 1959, Hopper organized a conference at the University of Pennsylvania to discuss creating COBOL (common business-oriented language). Hopper thought it could be a universal business language working on every new computer system built. She went to the US Department of Defense for funding. Out of the conference grew CODASYL (Conference/Committee on Data Systems Languages), a forty-person team of people from industry and universities. Five of the members were women. Somehow, Hopper coaxed competing groups to work together. Loosely organized and incredibly productive, the team quickly came up with a prototype. Input from users helped to improve it, much as happens in the open source movement today. Within ten years, COBOL became the world's most widely used program. It still runs on 80 percent of business computers today.

In 1967, the US Navy asked Grace Hopper to retire. No longer a naval officer, she kept working at EMCC, now part of Sperry Rand. In 1969, at age sixty-two, she was named, ironically, the first ever Computer Society Man of the Year. That same year, the navy called her back into active service to help them install and use COBOL on all their computers. This time, she stayed sixteen years.

Nuclear Submarine

In 1971, Hopper retired from Sperry Rand. Still eager to teach, she became an associate professor of management science at the George Washington University. Two years later, the navy promoted her to captain. She developed a fleetwide system of managing data for nuclear submarines, for which she received the Distinguished Service Medal.

Hopper spent her final three years in the navy touring and lecturing. When she finally retired in 1986 at age seventy-nine, she was the oldest naval officer. "I seem to do a lot of retiring," she said wryly. The worst thing about leaving the US Navy, she told David Letterman, was that now she had to go clothes shopping instead of just wearing her uniform. But once again, Hopper didn't stay retired for long. The Digital Equipment Corporation (DEC) hired her as a consultant and spokesperson. She traveled for DEC, talking about the exciting future of computers, until her death on January 1, 1992, at age eighty-five.

Because she was present from the beginning, Grace Hopper knew computers inside and out. An innovator and barrier breaker, patriotic and loyal, she saw early on that computers could be much more than fancy calculators. She wanted to open their power to people from all sorts of disciplines, and that meant "teaching" the computer to understand languages that regular people could write. In inventing the first compiler and leading the development of a universal business computing language, Grace Hopper opened the field of software to almost infinite possibility.

USS Hopper (ship named after Grace Hopper)

"Success is more a function of consistent common sense than it is of genius."

— An Wang, Lessons, 1986

11. Core Memories

王安
An Wang
(1920–1990)

Kunshan, Jiangsu

In 1926, a six-year-old boy named An Wang walked to his first day of school in the northern Chinese town of Kunshan, thirty miles upriver from Shanghai. Beside him walked his father, a teacher and practitioner of traditional medicine. They passed the foot of the town's one large hill, overgrown with flowering bushes and dotted with pagodas. Boats drifted on the canals, carrying fish from the city. Passersby greeted the father: when not teaching, he acted as their doctor, treating them with herbs and traditional medicines.

The boy, An Wang, was nervous about school. The first two classes were full, so his father wanted him to start at the third grade. He would be two years younger than his classmates—but his father said it was time for school. Obediently, the boy had left the family compound in Shanghai. No more running from one grandmother to the other in search of sweet mooncakes and stories.

An Wang

Shanghai Bund seen from the French Concession
1930

The oldest of five children, An Wang was born on February 7, 1920, in the great port city of Shanghai. At the time of his birth, China was so weak that parts of Shanghai were foreign territory or "concessions" ruled by the British, Americans, and French. Thirty-five thousand white foreigners controlled half the area of a city of three million.

An Wang's name means "peaceful king," but he was not born into peaceful times. He grew up, as he wrote in his autobiography, in a "China of feuding warlords and corruption, of Japanese brutality and fear." China had become a republic in 1911, but different factions battled in the streets and the countryside. The moat and broken-down city walls of Kunshan reminded the young boy that China's long history included many periods of warfare. But throughout all that time, his family had lasted. His father showed him a thick book in fine calligraphy that recorded twenty-three generations of family history, all the way back to the time of Marco Polo in the thirteenth century.

When An Wang was very small, his father traveled back and forth from the school where he taught in Kunshan to Shanghai to visit his young family. It was the boy's paternal grandmother who taught An about Chinese literature and traditions. Along

with sweets, she fed him stories teaching the Confucian ideals of duty, patience, moderation, and the golden rule. Above all, he later wrote, his grandmother taught him that "a sense of satisfaction comes from service to one's community."

When the family moved from Shanghai to Kunshan and An Wang entered school, he often felt lonely and isolated among the bigger boys in his class. Worse, he hated the rote memorization required for most of his studies. Mathematics was different. In math, thinking mattered. If he thought long and hard, he could usually come up with the answer.

In other subjects, Wang was less diligent. In junior high, he flunked his history courses and had to make them up in summer school. Luckily, he did so well on exams that he got away with his poor classroom performance. Meanwhile, he followed his own interests by reading about Western science. Isaac Newton fascinated him: How could one man have seen to the mathematical heart of gravity when everyone else accepted that things just fall?

In 1931, the Japanese seized Manchuria in China's northeast and began to bomb Shanghai. Wang's school organized political lectures and loud student rallies against the Japanese. The school required students to attend these rallies at least five times a year. Instead of making Wang feel patriotic, the mass meetings made him cynical about politics. Still, he started a student newspaper. It lasted only two issues. At the time, Wang had no idea that his interest in typesetting would later help him build a hugely successful company.

The Sino-Japanese War began in 1931, when Imperial Japan invaded the Chinese province of Manchuria and set up the puppet state of Manchukuo. In 1937, a skirmish called the Marco Polo Bridge Incident led to a full Japanese invasion of China. Until Japan's final World War II defeat in 1945, both the United States and Russia tried to help Nationalist China in its struggle against the Japanese invaders.

Marco Polo Bridge, 2013

Old library of
Shanghai Jiao Tong University

At thirteen, Wang moved back to Shanghai to live at the Shanghai Provincial High School, which had a top academic reputation. Too small for other sports, he took up Ping-Pong. He also built a radio from scratch and continued to excel at math and science, taught entirely from American textbooks. Three years later, he entered Jiao Tong University in Shanghai. The school was considered the Chinese MIT, and Wang was made class president because he had the highest entrance exam scores of his year. He played on the Ping-Pong team and translated articles from the magazines *Popular Science* and *Popular Mechanics* into Chinese.

During Wang's freshman year at university, he received the crushing news that his mother, "broken by years of fear and conflict," had died in Kunshan. That summer, while Wang was home with his grieving family, the Japanese army invaded Beijing. It was 1937, and for China, World War II had begun. As the Japanese army sliced through China, Wang cut short his summer vacation to hurry back to Shanghai. He made it just before warfare closed the roads. For safety, the university moved into the French concession. Eventually, other members of Wang's family joined him there. Along with tens of thousands of other refugees, Wang spent the next three years in the nine square miles of that protected area, while Japanese shells whistled overhead.

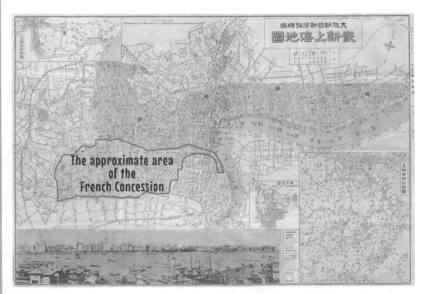

Map of Shanghai, 1932

Wang majored in electrical and communications engineering. His sense of patriotism and resentment of the Japanese occupation was rising. After graduating in 1940, he and seven classmates volunteered to build radio equipment for the Chinese army. The Nationalist government accepted their offer and transported the team by boat from Shanghai to British-held Hong Kong. Sometime after Wang left Shanghai, his father and sister died, and his younger brothers were scattered to live with other relatives. It was forty years before Wang saw any members of his family again.

Yangshuo, Guilin, 2011

One night, from a French-occupied town on the Yellow Sea, Wang and his team slipped behind the spread-out lines of Japanese soldiers. For three days and nights, they marched through the countryside into the Nationalist heartland. Then, by train and riverboat, they traveled upriver to the province of Guilin. There they set up in an old factory shop to make transmitters and receivers for the army. Their operation was like a start-up company running on a shoestring. At age twenty, Wang was put in charge of the team. Because they never knew what components they would be able to get their hands on, the young volunteers had to improvise, solving practical problems as they arose. About twice a week, Japanese bombers flew over, and Wang's team took refuge in nearby limestone caves. There they played bridge as the fat, low bombers rumbled overhead.

Though the challenges of his work stimulated Wang, he was dismayed by the arrogance and cruelty he observed within the army. Soldiers and officers bullied the peasants, robbing them of their harvest. Generals extorted taxes or dragged unwilling recruits into the army without providing food or uniforms for them. It was the opposite of everything Confucius had taught. Wang was not surprised in later years, when the peasants turned against the Nationalists and embraced the Communists.

Inside a DC-3

In 1944, as the Japanese army drew closer, Wang's unit evacuated to Chungking. Shortly afterward, Wang heard about an exam-based program to send highly trained Chinese engineers for apprenticeship in America. He jumped at the chance, applied, and placed second in the exam. In 1945, with the Japanese already retreating in the Pacific, Allied forces flew the group of young Chinese engineers in DC-3s over the Himalayas (called the Hump) to India. Strapped onto benches inside the frigid hull of a cargo plane, they gasped in the thin air. In India, their journey continued by train and then by sea.

Once he arrived in America, Wang thought through his options. Instead of accepting a company apprenticeship like other members of the group, he applied to graduate school at Harvard. Even without his university transcripts, he was accepted—in large part because Harvard was still short of men due to the war, still raging in Japan.

At Harvard, Wang did well in his courses. Although his spoken English was hesitant, his written English was good. Moreover, his years of practical experience helped him visualize connections between the academic and practical worlds. He could intuitively see how theory might work in practice.

In 1946, the Nationalist government of China ended its stipends of $100 a month to the Chinese engineers in the United States. So after taking a master's degree (he received two As and two A+s in his final semester), Wang looked for work. He took a clerical job in Canada for the Chinese government. But the work was so boring he decided to enter Harvard's PhD program in physics instead. His yearly stipend of $1,000 required him to work ten hours a week as a teaching assistant. Of this salary, Wang spent $7 a week at his boardinghouse.

Wang rushed through his PhD thesis. He couldn't afford not to. The subject was applied physics of nonlinear systems. Wang said later he wasn't particularly proud of his thesis work, but he managed to get it done in only sixteen months. In 1948, Wang received his PhD.

It was becoming clear that the Communists were winning the civil war in China, and going home was no longer a real option for Wang. He needed a job. The closest place to apply was the Harvard Computing Laboratory, just across campus. Wang went to work for Harold Aiken, inventor of the Mark I electro-mechanical computer, in May 1948.

Upstairs, the Mark II computer clattered so loudly it was impossible to carry out a conversation nearby. Wang stationed himself at one of the workbenches downstairs in the electronics laboratory. He had no background in computing, but neither did most people at the time. Aiken was working on a new machine, one that would be all electric, with no mechanical moving parts. Within a few days of Wang starting work, Aiken gave him a challenge that seemed impossible: Figure out a better way to use magnets to store memory in computers. And make sure the system he came up with relied on no mechanical moving parts.

Although Chinese Communists and Nationalists struggled from 1929 on, open war between them started in 1945. In 1949, the Communists won, and Mao Zedong announced the establishment of the People's Republic of China.

Founding of the
People's Republic of China

All computers share certain required components. They must have an **input unit**, a way of entering data and converting them to binary ones and zeroes. This can be a keyboard, a mouse, or, in the early days, paper tape. The **storage unit, or memory,** holds data (and programs) until the central processing unit (CPU) can act on them. The CPU is the brains of the computer. It controls and carries out arithmetic and logic operations to run programs on data. Finally, an **output unit** presents the completed work in a format humans can understand.

INPUT DEVICES — PROCESSOR — OUTPUT DEVICES
|
STORAGE MEMORY

Vacuum tube in 60s

Core memory module

Lorraine Chiu

At the time, people were trying all sorts of ways to store computer data, from punched cards to vacuum tubes. Each had its own problems. Magnets could store information by recording ones and zeros as different directions of magnetic flux. These could be read electronically by running a current through them, but doing so destroyed the information they held.

Then, one day, while walking across Harvard Yard, Wang had a flash of insight. All at once, he knew what to do. As the computer read the stored data, destroying it in the process, it could immediately and automatically rewrite it. Wang said later, "By destroying the memory—I know it." At first, it seemed crazy, as if every time you used a checklist, it erased and you had to write it down again. But Wang's method turned out to be faster and more stable than any other solution. His key insight—magnetic core memory—became the basis for computer memory for the next twenty years.

In 1948, attending a get-together for Chinese students and academics in the Boston area, Wang met Lorraine Chiu. Like him, she had been born in Shanghai, though she had relatives in Hawaii. She had been an English major at St. John's College in Shanghai, and then she had come to Wellesley as a special student to study Shakespeare. Like Wang, she found herself stranded by the civil war in China. The two grew close. Custom required them to get the blessing of their parents before marrying, but with communication to China shut off, that was something they couldn't do. After dating for almost a year, they married anyway. Their first child, Fred, was born in September 1950.

An Wang discussed with Lorraine two daring ideas. The first was to patent his invention. Academic researchers didn't usually do that, and Wang worried about a backlash from Aiken. He decided to go ahead anyway. Wang's second big decision was to go out on his own and try to start a company.

In 1951, only six years after arriving from China, An Wang withdrew his savings of $600 to establish his own firm. Later that year, Harvard allowed him to draw on his pension of just over a thousand dollars. Wang planned to build electronic components and core memories for companies and researchers who needed them. Although at first he had only one part-time employee, he chose the grand-sounding name Wang Laboratories.

An Wang and wife Lorraine

Wang's Chinese friends considered him reckless. There was prejudice against Asians, they warned. A company with a name like Wang would never get enough orders to support his new family. But Wang could be stubborn. He later said, "A small part of the reason I founded Wang Laboratories was to show that Chinese could excel at other things than running laundries and restaurants."

Wang set up production in a small office space above a garage in Boston's South End. To supplement his income that first year he also taught an evening course in electrical engineering at nearby Northeastern University. Meanwhile, Wang Laboratories sold magnetic cores, each shaped like a little doughnut, each holding one single bit of memory, for $4 apiece. By the end of the year, Wang had three employees. It was like the old days in Guilin, leading a team, making do with cheap materials, designing solutions in his notebook and then trying to make them work. But instead of bombers overhead, he only had to worry about money and fulfilling orders.

"When that insight did come to me, it was in a flash, and not as the logical conclusion of a conscious train of thought. This is the way most of my best ideas have surfaced—presented by my subconscious almost as a gift ..."
— An Wang, *Lessons*, 1986

Wang was confident, and his business grew. In 1955, he became a U.S. citizen. That year, he sold his magnetic core memory patent to IBM for $400,000. Meanwhile, his family also grew, with his son Courtney born in 1956 and his daughter Juliette in 1964.

To keep his company growing, Wang found that he had to be flexible, decisive, and quick on his feet. He partnered with a machine tool company to build a phototypesetting machine. Wang thought

Wang 700 Advanced
Programmable Calculator

he would have a stable line of business, but suddenly the partner company took over the manufacturing itself. So Wang decided to move his company into the brand-new calculator business. Doodling in his notebook, he came up with another important invention. Most calculators could basically perform only series of additions and subtractions. Wang developed a simple way, using logarithms, to perform much more complex operations. Now, if necessary, a calculator could instantly take not just the square root but the seventh root of a number like 4,817.623. The calculator itself was so large it rested on the floor. Scientists connected to it from keyboards at their own desks. The calculator sold for $6,500, and Wang patented his logarithm method.

Calculators allowed Wang Laboratories to grow from 35 employees in 1964 to more than 400 in 1967. The company developed specialized calculators for businesses and banks. It hired 80 sales people and opened offices in England, Belgium, and Taiwan. In 1967, Wang took his company public. He offered stock options to employees to help them benefit from the company's success. At the same time, he maintained family control over more than half the stock.

Wang 2200, 1973

But calculator prices began dropping rapidly, threatening profits. Wang decided to turn the company's attention to word processing. In this field, Wang would be competing directly with the giant IBM, which was 225 times Wang's size. To compete, he needed a better product. Wang sent engineers to interview secretaries. "People do not want technology," he wrote. "They want solutions to problems." Wang's engineers asked secretaries what they needed to make their work faster and more efficient.

Wang found solutions. In a first, his new word processors allowed people who were typing to make corrections they could see right on the screen in front of them. Wang's first word processors sold in 1976 for $30,000 apiece. After an ad run during the Super Bowl, orders soared.

In 1976, Wang moved his headquarters to the struggling mill town of Lowell, Massachusetts. Once more his workforce expanded. Over the next eight years, unemployment in Lowell fell from 15 percent to 4 percent. More and more, Wang was thinking about how to give back to the communities and institutions that had offered him opportunities. He and Lorraine donated $4 million to refurbish a center for the performing arts in downtown Boston. He founded a graduate school to teach software programming to engineers. He funded a program of Chinese studies at Harvard and a new walk-in health care center at Massachusetts General Hospital. His factory in Chinatown employed 300 people from the inner city. Always, he made his decisions quickly and with little fuss or fanfare. People described him as shy, formal, decent, and ethical.

Wang made sure his Confucian ethics were reflected in his company's philosophy. Their purpose, he reminded his employees, was to design equipment and services that would increase worker productivity and make jobs easier. "Find a need and fill it," he urged. He insisted on strong communication in the company and a sense of responding quickly to changing times. He always remembered the cruel and arrogant generals of China. Never, he insisted, would Wang Laboratories exploit either its employees or its community.

From word processors, Wang Laboratories went on to build more general workstations. A worker sitting at a desk could now handle data and words at the same time, on one machine, without connecting to a huge mainframe computer. But competition was tough, first from IBM, then from other manufacturers of desktop computers, and then from Japanese companies. In the late 1980s, the word processor market began to collapse with the rise of personal computers.

"When we enter society at birth, we receive an inheritance from the people who lived before us.... I feel that all of us owe the world more than we received when we were born."
—An Wang, *Lessons*, 1986

In 1984, *Forbes* magazine ranked Wang as the fifth richest American, with an estimated wealth of $1.6 billion.

Wang Theater on
Tremont Street in
Boston
exterior and lobby

Despite his watchful diligence, Wang made a pair of mistakes rooted in his Confucian philosophy of care for duty and family. For one thing, during an economic downturn, he borrowed money instead of selling more stock, because he did not want the family to lose voting control. Then, in 1986, he appointed his son Fred president of the company. With no background in engineering, Fred had a hard time earning the confidence of employees and customers. The company went into debt, and in 1989, Wang had to fire his son.

On March 24, 1990, An Wang died at age seventy of esophageal cancer. Two years later, Wang Laboratories declared bankruptcy. Purchased by a Dutch company, it disappeared. Other electronics companies suffered setbacks during the same period.

In the thirty-five years from 1951 to 1986, Wang Laboratories had grown from a one-man operation to a company with more than 30,000 employees and $3 billion in revenue. An Wang, a soft-spoken immigrant, led the industry with some of his inventions, particularly magnetic core memory and his logarithm-based method of building calculators. Just as important, he grew and steered a company through its challenging years of growth. Wang Laboratories led the development of computer memories, calculators, word processors, and computer workstations. Meanwhile, its founder maintained a sense of gratitude and loyalty to the places and institutions that had nurtured him. Wang rejuvenated the city of Lowell and boosted the arts in Boston. In the furiously competitive world of high technology, An Wang showed beyond a doubt that Chinese people could succeed in something beyond restaurants and laundries.

Wang Theater interior

"Optimism is an essential ingredient of innovation. How else can an individual welcome change over security, adventure over staying in safe places?"
— Robert Noyce

13. The Chip That Changed the World

Robert Noyce
(1927–1990)

In the image: "...n't be encumbered by history. ...off and do something wonderful." —Robert Noyce

In 1939, in a small town in Iowa, a twelve-year-old boy recruited all the kids in the neighborhood to build a grand project—a glider that would really fly. Bobby Noyce and his older brother Gaylord invested their savings of $4.73. A neighbor boy brought bamboo rods from his father's furniture store. A girl on the block sewed cheesecloth for the wings. Following a design they found in the encyclopedia, Bobby's team built a full-sized body with wooden struts and stretched cloth wings.

Now all they had to do was test it. Once the team levered the twenty-five-pound glider onto a garage roof, Bobby stepped into the pilot's slot. He hoisted the plane around him and tried to ignore the rapid beating of his heart. Then he took a deep breath. Eyes wide open, he raced to the end of the roof and jumped off. For a few glorious seconds, the glider soared. Then it landed with a bump, twisting its wings and collapsing. Bobby crawled out of the wreckage grinning.

Robert Noyce

Baby Noyce

Bob Noyce
in marching
band, 1940

Bobby Noyce, born December 12, 1927 in Denmark, Iowa, liked building things. He and his brother Gaylord made tiny hot-air balloons by wrapping paper on a wire frame. Under the open balloons, they laid oily rags. Then, on summer nights, they set the rags on fire and launched the glowing balloons from their second-story bedroom window. Luckily, none of the balloons ever started a fire in the surrounding cornfields.

"My hobby is handicraft," Bobby wrote in a school essay when he was eleven. "I like this hobby because it is useful. You can build things cheaply that are worth a lot." Making things cheaply was important, because during the Depression there wasn't much money to go around. All four of the Noyce brothers worked for pocket money, babysitting or shoveling snow. One of Bobby's jobs was delivering the morning newspaper, and on cold mornings the icy handlebars made his hands ache. So he rigged together an old car battery and headlight to carry in the basket of his bike. He slung the papers over his shoulder, and as he rode, he alternated one hand for steering and one hand warming up over the light.

In a scrapbook filled with articles from *Popular Science*, Bobby drew plans for ship models, an ice sailboat, and a motorized go-cart. He built a radio from scratch. He attached an old washing machine motor to a propeller and welded both to the back of his sled. He figured that would make the sled easier to pull uphill—he always said laziness was a great spur to invention. Unfortunately, Bobby attached the propeller backward: it pulled the sled the wrong way.

Bobby's father, the Reverend Ralph Noyce, was a Congregationalist preacher, and his mother was the daughter and granddaughter of ministers. During the Depression, as Bobby was growing up, the family moved from town to town, following Ralph's preaching jobs. Sometimes, parishioners paid the Reverend Noyce in crops instead of cash. Despite the Depression, the Noyce boys had a good time. They swam and rode their bikes and camped beside Lake Michigan. Bob played oboe in the high school band. He earned money wherever he could, and he was willing to take risks to make deals. He offered the neighbors a flat rate in advance to shovel their walks all winter, and then he prayed for a year of light snow.

Bob finished high school as class valedictorian just as World War II was ending. He attended Grinnell College on two scholarships—one for swimming and diving and one for being the child of an Iowa minister. He worked throughout college, painting balconies and cutting hair or sewing clothes for his classmates. He majored in math and physics.

Bob reveled in college life. He sang in the chorus and acted in plays. In 1948, he won the Midwest Conference Diving Championships. He also smoked, dated, drank beer, and stopped going to church. A few weeks before the end of his junior year, a group of his friends decided their spring house party should be a Hawaiian luau. They chose Bob and another local boy to steal a young pig to serve as dinner. That evening, Bob and his friend snuck across a field and snatched a twenty-five-pound suckling pig from a nearby farm. They carried it wriggling back to the party. Their housemates slaughtered the squealing pig in the shower and washed its blood down the drain.

Bob Noyce, 1944

In the morning, feeling sick about what they had done, Bob and his friend retraced their steps and offered to pay the farmer for the pig. But stealing a pig was a felony, and there had to be punishment. Grinnell suspended the miscreants for the first semester of their senior year.

It was probably the low point of young Bob Noyce's life. In disgrace, he left campus and moved to New York. There he managed to get a job as an actuary. He spent his days working on insurance tables that predicted when people would die. The work was depressing, and Bob worried about his future. He volunteered to join the U.S. Air Force, but when recruiters told him he could never be a pilot because he

Noyce with model airplane

Transistors

William Shockley, John Bardeen, and Walter Brattain invented the transistor in 1947. Transistors are made of a semi-conducting element like silicon or germanium, with small amounts of other elements diffused or seeping into them. These impurities allow electrons to flow through the semiconductor in some conditions but not others. Changing the current flowing through the device allows it to serve as either an amplifier—boosting the current—or a switch. Transistors made integrated circuits and modern electronics possible.

An early transistor

was colorblind, he backed out. Instead, he applied to graduate school in physics at MIT.

When January arrived, Bob returned to Grinnell. That spring, he encountered the device that would hold his interest for the rest of his life—the transistor. When Bell Labs publicly announced the invention of the transistor, Grinnell physics professor Grant Gale requested a sample device from one of the inventors, his old classmate John Bardeen. Together, Gale and Noyce read every technical article they could find about transistor physics. Bob later said, "I couldn't grasp how it worked immediately...." The study of transistors became a lifelong passion and the basis of Noyce's later success as an innovator.

In September 1949, Bob drove his old Ford to Cambridge, Massachusetts, to start graduate school at MIT. There, the country boy from a small college buckled down and studied hard. By the second year, he got a job as a teaching assistant. He sang as a baritone in a Boston choral group. Best of all, he learned to ski. He and his friends drove to New Hampshire, attached skins to the bottom of their skis (it worked better than wax), climbed up the slope, and skied down. On one such outing, Bob hurtled over a ski jump and shattered his left humerus, the long bone in the upper arm. He spent two weeks in traction and had surgery to screw the bone back together. For the rest of his life, his arm carried a long, broad scar like a zipper.

For his PhD thesis, Bob studied how electrons behave at the surface of insulators. He learned about electrons, holes, and quantum mechanics. In 1953, after four years of graduate school, Bob completed his thesis. During his final spring of graduate school, while singing in the musical *South Pacific* at Tufts University, he fell for the costume mistress, a young Tufts graduate named Betty Bottomley.

That summer, Ralph Noyce married the young couple in Sandwich, Illinois. From there, they drove to Philadelphia, where Bob took a job for $6,900 a year at Philco. He had chosen the television manufacturer over better-paying jobs at IBM and Bell Labs because he believed they really needed his expertise. He did experiments to improve the etching and electroplating required to manufacture a new germanium transistor. He also got his first taste of management. As a manager, he was easygoing, and as one man who worked for him said, Noyce was "very easy to talk to, very helpful."

Bob Noyce with kids Billy and Penny (author), 1957

During their three years in Philadelphia, Bob and Betty had two children, Billy and Penny. Bob traveled often to meet with Philco's military customers. Gradually, his first excitement at working for Philco wore off. Philco was struggling. It stopped investing in research and instead chased after government contracts. Bob hated the "waste, make-work, and lack of incentives" of government work. He grew restless.

Then, in January 1956, Bob Noyce got a fateful call from William Shockley. As Bob said later, "It was like picking up the phone and talking to God." Shockley had led the Bell Labs team that invented the transistor. His intuition for electronics was so acute, people said it seemed he could *see* electrons.

Bob Noyce with kids Polly and Margaret, 1963

Shockley invited Bob to join a new electronics company. At Shockley Semiconductor, Noyce could work on cutting-edge technology with the best minds in the business. And it would be in California. "All Iowans think California is heaven," Bob once said. Shockley asked Bob to go to New York to take a series of intelligence and personality tests. His test results predicted that he would be good in the lab but would never make an effective manager.

In February 1956, Shockley paid for Bob and Betty to fly to San Francisco so he could interview Bob in person. The morning they touched down, they drove down the peninsula between the San

William Shockley

Francisco Bay and the coastal hills, between apricot orchards and the sulfur flats of the bay. They looked at houses, and Bob, ever confident, made a down payment on a small house in Los Altos. In the afternoon, he went for his interview. He got the job.

True to his word, Shockley assembled an impressive team of scientists. Among them was a physical chemist, Gordon Moore, who became Bob's closest partner. The group was young, multinational, and brilliant.

Shockley had an outsize personality. He loved to climb mountains and do magic tricks. He considered himself a teacher and even a father to the young men he gathered around him. He also meant to keep a close eye on them—not to let them go off on their own and invent something important without him. Shockley made sure his name was on every paper and every patent the group produced.

The team quickly set to work. Shockley had decided they would build transistors out of silicon, the major ingredient of sand and one of the most plentiful elements on Earth. It is primarily because of Shockley's choice that today the Santa Clara Valley is called Silicon Valley instead of Germanium Valley. The team "doped" the silicon through a process known as diffusion, where the silicon is cooked with impurities in a furnace at the right temperature to let them seep into the silicon. Doping adds a few atoms that have either one more electron or one fewer electron in their outer orbit than silicon does. These make what are called n- and p-regions. The slight lack or excess of electrons allows the silicon to conduct under certain conditions and not others.

Noyce led a team of six PhD scientists. He didn't think of himself as a manager. He was doing research and soaking up insight from Shockley. Noyce himself was a good teacher, experienced, approachable, and modest. "He had a very quiet leadership style, a gee-whiz-aw-shucks-farm-boy approach that was very attractive," said one colleague. The scientists gave each other mini-seminars so they would understand one another's work. Noyce wrote papers and won patents for advances in transistor production.

Shockley, however, determined the direction the research took. In August 1956, Bob had a brainstorm about a new kind of diode, which he called a "negative resistance diode." Excited, Bob took his notebook to Shockley. But Shockley showed no interest, and Bob dropped the diode idea. Seventeen months later, the Japanese scientist Leo Esaki published an article describing virtually the same device as the one sketched in Bob Noyce's notebook. He called it the "tunnel diode." When he saw Esaki's article, Bob brought his lab notebook to show his friend Gordon Moore, saying, "If I had gone one step further, I would have done it." In 1973, Esaki and a colleague received the Nobel Prize in Physics for the invention of the tunnel diode, "the first quantum electron device."

Two and a half months after the episode with the diode, William Shockley awoke to a momentous phone call of his own. Along with Walter Brattain and John Bardeen, he had won the Nobel Prize for inventing the transistor.

Shockley returned from the award ceremony in Sweden carrying little gifts for everyone in the lab, with the biggest one for his favorite, Bob Noyce. But he also returned with even greater faith in his own genius. He became more erratic, suspicious, and belittling to those who worked for him. He pulled five scientists from Bob Noyce's silicon transistor project, which was making progress, to work on a notion of his own, a four-layer diode that Shockley never managed to produce in quantity.

By 1957, the company was still not making money. Working for William Shockley continued to grow more difficult. Although he could still be charming, Shockley attacked people when they made mistakes and humiliated them when he thought they weren't smart enough.

tunnel diode

A diode is an electronic component, made of doped semiconductor, that generally allows current to pass in only one direction. Such a diode can act as a one-way valve. What Bob Noyce sketched out in his lab notebook was a diode whose silicon was doped with a thousand times more impurities than usual. Such a device, Bob predicted, would show a startling new behavior. As low voltages gradually increased, current would increase in the forward direction, just as usually happened with diodes. But at higher voltage, current would suddenly drop in a quantum effect known as tunneling. Only when voltage was increased still further would the forward current rise again. Tunnel diodes have been used in television tuners, in high-radiation environments, and in oscilloscopes.

Bardeen, Shockley,
Brattain, 1948

The young scientists began to hold back and doubt their own ideas.

Seven of Shockley's recruits quietly decided to leave the company. They tried to convince Noyce to join them, but Noyce still felt loyalty to Shockley. Moreover, he needed a steady job. He and Betty had just had their third child, Polly.

At that time, there was no system of venture capitalists waiting to invest in start-up companies. But eventually, the group found a pair of bankers, Arthur Rock and Bud Coyle, who agreed to help them find a million dollars to start a new company if they could show they had a leader. So Sheldon Roberts called Bob Noyce for one last attempt to convince him to join them. In the end, Noyce agreed to meet with the investment bankers.

Shockley Semiconductor celebrates
Shockley's Nobel prize.
Noyce raising a glass in center.

The next night, the whole team met at the Clift Hotel. The more they talked, the more Noyce liked the idea of the team of eight striking out on their own. Arthur Rock saw at once that the other members of the group looked up to Noyce as a leader. That evening, the group committed themselves to starting a new company. The eight scientists and two bankers signed and shared ten $1 bills to seal their pact.

Arthur Rock looked for a company to house the new semiconductor start-up. Thirty companies turned them down. After all, who were these eight young men who considered themselves too good to work for a Nobel prizewinner? Finally, Sherman Fairchild, a millionaire inventor, offered the group a chance to start a division of Fairchild Camera and Instrument. Each of the eight put up $500 of earnest money in return for a hundred shares of stock. (Bob Noyce had to borrow this money from his grandmother.) Fairchild Camera and Instrument would loan them more than a million dollars to get started in return for a chance to buy them out later.

Shockley never forgave Bob Noyce for his betrayal. When the eight scientists left, Arnold Beckman, Shockley's financial sponsor, warned them, "This will be looked on as a shameful act." True enough, the eight defectors soon became known as the Traitorous Eight. But before long, the title became a badge of proud membership in an elite group. As the semiconductor industry expanded in Silicon Valley, so did the tradition of young scientists and engineers looking around at the walls of a company, taking a deep breath, and striking out on their own.

The Traitorous Eight
from left to right: Gordon Moore, Sheldon Roberts, Eugene Kleiner, Robert Noyce, Victor Grinich, Julius Blank, Jean Hoerni and Jay Last

On October 4, 1957, the Soviet Union had launched Sputnik, the first man-made satellite to orbit the earth. That America's Communist rival could achieve such a feat sent waves of anxiety across the nation. President Eisenhower vowed that the United States would launch its own satellite within months. The space race, with its vast requirements for electronic guidance, began.

At the new Fairchild Semiconductor, Bob Noyce served as the lab's technical head, but the atmosphere was egalitarian and free, very different from Shockley's lab. Word spread, and soon other Shockley scientists and technicians began moving to Fairchild.

Fairchild's big chance came when they learned that IBM wanted a silicon transistor for a computer to guide a long-range bomber. Noyce listened to the specs for a heat-resistant transistor that would be faster than anything on the market. Although his team had not yet built a single transistor, Noyce told his IBM contacts, "Sure. We can do that." He split the engineers into teams. Sheldon Roberts grew the silicon crystals and sliced them into dime-sized wafers.

Gordon Moore and Jean Hoerni diffused the doping impurities into the silicon. Jay Last and Bob Noyce used photolithography, etching with light, to mark tiny individual transistors on the silicon wafer. Blank and Kleiner supervised a group of women who cut the transistors apart, wired them into containers, and packaged them.

Four months after signing the contract, Fairchild Semiconductor delivered one hundred new transistors to IBM. Theirs was the first double diffusion transistor on the market, and the team had proved themselves to their first major customer. Bob Noyce's optimism had paid off.

"Don't be encumbered by hostory, go out and do something wonderful."
— Bob Noyce

The Integrated Circuit

By this time, 1958, Fairchild Semiconductor had hired a general manager, Ed Baldwin, and Bob Noyce could focus his full attention on research. His mind bubbled with ideas. He stayed up long after Betty and the children were in bed, filling pages of his lab book with calculations. He spoke at technical conferences, bounced ideas off Gordon Moore and other friends in the lab, and filed for seven patents. His ideas came primarily through intuition. He would pose himself a problem, think about the fundamentals of the physics involved, and then put it out of his mind.

When an idea came, Noyce asked himself only two questions: "Why won't this work?" and "What fundamental laws will this violate?" Although many of his intuitive notions went nowhere, some led to important breakthroughs.

But no matter how details of semiconductor manufacturing improved, one problem stood out in the electronics industry in the late 1950s. Circuits were becoming more complex. They often had hundreds or even thousands of components, each of which had to be wired to tens of others. An assembly line of young women in white coats did this painstaking work, connecting thousands of wires thinner than a human hair with tiny tweezers under a microscope. The more the wires, the greater the possibility of error and the slower the circuit. Engineers referred to this problem as "the tyranny of numbers."

Fairchild's breakthrough leading to a solution grew out of another problem. Customers were returning transistors that had failed. Fairchild engineers discovered that, as workers sealed the cans that protected the transistor, tiny pieces of metal broke off inside and bounced around, shorting out the transistor. Jean Hoerni decided that the surface

Noyce with his Fairchild team

of the transistor needed better protection. In 1958, he found a way to lay a thin layer of silicon oxide over a wafer of silicon, like icing on a cake. Tiny holes in the icing still allowed him to diffuse impurities into the silicon.

This icing method became known as the planar process, and it made a big impression on Bob Noyce. To him, it was like "building a transistor inside a cocoon of silicon dioxide so it never gets contaminated …like setting up your jungle operating room. You put the patient inside a plastic bag and you operate inside of that, and you don't have all the flies of the jungle sitting on the wound."

Robert Noyce with a chip design, 1959

Bob grew intrigued by the possibilities this new manufacturing method might open. Starting in January 1959, he sketched a series of ideas in his lab notebook. He mused that the protective coating of silicon dioxide with tiny holes in it would allow one to make precise metal connections between different parts of the underlying silicon. One could drop molten metal on top of the icing, but only through the tiny holes would the metal reach down to touch the actual semiconductor surface. Metal was a conductor, basically a wire. That meant you could "print" tiny and precise wiring directly onto the semiconductor. In fact, different electronic components could be built on different areas of one small piece of silicon and connected through the printed wires.

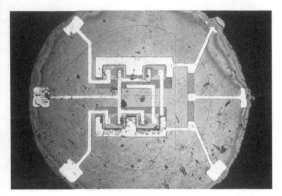

First commercial integrated circuit

This was the idea of the integrated circuit, the computer chip that is now found in every electronic device, in computers, music players, cars, microwave ovens, televisions, and Mars rovers. As Bob said later, the invention came by thinking, "Let's see, if we could do this, we can do that ...a logical sequence. If I hit a wall, I'd back up and then find a path, conceptually, all the way through to the end." He filed for a patent in July 1959.

All his life, Noyce saw his invention of the integrated circuit, or microchip, as an improvement in a manufacturing process, not as a scientific breakthrough. Others felt differently. Years later, John Bardeen, co-inventor of the transistor, called the invention of the integrated circuit "as important as the wheel."

Jack Kilby

Meanwhile, Jack Kilby, an inventor at Fairchild's huge rival, Texas Instruments, had come up with a design of his own. He built a circuit on a single piece of germanium. Tiny gold wires like spiderweb fibers flew off the surface to connect the components. The wiring meant the device could not be mass-produced, but Texas Instruments announced the invention as the first integrated circuit. After years of court battles between Fairchild and TI, Noyce and Kilby were eventually credited as co-inventors of the integrated circuit. Any company wanting to build one had to pay licensing fees to both companies.

As for Bob Noyce and Jack Kilby, they respected each other's work and were happy to share the credit. Over the years, they shared a Franklin Medal, a National Medal of Technology, a National Medal of Science, and a Draper Prize, sometimes called the Nobel Prize of engineering, for their invention. In the year 2000, eight years after Bob Noyce's death, Jack Kilby even won a Nobel Prize for the integrated circuit. The Nobel Prize only goes to living scientists, so although Kilby, the big soft-spoken Texan who kept inventing all his life, mentioned Noyce in his Nobel acceptance lecture, this was one prize Noyce didn't share.

Noyce family, 1963

Fairchild Semiconductor grew rapidly. After two years, Fairchild Camera and Instrument bought the company. Each founder received $300,000 in return for his $500 investment. Bob Noyce paid back his grandmother and sent his parents on a vacation to Europe. He bought a new car to replace the beat-up old family Chevy with a hole in the floor.

Bob was now general manager of Fairchild Semiconductor. He wanted the company to be as open and egalitarian a workplace as possible. Fairchild had a common dining room where hourly employees ate with their bosses. The company provided voluntary paid overtime, management classes, and health care. Researchers in the lab were given freedom to pursue projects they found interesting. Bob had learned from the episode of the tunnel diode. He believed that the role of management was to enable and coach people to do what they did best.

In the 1960s, Fairchild grew at a rate of about a hundred employees a month. By 1962, it had 3,000 employees. Noyce traveled often. He flew to headquarters in Syosset, New York, every three weeks. He also did business in Hong Kong, Japan, and Italy. He brought home gifts—elegant Japanese dolls and painted screens. On winter weekends when he was home, he and Betty drove the kids—now four of them—to the Sierras to ski.

As Fairchild grew, some of its top employees, including some of the eight founders, left to start their own electronics companies.

Bob had always loved singing. In Los Altos, he started a madrigal group that met on Wednesday nights. When he was home, he conducted the group, but he was often traveling. Once someone asked a group member if she knew Bob Noyce, and she answered, *"Oh yes, he's our semiconductor!"*

Before long, these new start-ups became known as "the Fairchildren." Engineers and scientists left because they wanted freedom and the chance to get rich. Moreover, Fairchild was growing large and bureaucratic. The semiconductor division was the most profitable part of Fairchild Camera and Instrument, but instead of reinvesting profits in the semiconductor vision, Fairchild management siphoned them off to prop up other parts of the company.

By 1967, Bob began to think of leaving, too. After a downturn in the market, the one boss Bob most respected was fired. Bob himself was considered as president for all of Fairchild, but the board decided that, at forty, he was still too young. It was just as well. Bob wrote to Sherman Fairchild, "As [the company] has gotten larg-

Intel original building in Mt View

er and larger, I have enjoyed my daily work less and less." He wanted to start again, with a new company that would stay small and inventive. And he wanted Gordon Moore, head of research and development for Fairchild Semiconductor, to come with him. It took some effort to convince Moore to take the leap, but in July 1968, Bob Noyce and Gordon Moore both resigned from Fairchild.

Noyce and Moore
at Intel, Santa Clara,
1970

Bob and Gordon named their new company Intel. Although Bob took the title of president to satisfy outsiders, the two considered themselves equal partners. Engineers, many of them from Fairchild, flocked to the new company. So did investors. Arthur Rock raised $2.5 million for the company in forty-eight hours. Bob had typed out a three-page business plan, but none of the investors asked to see it. As Warren Buffet, then on the board of Grinnell College, said, "We were betting on the jockey, not the horse." Grinnell's early investment in Intel made it one of the wealthiest small liberal arts colleges in the United States.

Originally, Intel focused on building computer memories. It brought out its first working product, a 64-bit random access memory, in May 1969. Then it introduced a product called the 1103, and Noyce convinced most of the large computer companies to buy it. But most important of all was the microprocessor, invented by Intel employees Ted Hoff, Federico Faggin, and Stanley Mazor. The microprocessor was essentially a tiny computer on a chip. Soon, Intel abandoned memories to focus on these complex, programmable chips. Bob gave talks predicting that soon there would be computers in cars, ovens, watches, and telephones.

Robert N. Noyce Building, Intel

Outside the company, Bob Noyce pursued other adventures. He got his pilot's license and even bought his own plane. He took the family skiing whenever he could. On an Easter trip to Aspen in 1968, he broke his leg so badly that even after surgery he had a draining infection that lasted months.

In 1971, Intel went public, offering its stock in public markets for the first time. Shares in the company sold for five times what they had when the company started. To share the wealth, the company extended a stock purchase plan to all its employees, "even janitors," as Bob proudly said.

Noyce and Moore

Despite Bob's wish for a company that would stay small and agile, Intel grew far faster than Bob and Gordon could have imagined. The 8080 microprocessor became the industry standard. Profits exploded. Bob's role outside the company grew. He listened to customers and testified before government committees. Over time, he became a spokesman for the entire electronics industry. At some point, people began referring to him as "the mayor of Silicon Valley."

In 1974, Bob's marriage to Betty ended, and Betty moved to Maine. A few months later, Bob began dating Intel's head of human resources, Ann Bowers. In late 1975, the couple married. Shortly afterward, Ann left Intel to become the vice president for human resources at a new start-up called Apple.

Bob Noyce and Steve Jobs

Steve Jobs, Apple's founder, became a friend, dropping by on his motorcycle for dinner. He considered Bob Noyce the "soul of Intel" and looked to him as a mentor. The two of them often went down to Bob's basement to play with electronics. Bob taught Steve to ski better, often taking him on plane flights. Once, flying Steve home, Bob put the landing gear up instead of down as they approached the runway. The plane landed in a terrifying skid. Steve imagined the headlines: "Bob Noyce and Steve Jobs Killed in Fiery Plane Crash." Steve said, "It was only due to [Bob's] excellent piloting that we survived."

In 1975, Bob Noyce stepped down as president of Intel, making room for Gordon Moore, while Noyce became chairman of the board. Bob spent more time investing personally in other companies—lasers, bar codes, a new ski design—and speaking for the electronics industry as a whole. Now he traveled for enjoyment. He and Ann visited New Guinea and Tibet. They took scuba diving vacations with other couples, and Bob invented a box to hold his camera underwater. Every winter, Bob went helicopter skiing on glaciers in Canada. He and Ann rode horses on their new ranch on the California coast. Bob took more flying lessons and bought a jet.

Over time, Noyce and other electronics CEOs grew more and more worried about competition from Japan. Japan was already taking over consumer electronics and the car business. Were semiconductors next? Noyce estimated that between 1984 and 1986, the American electronics industry had lost $2 billion in earnings and 27,000 jobs to Japan. Moreover, in Japan, the government helped fund electronics research. Along with others—most notably National Semiconductor's Charles Sporck—Noyce began to lobby for a similar effort in the United States. Finally, Congress agreed. They would create a government-industry research consortium, to be called Sematech, in Austin, Texas.

Next came the search for someone to lead the new venture. Finding a widely trusted leader willing to work for the whole industry instead of one company was nearly impossible. Finally, Ann told Bob, "If you think this is so important, you should do it yourself."

At the age of sixty, Bob left his beloved California and moved to Texas to build his third start-up. This one was different. It meant persuading fierce competitors to lend their best engineers for a year or two to a cooperative effort—while paying for the privilege. Noyce helped establish Sematech's principles for doing business. He flew around the country, using all his charisma to share his vision of why cooperating was so important.

After two years, Sematech had stabilized and was making an important contribution. Bob Noyce announced that he would be moving on. On June 1, 1990, Sematech planned a surprise for him. That morning, when he arrived at work, every employee greeted him wearing a T-shirt quoting the headlines of a recent column in the *San Jose Mercury News*: "Bob Noyce, Teen Idol."

Two days later, on June 3, 1990, Bob took a morning swim before setting off for a weekend of flying lessons. As he climbed out of the pool, he told Ann he felt dizzy. When he lay down on the bed, his heart stopped.

Bob Noyce's sudden death sent a shock through the industry. His colleagues staged two large memorial services for him in in Austin, Texas, and in San Jose, California. The *San Jose Mercury News* published a special section of people's memories of Bob. Many related how he had inspired them, to build a harpsichord, to study Japanese, to ski down a frightening slope. Bob Noyce, the boy who wanted to fly, had always inspired people to fly higher than they believed they could.

A corner in the Intel Museum, Santa Clara, CA.
The picture on the left has Robert Noyce and
Gordon Moore at the front.

"The number of transistors on a chip doubles every twenty-four months."

— Gordon Moore, 1965

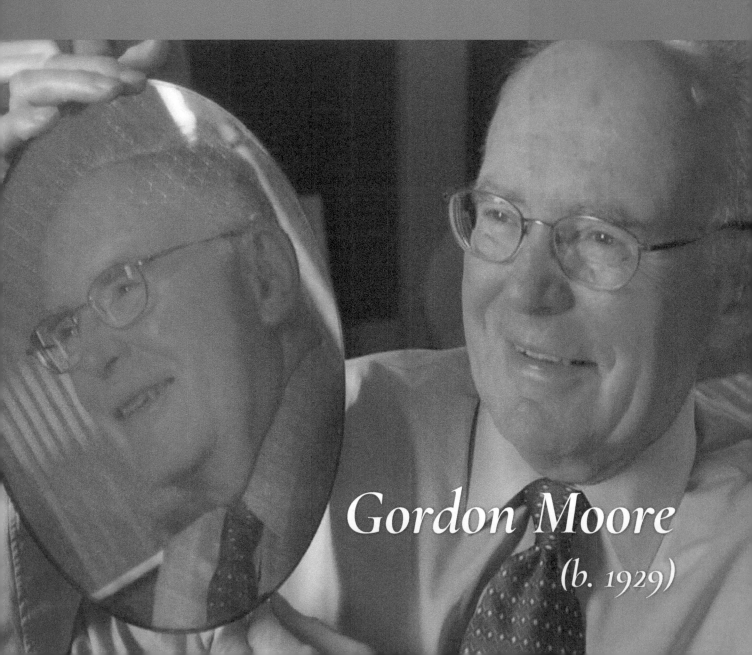

14. Electronics Visionary

Gordon Moore
(b. 1929)

Baby Moore

When Gordon Moore was born on January 3, 1929, there were no personal computers, no cell phones, space capsules, video games, or even televisions. As Gordon was growing up, no one guessed that this quiet, introverted boy would help create a new world of electronics. No one then <u>could conceive of</u> computers whose parts would become ever smaller, cheaper, and more powerful—a vision that became known as Moore's Law.

Gordon lived on the California coast, in the small fishing and ranching town of Pescadero. His grandfather ran the general store, selling picks and vegetables and underwear. Gordon's father was a policeman, breaking up fights and chasing smugglers who snuck illegal alcohol ashore from darkened boats.

Electronics is the science of how electrons flow through a vacuum, a gas, or certain solid materials, and the devices and systems that use this electron flow.

Pescadero is Spanish for "fishmonger," or someone who sells fish. (picture above, Pescadero State Beach, CA)

Gordon Moore

Gordon Moore's great-uncles and his grandfather Walter Henry Moore, second from left.

Gordon's grandfather's store

Walter Moore, Gordon's father

At age five, Gordon rode a bull calf in the local rodeo. He held on to the strap so hard that when the calf bucked him off, he couldn't get his hand out. His arm broke. After that, Gordon decided not to be a cowboy.

Gordon enjoyed exploring the woods, fishing for crayfish, and building forts with other kids. He and his friends fished in Pescadero Creek for baby steelhead, which they called trout, using salmon eggs from his grandfather's store. "Six inches was a big one," Gordon says. At school, he didn't talk much. His teachers thought he was "slow" and wanted him to repeat first grade. But Gordon's father didn't want his son to waste time "playing in the sandbox" for another year. So he marched down to the school to argue, and Gordon entered second grade on time.

The family's days in tiny Pescadero ended when Gordon's father was promoted to county sheriff. They moved away from the coast, across the mountains to Redwood City, a growing town set among plum and apricot orchards. In his new school, Gordon's teachers misjudged him again. They placed him in a special pull-out class for students with language delays.

One of the best days in Gordon's life came the year he turned eleven, when his friend Donald Blum received a chemistry set as a present. Doing experiments with Donald, Gordon fell in love with chemistry. Soon he was saving money to buy his own chemicals and beakers. "In those days you could buy almost anything," Gordon says. Mixing liquids that bubbled or changed color was fun, but big blasts were best of all. Making gunpowder became his specialty. Gordon built a cement floor in the shed behind his house and spent hours there alone after school, mixing chemicals and concocting rocket fuel. He loved colorful flames, flashes of light, and any sort of explosion. Once he badly scorched his hands, but luckily, his parents didn't notice.

Gordon Moore and
Walter Moore

When Gordon was in high school, his older brother, Walter, was drafted into the army to fight in World War II. Back at home, Gordon played halfback on the football team, swam, and did gymnastics. On weekends, he fished or hunted with his cousins. In English class, he said, "I could diagram a sentence and knew what a pronoun was, but I wasn't a voracious reader. I was not interested in *Wuthering Heights*, things like that." Math and science were his best subjects. He already knew he wanted to be a chemist, "... whatever that was. I knew you mixed things together and funny things happened."

Once, Gordon's father brought home a little bottle of yellow liquid. The police had found it with some safe-cracking equipment. Was it an explosive? Gordon's father asked. To find out, Gordon soaked a bit of filter paper with the liquid and struck it with a hammer. It made a "beautiful bang." Yes, he told his father, the liquid was nitroglycerine. "I'll take care of it," Gordon said, and he made the rest of the nitroglycerine into dynamite.

Gordon as swimmer

Gordon became the first member of his family to go to college. He started at San Jose State College so he could save money by living at home. After two years, he transferred to the University of California at Berkeley, where he could study with some of the top chemists in the world. One time he signed up for an advanced, graduate-level course. On the midterm exam, he got a zero. Shocked but not discouraged, he buckled down and studied harder. On the final exam, he received the second-highest grade in the class.

Betty and Gordon Moore wedding with parents

In his senior year, Gordon began doing original research with his professor, George Jura. He investigated why different colors appeared when charged molecules were adsorbed into a silica gel. At the time, he didn't know that he would spend much of his life working with silicon, an element found in sand. What he did know was how much he liked figuring things out for himself. He loved research because he got to do experiments and learn things nobody else knew. He published his first scientific paper.

To learn more about chemical research, Gordon decided to go to graduate school at the California Institute of Technology, Caltech. But first he asked his college sweetheart, Betty Whitcomb, to marry him. The couple had met at a student government conference and had been dating for several years. On an August evening, they married by candlelight. The next day they drove to Pasadena, where Caltech was located. The year was 1950.

At Caltech, Gordon found a spot in the laboratory of Richard McLean Badger, who studied how atoms bind together into molecules. The lab researchers used infrared light to examine the shape of chemical bonds between atoms. Humans can't see infrared light, but special instruments can easily detect it. Professor McLean Badger mostly left Gordon alone to work as he saw fit, and Gordon happily worked long hours in the basement of the chemistry lab, improving instruments and making careful measurements. His quiet, methodical approach worked well. In less than three years, much faster than usual, he earned his PhD degree. (He thinks he took his oral exams for his PhD the same day Robert Noyce did at the other end of the country.) In his thesis, Gordon included his tongue-in-cheek prescription for inspiring more students to become chemists: "A laboratory course in explosives and pyrotechnics [fireworks] should be included in the high school curriculum."

With his new degree in hand, Dr. Gordon Moore found a job at a US Navy—funded lab in Maryland. There he continued his work on infrared spectra. He blew glass for his instruments and built furnaces to heat his chemicals. In 1956, his son Ken was born. At that time Gordon had no thoughts of going into business. He was still shy and quiet. Before giving a talk to a group of scientists from all over the country, he suffered from an upset stomach for days. Finally, he calmed himself down enough to speak. "I was so darn nervous," he said later, "but I learned."

Although Gordon enjoyed research, he began to wonder whether it had any practical use. His major output was scientific papers that only a few experts ever read. Once Gordon calculated how much the government was spending on his writings: $5 per word! "I wondered," Gordon said later, "was the government getting its money's worth?"

Then, one evening, William Shockley phoned. Shockley was a famous physicist, known as the inventor of the transistor, which was beginning to replace vacuum tubes to run computers and other electronic devices. Now Shockley planned to start a company in California to build and sell new, improved transistors. He intended to hire only the brightest physicists, chemists, and electrical engineers. Would Gordon Moore be interested? Gordon jumped at the chance to return to California. He was eager to work with a famous scientist, "actually making a product and selling it."

As he had with Robert Noyce, Shockley first sent Moore to take an intelligence test. Later he showed the two men their results. They were remarkably similar: the two new employees were bright and would be good researchers, but they would never be managers.

In *The Power of Boldness*, Moore wrote, "A transistor is the building block of digital logic and memory circuits. It works much like an electric light switch: current is allowed to pass when the switch is in the open position; the flow of current is stopped when the switch is closed."

For a salary of $750 a month, Gordon Moore joined Shockley Semiconductor. He arrived at work on a Monday and received a badge with employee number 18. Noyce, employee number 17, had arrived the previous Friday.

At the time, 99 percent of the world's transistors were made of an element called germanium. Shockley wanted to leap ahead by building his transistors out of silicon. Gordon helped design the lab, blow glass, and set up equipment. Then he began to learn the special chemical techniques the new business would need. He learned to "print" onto thin layers of silicon. To do this, he heated the elements boron or phosphorus in a high-temperature furnace. Then he let the atoms of the heated elements, now in gas form, diffuse into the surface of the silicon.

At first, Shockley Semiconductor was an exciting place to work. Brilliant young scientists challenged one other, pushing the edges of physics and chemistry. In 1956, their boss, William Shockley, shared the Nobel Prize in Physics for helping to invent the transistor with John Bardeen and Walter Brattain.

But Shockley turned out to be a terrible manager. He kept pulling men (all the company's scientists and engineers were men) away from their own projects to work on his latest new ideas. He grew angry whenever a new idea didn't work out. He didn't trust his employees. The company was fast running through money, and it still had no product to sell. Once, convinced that someone had stuck a pin in a doorway to hurt him, Shockley demanded that every employee take a lie detector test.

Gordon Moore and seven other young scientists from the transistor project, including Gordon's future partner Robert Noyce, decided they could no longer work for their suspicious and controlling boss. With help from a New York banker, they looked for another company to take them in. When Shockley heard rumors of the defection, he called in his young scientists one by one to question them. Moore, who had always been so steady and reliable, broke the news that eight of them were leaving. "I saw him a little while later," Gordon says. "He left the building with his head hanging down walking out the door. It's never fun firing anyone, especially your boss."

Shortly afterward, the eight scientists resigned as a group and started Fairchild Semiconductor within a larger company called Fairchild Camera and Instrument. Starting Fairchild was risky. None of the men had business experience, and they had no idea how to start a company. What they did have, they thought, was a pretty good idea of how to make transistors. "There were half a dozen steps," says Gordon. "So we just parceled them out, put a person in charge of each one, and went to work."

Robert Noyce and Gordon Moore
in front of
Fairchild Camera and Instrument

Moore was the new company's most experienced chemist. To get started, he designed and built furnaces with materials he ordered from Sweden. Using the new furnaces, he refined methods for diffusing impurities into silicon. The impurities helped silicon act as a semiconductor. Many of the Fairchild's early transistors failed, but Gordon persisted. He once said, "If everything you try works, you aren't trying hard enough." Before long, Moore became Fairchild Semiconductor's director of research and development.

Gordon Moore worked very closely with Bob Noyce. Their work styles fit each other well. Often, Bob generated wild ideas and Gordon decided which of them to pursue with careful work in the lab. In one case, Gordon's persistence led to a patent the two inventors filed together. The patent was for using aluminum to make contacts for both p- and n-type silicon. Aluminum soon became the standard in the industry for making these contacts. Still, Moore considers himself more a maker than an inventor. His specialty

P-type silicon has small amounts of boron added, and n-type silicon has small amounts of phosphorus. Both impurities allow electrons to move more easily through the silicon, allowing it to conduct electricity under certain conditions.

was carefully adjusting manufacturing conditions to make products better and more reliable.

As a manager, Gordon says he was a lot more like his thesis adviser, Richard McLean Badger, than William Shockley. He avoided conflict. "I had a kind of hands-off management style," he says. "I have a bad habit that if I agree with someone [about a research approach], I don't say anything." If he disagreed, he tried to come up with a better idea for the person to work on.

Moore on trail

In hiring young engineers and scientists, Moore didn't expect a perfect match. Texas Instruments had turned down the young Hungarian physicist Andy Grove for a job because his PhD thesis was about how fluids move around a sphere, nothing to do with electronics. But Gordon himself had come to semiconductors from another field. For him, it was the quality of a candidate's thinking, not the topic, that mattered. He hired Grove, who later became Intel's third president.

By this time, Gordon and Betty Moore had another son, Steve. As the boys grew, Gordon helped them build go-karts and watched them begin to work on larger cars. The family bought a cabin in the Sierras and went hiking and fishing in the mountains. "Gordon loves fishing," a friend once said, "but he doesn't do it for relaxation or meditation. He does it because he wants to get the fish." Gordon insists that trying to outwit the fish is relaxing, because the fisherman stops thinking about anything else. The busier Silicon Valley grew, the more Gordon enjoyed slipping into the woods or out onto the water in his fishing boat.

Meanwhile, inventions and new processes rapidly drove the electronics industry forward. By the early 1960s, Fairchild Semiconductor was making integrated circuits, which were chips of silicon with entire circuits embedded inside. Gordon's team kept finding ways to fit more circuits onto each chip. In 1965, Gordon graphed the progress of the industry. He noted that the number of transistors on a chip had doubled every year. He predicted that the yearly doubling would continue for the next ten years. It was a bold prediction. At that time, thirty components could fit on a chip. Moore was claiming that in ten years, that number would be 60,000. And he was right! At that point, Moore revised his prediction to say that the doubling would now happen every two years.

This prediction, which people began to call Moore's Law, became a goal and standard for the entire electronics industry. Competing companies invested huge amounts in research. They developed new processes to crowd more transistors onto the same size

Moore's Law is not a true scientific law like the Law of Gravity. Instead, it is a prediction that has inspired generations of chemists and engineers.

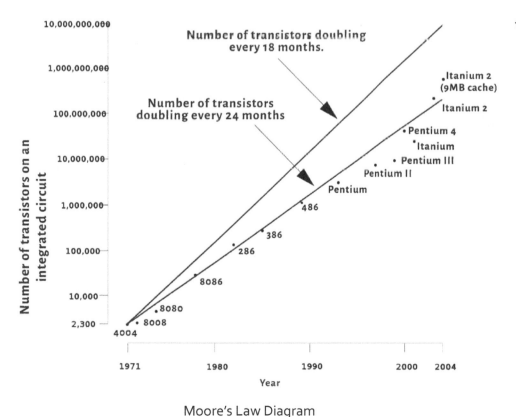

Moore's Law Diagram

chips every year. No other industry in the history of the world has ever made so much progress so quickly for so long.

From left: Vic Grinich, Gordon Moore, Bob Noyce, Julius Blank

Most importantly, as the number of components increased, the cost per component fell rapidly. Computing power became affordable, and that began to change everything—how people lived, how they worked, and how they got information. Gordon once said, "We are the real revolutionaries in the world today—not the kind with the long hair and beards." He had a point. The dropping costs of silicon chips brought computing power to every corner of the world. Microwave ovens, cell phones, personal computers, the Internet, digital cameras, the space program—all relied on those ever more complex, ever cheaper chips.

1970's Moore and Noyce reviewing papers

Fairchild Semiconductor grew rapidly. All the founders became wealthy. Still, many of them grew restless inside the bureaucracy of a large, New York-based company. They were Californians now, and they sought new adventures. One by one, the founders left to start their own new companies. People in Silicon Valley called the new companies "the Fairchildren."

By ten years after Fairchild's founding, only Robert Noyce and Gordon Moore remained of the original eight founders. They, too, felt frustrated by the demands and directions sent down by distant New York bosses. Moreover, New York was planning new directions. Gordon loved his job, but he was afraid that might change under new management. He always called himself an "accidental entrepreneur." Some people, he said, "can make a business out of almost anything. But the accidental entrepreneur like me has to fall into the opportunity or be pushed into it." Ten years earlier, Moore had helped convince Bob Noyce to leave Shockley. This time, it was Noyce who lured Moore away from Fairchild.

The new company, they decided, would make special memory chips for computers. Moore and Noyce would be equal partners. They considered naming the new company "Moore-Noyce," but that sounded like "more noise," a bad thing in electronics. Finally, they named the new company Intel. To satisfy outsiders who wouldn't understand a two-headed company, Noyce became president and Moore vice president. Besides, Gordon said, "I wouldn't have known what to do with him if he worked for me."

Andy Grove, Robert Noyce & Gordon Moore

Intel quickly set about hiring engineers. The first to come was Andrew Grove, the Hungarian engineer who esteemed Gordon Moore enough to follow him anywhere. Gordon became Intel's "Mr. Inside," the head of research. Robert Noyce became "Mr. Outside," courting customers and investors. Andy Grove became the manager who kept the company running efficiently even as it grew. With their outgoing personalities, Noyce and Grove were more visible, but people in the industry knew it was Gordon Moore who drove constant improvements in Intel's products through his leadership in the lab.

New circuit designs, continuous advances in manufacturing, and new inventions all helped Intel grow very fast. Intel strove also to be at the forefront of the industry. Being first meant being willing to take risks. Moore said that he wanted Intel to be like "a rifleman who shoots at a blank wall, finds the bullet hole, and then paints the target around it." If Intel was first to build a new kind of circuit, they would set the target for the industry, and other companies would have to scramble to catch up.

Companies sell stock to help fund their growth. Owning a share of stock means you own a small piece of the company that issued it.

Within two years, the company's value had more than doubled, and it offered public stock for the first time. Intel produced a series of memory chips, then a microprocessor and a microcomputer. The company

Factory workers in bunny suits

A microprocessor includes all the functions of a computer's central processing unit (CPU) on a single chip. It can be programmed to do different things, and its small size helps make it cheap and reliable.

built huge, expensive new factories, called "fabs," where workers climbed into "bunny suits" and worked in clean rooms designed to keep even the smallest speck of dust from falling on the delicate microchips.

When competition from Japan ate into the memory business, Intel turned its focus to microprocessors and building the hardware brains inside computers. It began an advertising campaign called "Intel Inside," convincing consumers to prefer computers with Intel chips to those with any other kind.

In 1975, Noyce stepped down as president of Intel, and Gordon Moore took his place. As president, Moore continued to drive the company to invest huge amounts in research and constantly come up with better, more powerful chips every year. Some projects, like one to make digital watches, failed, but the company always recovered. As Gordon has said, "Failures are not something to be avoided. You want to have them happen as quickly as you can so you can make progress rapidly."

Another failure was a side project Moore convinced Noyce to try. It started with the observation that Pacific salmon, after two to five years at sea, return to the river where they were born. Wat if you stocked a stream with fingerling (baby) salmon from a fish hatchery? Would the baby salmon imprint on the stream and come back in such large numbers they could easily be caught? In theory, the baby salmon might learn the smells and tastes of a stream's chemical "fingerprint" and seek them out again when it was time to breed. They tried the experiment on a coastal creek. Gordon figured a 5 percent return rate would be fantastic, but they never got returns of more than 0.05 percent of the fish. Maybe the fingerlings were too old when they started downstream, or maybe they just got lost at sea.

Intel CPU Core i7

In 1987, after twelve years as Intel's president, Gordon became chairman of the board, while Andy Grove took over as president. Until his final retirement in 2002, Gordon continued to plan new directions for Intel. He helped to choose which research programs to pursue.

Intel stock made Gordon Moore a billionaire. Still, he continued to work every day and to live modestly. His favorite recreation was fishing off the California coast and around the world. Sometimes he and Betty returned to a place that had been remote and beautiful a few years before, only to find it clogged with hotels and shops. Gordon began to wonder what would be left for future generations.

Gordon also sought ways to share his wealth. In 2000, he and Betty donated $5 billion to establish a charitable foundation. They focused on the environment, basic science, nursing, and higher education. The Gordon and Betty Moore Foundation has made major contributions to Caltech, where Gordon earned his PhD. It has also bought vast tracts of land in the Andes and the Amazon basin to protect wild regions from development. It founded the Public Library of Science, known as PLOS, and helped establish the field of marine microbiology, the study of tiny ocean organisms.

Meanwhile, Moore's Law marches on. More transistors have now been built than there are grains of sand on all the beaches in the world. Two and a half billion people own smartphones today (2018). These smartphones have 1,700 times more computing power than the first huge computers that filled a room. They are 40 million times smaller and cost 17,000 times less. Gordon Moore used to compare this progress to car manufacturing. Already in 1975, he pointed out that, "If the auto industry had made advances [similar to those in the electronics industry], we could cruise comfortably in our cars at 100,000 miles an hour, getting 50,000 miles

How many transistors have been built? More than one sextillion. That's 100,000,000,000,000,000,000,000.

per gallon of gasoline." And rather than pay for parking for just one evening, it would be cheaper to throw out the car and buy a new one at midnight.

If transistors were people, each of Intel's latest chips would have more transistors than the population of China (1.5 billion, 2015).

Even Gordon agrees that Moore's Law can't last forever, saying, "All exponentials like that have to come to an end. There's not enough stuff in the universe to keep it going forever." Some electronic components are now only a few atoms thick. Tomorrow's inventors and engineers will have to find new ways to make electronics faster, cheaper, and more powerful.

Today, Gordon and Betty Moore spend much of their time in Hawaii. They have a beautiful house looking out over the Pacific Ocean. Outside are fish ponds filled with koi, the giant, decorative Japanese carp. Gordon feeds them every day and has names for his favorites, like Skinny and Monstro.

The quiet boy who loved fishing grew up to help lead the electronics revolution. He formulated a vision that inspired an industry. Never flashy, he seldom attracted attention. Instead, he worked to make his vision real by steadily improving the way computer chips were manufactured. Today his generosity is helping the world preserve the best of wild nature even as computers and the Internet bring power to people all over the world.

"Do not pass Go.
Do not collect $200."

15. Fun and Games

Monopoly to the Super Soaker

(1879–Present)

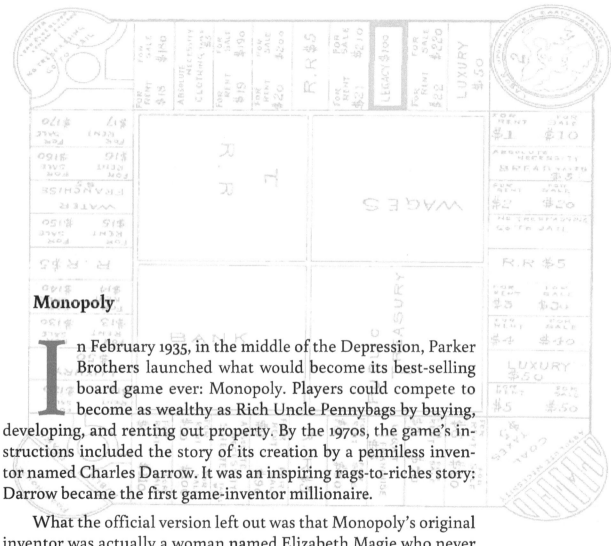

Monopoly

In February 1935, in the middle of the Depression, Parker Brothers launched what would become its best-selling board game ever: Monopoly. Players could compete to become as wealthy as Rich Uncle Pennybags by buying, developing, and renting out property. By the 1970s, the game's instructions included the story of its creation by a penniless inventor named Charles Darrow. It was an inspiring rags-to-riches story: Darrow became the first game-inventor millionaire.

What the official version left out was that Monopoly's original inventor was actually a woman named Elizabeth Magie who never came away with more than a few hundred dollars for the game. Magie called it The Landlord's Game. Her purpose was to show the unfairness of the very money-grubbing competition the game displayed. All the players started in the same condition, but some, through luck and ruthlessness, acquired property that led them to become tycoons while driving their companions into poverty.

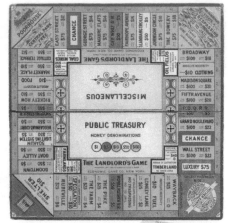

The Landlord's Game

Elizabeth Magie (1866–1948), known as Lizzie, was an unusual woman. She was born in Macomb, Illinois, soon after the end of the Civil War. Her father, James Magie, had been an abolitionist and colleague of Abraham Lincoln. During Lizzie's childhood, her father ran unsuccessfully for the Illinois legislature. Lizzie Magie inherited her father's interest in political change and the economic theories of Henry George.

Henry George was an influential American economist. In 1879, he published a book called *Progress and Poverty*. The book became so popular that in the 1880s, only the Bible sold more copies. George asked why, as societies grew more prosperous, the fate of the poor only grew worse. The reason, he said, was that a few rich people owned the land. George argued that while workers should be able to own whatever they made with their own hands, land and natural resources should always be owned in common. The solution to vast inequality, he argued, was a single tax on the value of land. He also advocated equal pay for women.

George's ideas helped to fuel the Progressive movement in American politics, and they made a great impression on Elizabeth Magie. She first learned of George's ideas around the same time her family faced a financial crisis. In 1879, when Lizzie was only thirteen, her family lost most of its money, probably in a bank panic. Lizzie had to leave school and find work. She became a stenographer, mastering that strange new device the typewriter. Her earnings were $10 a week.

Around 1890, the Magies moved to Washington, DC. Lizzie worked as a stenographer and secretary at the Dead Letter Office, but she also took time to develop her creativity. She

Henry George

wrote poetry and short stories, and she played small comedy roles in Washington theaters. At the age of twenty-six, she invented and patented a device to help paper move more easily through the rollers of a typewriter. In the evenings, she taught classes on Henry George's economic theories.

Around 1902, at the age of thirty-three, Magie created the first version of The Landlord's Game. Explaining the game in a 1902 issue of the *Single Tax Review*, she wrote, "It is a practical demonstration of the present system of land-grabbing with all its usual outcomes and consequences." Players proceeded around a board, buying property. If they landed on another player's property, they went to jail until they paid a fine. Players could rest in a public park, pay luxury tax, or end up in the poorhouse. The purpose of the game was to teach about the evils of monopoly and the benefits of the single tax.

Lizzie Magie with Monopoly

Playing with friends, Magie improved the game and won a patent for it in 1904. She developed a second set of rules for a version called Prosperity, where all players benefited from the creation of wealth. In 1906, Magie and two other Georgists formed The Economic Game Company and began to manufacture an improved version of The Landlord's Game. Now it had spaces for oil fields, timberlands, coal mines, and farmlands, all the kinds of natural resources Georgists believed people should share.

The Economic Game Company tried to sell the game rights to Parker Brothers, who turned it down. On the other hand, the Newbie Company in the United Kingdom published a version called Brer Fox and Brer Rabbit. At the same time, in harmony with her beliefs, Magie freely shared the game with friends, schools, college students, and professors. Among the first players were the residents of a utopian community in Arden, Delaware. Residents created their own handmade copies with crayons on wood or cloth. Instead of grouping properties by numbers, as

Brer Fox and Brer Rabbit

Magie had, they began to group them by color. By the 1920s, most people called the game simply Monopoly.

In 1906, Lizzie Magie moved to Chicago. Wanting to earn more than she did as a stenographer, she thought of a daring publicity stunt to bring attention to her skills. At age forty, she bought a newspaper ad that mocked marriage by offering herself—not as a wife, but as an employee—to the highest bidder: "Intelligent, educated, refined; true; honest, just, poetical, philosophical...womanly above all things...height 5 feet 3 inches...rare and versatile dramatic ability...deeply and truly religious—not pious...crackerjack typewriter, but typewriting is hell."

The ad led to proposals of marriage, vicious letters attacking Lizzie's morals, and a meeting with the writer Upton Sinclair. But they also led to a job as a newspaper reporter. Meanwhile, Magie continued to invent games with names like Mock Trial, which Parker Brothers published.

In 1910, at the age of forty-four, Lizzie surprised many people by marrying Albert Phillips, ten years her senior. She began to go by the name E. M. Phillips. In 1923, she renewed her patent on The Landlord's Game, which continued to be played throughout the Northeast. Fraternity boys played it at Williams College, and a group of Quaker players in Atlantic City substituted in the names of their local streets.

Charles Darrow

One evening, Charles and Olive Todd of Philadelphia taught a homemade version of the monopoly game to a friend named Charles Darrow and his wife, Esther. Darrow enjoyed he game so much that he asked for a written copy of the rules. Surprised, Todd made his friend a copy not just of the rules he had learned verbally, but of the entire game. Darrow was an unemployed salesman, and he needed money to help provide care for his brain-damaged son. Seeing possibilities, he took the game home and tweaked it. He asked his friend, a political cartoonist named Franklin Alexander, to draw in a couple of cartoon characters. Then he patented the game board and offered the game to Parker Brothers.

The game company turned him down, so Darrow manufactured and sold copies of Monopoly on his own. He sold so many over the 1934 Christmas season that Parker Brothers changed its mind. In 1935, the company bought rights to the game from Darrow, offering him a royalty on every copy sold. The game sold as fast as Parker Brothers could print it—1.8 million copies by the end of 1936, during the midst of the Depression.

Although Darrow insisted he had invented the game on his own, Parker Brothers lawyers soon learned of Elizabeth Magie's 1923 patent. In 1935, George Parker, head of the company, traveled to Arlington, Virginia, to talk the inventor into selling her rights. Buyer and seller were both almost seventy years old. Parker offered $500. Magie agreed—but only if Parker Brothers pledged to sell both versions of the game, Monopoly and Prosperity, and only if they bought two more of her games. Parker agreed. But Magie ended up with a bad deal. Although Parker Brothers produced copies of Prosperity, they did not promote it. Along with Magie's two other games, Prosperity remained obscure. Not only that, the company promoted the tale of Charles Darrow as Monopoly's sole inventor. Magie's vision of her games awakening the public to Henry George's economic vision came to nothing. Monopoly players gleefully raked in the pretend money and enjoyed driving their opponents into bankruptcy.

Magie died without fanfare in 1948 at age eighty-two. Through the end of 2017, more than 250 million copies of Monopoly had been sold worldwide. Monopoly players' tokens have included a shoe, thimble, wheelbarrow, iron, top hat, T. rex, penguin, elephant, purse, bag of money, and many more. The game has

The most landed-on squares in Monopoly (not counting Jail) are Illinois Avenue, Go, New York Avenue, B&O Railroad, and Reading Railroad.

Monopoly pieces

been played in innumerable versions—a Beatles version, sports team versions, versions for different cities—and in at least twenty-seven languages.

Scrabble

The famous crossword game Scrabble, which has sold more than 150 million sets, has a much less murky origin story than Monopoly. It combines language skill, luck, and an understanding of probability in a way that attracts both techies and people who love words. Its wooden tiles click satisfactorily as the player mixes them, and every player has ground his or her teeth sometime on coming up with a set of seven letters that are either all vowels or all consonants.

Alfred Mosher Butts

Alfred Mosher Butts letter
frequencies (extract)

Scrabble's inventor, Alfred Mosher Butts (1899–1993), graduated from the University of Pennsylvania in 1924. He worked as an architect until the 1930s, when the Depression meant there was very little new construction. Butts was a fan of chess, jigsaw puzzles, and crosswords, so he decided to invent a game of his own. He took an analytical approach. Games, he decided, could be divided into three groups: number games, games like chess that required moves, and word games. The best games combined chance and skill.

Alfred settled on a game that had elements of anagrams (rearranging a set of letters to make words) and crossword puzzles. Along with words, he brought in an element of numbers by requiring players to keep score. To make the game fair, he wanted the ideal number of tiles for each letter. Alfred remembered a story he had read by Edgar Allan Poe in which the hero breaks a cipher by figuring out how frequently certain letters are used in English. Following Poe's lead, Alfred Butts sat down with the morning newspaper and carefully counted how many times each letter appeared. For the one hundred tiles in his game, he printed letters in the same percentages he found in the newspaper. He made one exception. S was too easy to play, so Butts cut the number of S tiles to just four. He gave ten points when players played rare, difficult letters like Q or Z, but only one point for letters like E or T and no points at all for the two blanks, which were wild.

At first, Butts called his game Lexico. Then he added a game board with some spaces providing extra points, and he changed the game's name to Criss-Crosswords. It was 1938, and Monopoly was already selling by the millions. Butts tried to sell Criss-Crosswords to game makers like Parker Brothers and Milton Bradley, but they weren't interested. So instead, Butts manufactured and sold a few hundred sets himself. The price was $2 plus 25¢ for shipping.

In 1948, a man from Connecticut named James Brunot who happened to be an early owner of Criss-Crosswords got in touch with Butts and asked to buy the rights to manufacture the game. In return, Brunot offered Butts a small royalty on each set he sold. Butts, who was working as an architect again, accepted. Brunot rearranged the extra-score spaces on the board and changed the game's name to Scrabble, a word that means to scratch, scrape, or scribble. He also added a fifty-point bonus for anyone who could play all seven letters at once.

Today, Scrabble is played on a board that is fifteen by fifteen inches with 225 squares; some squares are marked to double or triple the score for a letter or a whole word. There are one hundred letter tiles. Players draw seven tiles and place them on a rack in front of them. In turn, each player places a word on the board, connecting with other words. The score for each turn is found by adding up the points on each letter played and every letter in word that letter adds to. The most points ever earned in a single play is 365 points for QUIXOTRY, played across two triple-word scores and meaning "behavior inspired by romantic beliefs without regard to reality," according to yourdictionary.com.

To manufacture Scrabble, James Brunot retired from his day job. He and his wife rented a little red farmhouse in Dodgington, Connecticut, where they gathered a small team to begin building twelve Scrabble sets an hour. Sales grew, but slowly. The Brunots lost money. Butts earned three cents a set. Then luck intervened. According to the story Hasbro tells, Jack Straus, the president of Macy's, played the game on vacation, liked it, and was peeved not to find it in his stores. Macy's stocked the game, and its popularity took off. The Brunots hired thirty-five workers to turn out 6,000 sets a week. It wasn't enough to keep up with demand.

In 1952, the Brunots licensed the game to the Selchow and Righter Company, which ramped up production and marketing. By 1954, Selchow and Righter had sold more than 4 million game sets. Hasbro bought rights to the game in 1989. Alfred Butts said of his eventual million dollars in Scrabble earnings, "One-third went to taxes. I gave one-third away, and the other third enabled me to have an enjoyable life."

Today, Scrabble continues to be a favorite around the world. It is played in thirty-one languages, including Braille. Most people play friendly games at home, but there is also an intensely competitive world of tournament Scrabble, where people play for thousands of dollars. Four thousand Scrabble clubs exist in the United States, but many tournament champions come from other countries. Thailand, which encourages Scrabble as a way of learning English, does particularly well. Ironically, Thai players don't necessarily understand English very well, but they work to memorize the official Scrabble dictionary, which starts off with 101 two-letter words. Most of them you've never heard of. Computers are good with dictionaries, too. In 2006, in a

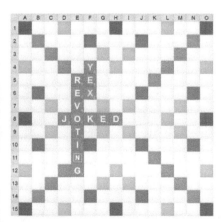

Scrabble game using Quackle, an open-source program

thirty-eight-game marathon, an open-source computer program named Quackle defeated David Boys, who had been Scrabble world champion in 1995. The final score was Quackle 36, Boys 2.

Snowboarding

One winter day in 1963, a seventh-grade boy named Tom Sims (1950–2012) bent over his workbench in woodshop class in Haddonfield, New Jersey, drawing the design for his next project. Born in California, Tom had moved with his parents to the New Jersey at the age of two. It was on a trip back to Los Angeles at the age of ten that he saw his first skateboarders. He fell in love with the sport and brought it home to his New Jersey neighborhood. There was only one problem: skateboarding didn't work on icy streets. Now he was going to solve that by building a board that would slide on snow and ice.

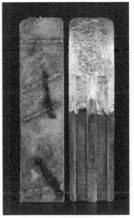

Tom Sims'
first board, 1963

Tom's new "ski board" was simple, even rough. Built of one long flat board, it had one end that curved upward, two grooves to help it stay on track, and roughened areas of the surface where he would place his feet. Tom tried it out, but we don't know how much he actually skated on it. Soon he was on to other projects—for a while.

Tom Sims never thought of patenting his invention, but others did, both before and after him. In 1939, Swedish immigrants Gunnar and Harvey Burgeson patented a curved sled. The rider stood on the sled with his back foot strapped in, and the sled had both a rudder in back and a rope in front to allow steering. The sled grew out of a design by their friend Vern Wicklund, who as a teenager in Minnesota had stood on a sled using a stick for steering. The three friends tried to sell their boards but found no buyers.

Burgeson
snowboard

The next person to invent a snowboard was an indulgent father from Muskegon, Michigan, named Sherman Poppen. On Christmas Day in 1965, his two young daughters were getting bored after

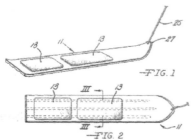

Snurfer patent
diagram excerpt

Brunswick Advertising

opening their presents. The girls had just received a pair of short, fat plastic skis, and Poppen decided to fasten them together side by side, about six inches apart. He attached a rope to the front and led the girls outside, where they had a great time sliding in the snow. Poppen's wife thought up the name Snurfer, for snow surfer.

Soon other kids in the neighborhood were asking for Snurfers so they could try sliding down the snow-covered sand dunes that bordered Lake Michigan. To meet the demand, Poppens collected old water skis from Goodwill and junk sales. He routed grooves into the bottoms and added a strip of metal around the edge. Within a few months, he patented his board, winning the rights to any downhill device with metal edges. In 1966, Poppen licensed his Snurfer to the Brunswick Corporation. The boards, now made of laminated wood, sold well—more than a million before the 1960s were over.

The local community college began hosting a yearly snurfing competition. In 1979, a young man named Jake Burton Carpenter (1954 -) showed up with his own board, which he called a Burton Board. Burton helped to make the sport popular, and in 1982, the National Snow Surfing Championships were held in Burton's home state, Vermont. Poppen recalls of Burton: "When he got started and Burton was calling his board Snurfboards, and mine was a Snurfer...I hired an attorney to tell him that, hey, that name is trademarked. Well, I wish I hadn't done it now, because that's when the sport became snowboarding."

Jake Burton, as he is usually known, grew up in upstate New York. He planned to be a competitive skier at the University of Colorado in Boulder, but a bad car accident ended that dream. Instead, he got a degree in economics from New York University. Then he moved to Londonderry, Vermont, and thought again about the thrill of a downhill rush on snowy slopes. He improved on the Snurfer by adding such features as a rigid binding to hold the rider's boot. Then he came up with the term snowboarding. Burton promoted the snowboarding lifestyle, and since 1980s, Burton Snowboards has been one of the world's largest snowboarding manufacturers.

But back to Tom Sims. After graduating from high school, he became a skateboard designer and a professional skateboarder. In the mid-1970s, he founded a company called Sims Skateboards in Whittier, California. The company built and sold skateboards, and it sponsored competitive skateboarders. Soon it branched into making snowboards, too.

Tom Sims freestyle

In the 1980s, Sims competed in snowboarding competitions. Instead of sticking to slalom races, he helped to introduce freestyle snowboarding, swooping over natural and artificial obstacles to perform skateboarding-like tricks. He led the push to include the half-pipe in competition, making possible the flips and airborne twists we see today. Sims Snowboards introduced lighter snowboards for women and high-backed bindings that allowed better control for tricks.

Tom Sims became a world champion snowboarder in 1983. Two years later, he was the stunt double for Roger Moore during a snowboarding scene in the James Bond movie *A View to a Kill*. He continued to innovate and publicize the sport until his death from cardiac arrest at the age of sixty-one.

Snowboarding

In the 1980s, many ski resorts did not allow snowboarding, which was seen as a fringe sport practiced by irresponsible young men. But gradually the sport won more followers. It was safer on the knees that skiing, and many people loved snowboarding's comfortable boots and the floating sense of surfing on snow. In 1998, snowboarding appeared for the first time as an Olympic sport in the Winter Games in Nagano, Japan.

The Super Soaker

Lonnie Johnson

The inventor of America's favorite squirt gun—though "squirt" is much too weak a word—is an engineer named Lonnie Johnson. Born in 1949, Lonnie grew up in still-segregated Mobile, Alabama. He was the third of six children. His father was a World War II veteran and his mother a nurse's aide. Lonnie was a curious kid, and his parents encouraged him, though they occasionally had doubts. They weren't delighted when he took apart his sister's doll to find out what made her eyes close. Once he mixed up some rocket fuel from a recipe he found in a library book. The mixture of saltpeter and sugar filled the house with thick black smoke and burned a kitchen chair. In response, as Lonnie later told an interviewer, "My parents got me a hot plate and said, 'Do that kind of stuff outside.'" Lonnie's father showed him how to connect wires and to repair irons and lamps.

Neighborhood kids called Lonnie Johnson "the Professor," and he led them in building projects. He built a go-kart out of a lawnmower engine and steered it with a piece of string. Another time, a policeman stopped Lonnie on the road when he was riding his bike with a pile of scrap metal tied to the back. Lonnie was scared, but the officer, intrigued, just wanted to know what he was up to. So Lonnie took him home and showed him the robot he was building—just like the ones he saw on TV. Johnson later told the BBC, "Nobody had told me that the robots I saw on shows like *Lost in Space* had actors inside them!"

Lost in Space, 1966

Lonnie's robot, named Linex, stood three-and-a-half feet tall and ran on compressed air. He could rotate his shoulders and swivel his elbows and wrists. His memory consisted of sounds like the beeps of telephone buttons recorded on a tape recorder inside the robot. Lonnie controlled the tape recorder with a unit built from his sister's walkie-talkie, and Linex responded to the sounds with different movements.

Building Linex took most of Lonnie's senior year of high school. All the teachers at his school, Williamson High, were black, and Lonnie and his fellow seniors were the last segregated class to graduate. Lonnie exhibited Linex at the 1968 statewide Junior Engineering Technical Society science fair at the University of Alabama. It was the first time his school had ever participated in the competition, and he walked away with first prize but no congratulations or interest from university officials. As Johnson later recalled, "The only thing anybody from the university said to us throughout the entire competition was 'Good-bye, and y'all drive safe, now.'"

Only five years earlier, in 1963, Alabama Governor George Wallace had stood In the doorway of the University of Alabama to block the first black students from entering.

Lonnie's robot invention and his high math scores won him an Air Force scholarship and a scholarship to Tuskegee University. Attending Tuskegee delighted him because George Washington Carver was one of his heroes. Johnson graduated from Tuskegee with a bachelor's degree in mechanical engineering in 1973 and a master's in nuclear engineering in 1975. While working on his master's, he signed up for the Reserve Officers Training Corps, ROTC. He also found time to marry. Together, he and his wife, Linda Moore, eventually had four children.

After graduation, Johnson's first job was as a research engineer at the Oak Ridge National Laboratory in Tennessee, working on cooling systems for nuclear reactors. Then his career alternated between enlistments in the U.S. Air Force, serving at bases in New Mexico, Nebraska, and California, and years doing research at NASA's Jet Propulsion Laboratory in Pasadena, California. His stints at NASA lasted from 1979 to 1982 and again from 1987 to 1991. In both the USAF and NASA, Johnson refined nuclear power sources for spacecraft. These included the unmanned Galileo mission to Jupiter and its moons, the Mars observer project, and the early stages of the Cassini mission to Saturn. For the air force, Johnson developed components for the stealth bomber. NASA gave him numerous awards for his contributions to spacecraft system design.

Lonnie kept tinkering, too. Around 1982, when he was about thirty-three years old, he was experimenting with a new, environmentally friendly type of refrigeration that would use water instead of Freon. Freon was a chlorofluorocarbon (CFC) that was destroying the earth's ozone layer, leaving living things more vulnerable to the sun's ultraviolet rays. Fiddling with his tubes at home one evening, Lonnie made a nozzle and attached it to the bathroom sink, where he was doing an experiment. Out shot a strong stream of water, and Johnson suddenly felt inspired at the thought of an extra-powerful water gun.

A few months later, Johnson set up a shop in the basement of his home in Omaha, Nebraska, complete with lathe and milling machine, to work on the prototype for his toy. He gave his first plastic gun to his seven-year-old daughter Aneka. None of the other kids on the air base could get close to her with their puny squirt guns.

Johnson wanted to manufacture the guns himself, but a factory estimated it would cost $200,000 to make the first thousand guns. That was money Johnson didn't have. In 1986, he received a patent for his water gun, now improved with an attached air reservoir. Still, he could find no one interested in manufacturing it until 1989, when he attended a toy fair in New York. There the

Super Soaker

vice president of a small company called Larami invited him to visit company headquarters in Philadelphia. But he wasn't too encouraging. "By the way," he told Lonnie. "Don't make a special trip."

With his newest prototype, Johnson made a special trip to Philadelphia a couple of weeks later. He wowed the officers of the company by shooting water across the conference room. Larami agreed to make the gun, and together the team worked hard to bring the price down to $10. That was still far more than anyone had ever paid for a squirt gun. Larami named Johnson's invention the Power Drencher and put it on the market in 1990. It had been eight years since Aneka played with the first model.

Sales were slow but not too bad. The next year, Larami renamed the toy the Super Soaker and invested in television advertising. That year, 1991, the company sold 2 million units. The Super Soaker became America's best-selling toy that year. Johnson left his work at NASA and founded a company called Johnson Research and Development. Royalty income from the Super Soaker, he figured, could fund other kinds of research he wanted to do.

In 1995, the giant toy-maker Hasbro bought Larami. Johnson got to work making new models of the Super Soaker. Since 1991, nearly 125 types of Super Soakers have been on the market. Johnson also invented a range of Nerf dart guns, which shot soft foam projectiles across a room. He used the money to expand his company in Atlanta, Georgia. Eventually, he hired thirty employees.

Super Soaker HydroBlitz

Among Johnson's inventions: a diaper that plays a nursery song when wet. It never became a commercial success.

Besides creating new toys, Johnson R & D has focused on Lonnie Johnson's other technical interests, and in the process spun off two other companies. At Excellatron Solid States, Johnson developed rechargeable lithium thin-film batteries that can be stored safely from $-55°$ to $300°C$ and last a long time. The battery technology has applications both for the military and for medical devices. Johnson Electro-Mechanical Systems focuses on Johnson's thermo-electrical converter system, which *Popular Mechanics* called one of the top ten inventions of 2008. The system, made entirely of solid-state materials, pushes hydrogen through two membranes, releasing electricity. To further develop this technology, Johnson is collaborating with the Palo Alto Research Center (PARC). Altogether, Lonnie Johnson has been granted nearly a hundred patents, with others currently in the application pipeline.

More than a billion dollars' worth of Super Soakers have sold worldwide. But in 2013, Johnson had to sue Hasbro for his fair share of the proceeds. He accused the toy company of violating a 1996 agreement to pay him 2 percent royalties for "three-dimensional products" based on the toy's appearance. In the end, Hasbro settled the case, compensating Johnson with $72.9 million for underpaid royalties for the years 2007 to 2012. Once again, Johnson poured the funds into further research.

As he nears the age of seventy, Lonnie Johnson loves to visit schools and talk to kids. He knows what it was like to grow up in a society that had low expectations for him. His water guns get the kids' attention, but his real message is inspiration. Johnson has told the BBC, "Kids need exposure to ideas, and they need to be given an opportunity to experience success. Once you get that feeling, it grows and feeds itself—but some kids have got to overcome their environments and attitudes that have been imposed on them."

"All children are scientists, but ...I think it gets lost because people forget about the excitement and the joy of discovery."

— Lydia Villa-Komaroff, 2014

16. DNA Wrangler

Lydia Villa-Komaroff
(b. 1947)

Before the 1920s, childhood diabetes was a fatal disease. Affected children lacked a hormone called insulin. Without it, they could no longer process sugar in their blood. Their urine had the sweet smell and taste of spilled sugar. Unable to build fat or muscle from the food they ate, they wasted away. In the end, with very high blood sugar levels, they lapsed into coma and died.

A child with diabetes before (above) and after (below) insulin treatment

The purification of insulin changed all that. In the early 1920s, Canadian doctors and scientists managed to extract insulin from the pancreas first of dogs and then of unborn calves. In 1922, they tried their compound on a dying fourteen-year-old boy. He had a severe allergic reaction to his first injection. Undaunted, they further purified their substance. The boy's response to the second dose was almost miraculous. His blood sugar returned almost to normal, and he stopped spilling sugar in his urine. He gained weight and strength.

Lydia Villa-Komaroff

The name *insulin* comes from the Latin word *insula,* meaning "island." It refers to the Islets of Langerhans, collections of cells in the pancreas that produce insulin.

Soon Eli Lilly and other companies were manufacturing and selling the lifesaving new drug, called insulin. The major problem was that many patients developed immune reactions to the insulin over time. That was because the insulin came either from calf or pig pancreases. The human body identified the animal insulin as a foreign protein and made antibodies against it. Patients needed higher and higher doses of insulin to keep their blood sugar in control.

To address the problem of resistance to animal insulin, scientists sought a way to "convince" bacteria to make human insulin. This advance, when it came, helped launch the biotechnology industry. A key actor in the development of "recombinant" human insulin was a Mexican American biologist named Lydia Villa-Komaroff.

Lydia Villa's family. Lydia stands in white next to her father.

Born on August 7, 1947, Lydia grew up in Santa Fe, New Mexico. Her mother's ancestors had come from Spain with the conquistadors. Her father was a mestizo, or part Indian, born in Mexico. When Lydia was a child, few Mexican American girls were expected to have careers, but her parents were different. Both of them had been the first in their families to go to college. Her father was a teacher and musician who played violin and guitar. Her mother, a social worker who had once dreamed of being a botanist, worked when Lydia was a child. Then there was her uncle Ismael, a chemist. Once he showed Lydia a research paper he had published. "This was easier to write than an English paper," he told her. That caught her ear, because she found writing English papers *hard.* At the age of nine, she decided to become a scientist.

As the oldest of six children whose mother worked full-time, Lydia helped raise her younger siblings. So another thing about science that attracted her was the idea that scientists get to work in roomy white labs, alone. That would be a contrast to her small house, always full of brothers, sisters, and cousins. Lydia wanted space! Later she learned that most good science involves close work with and among colleagues.

Lydia's first science experiment was one she conducted with her younger brother. They went around the house firing a squirt gun at all the lightbulbs. They discovered that the jet of cool water had no effect on lightbulbs that were turned off. But every lightbulb that had been on a while and was hot burst with a satisfying pop!

Lydia, 6 or 7 and brother Richard, 5 or 6

When Lydia was thirteen, her mother went back to school to take a course in statistics. Lydia's mother had struggled with math ever since missing a year of school with rheumatic fever (an infection that affects the heart) as a child. But she battled her way through the statistics class and passed. Lydia never forgot her mother's determination and persistence.

During junior high, Lydia had the chance to attend a summer program funded by the National Science Foundation. She and other middle-school students did experiments on a college campus in Tyler, Texas. She enjoyed the camaraderie among the students and loved the chance to use her brain and hands together. The experiments themselves had to do with the physiology of the adrenal gland, which they extracted from rats. Lydia brought some of the rats home, where a few of them escaped. For years afterward, people reported spotting unusual black-and-white rats running through the neighborhood.

Black-and-white rat

When Lydia went to college at the University of Washington in Seattle, she meant to major in chemistry. But she struggled in her first chemistry course. Halfway through, she went to see an adviser. "Of course, you're having trouble!" he said. "Chemistry's not for girls." Lydia was innocent enough to accept his verdict. After that, she changed her major four more times before settling on biology. What most attracted her was developmental biology: How did a single cell develop into a whole human?

In high school, Lydia had earned top grades without much effort. She hadn't really learned to study. However, once she got to college, her grades were uneven. Her new adviser told her that to really make a mark in developmental biology she would have to go to graduate school, but she didn't seem to be on that path.

Anthony Komaroff

Then a medical student named Anthony Komaroff bumped into Lydia in a hallway. As an apology, he asked her out, and soon the two became serious. Anthony planned to do research at the National Institutes of Health (NIH) in Washington, DC, after graduating. So, in 1967, Lydia transferred to a small women's college in Baltimore, Goucher College. There the faculty gave her plenty of personal attention, and she thrived. They helped her get a job in the NIH lab of Loretta Levy, a microbiologist who Lydia says taught her "everything—from pipetting on up." With Dr. Levy, Lydia studied how molecules on the surface of bacteria help cause disease. Today, Dr. Villa-Komaroff urges science students to study in groups when they can and to get involved in research as soon as possible.

When Lydia graduated in 1970, she married Anthony Komaroff. Since they planned to move to Boston together, Lydia applied to every graduate school in Boston—except for MIT. MIT, she thought, was just a "bunch of guys running around with slide rules doing math." But Loretta Levy admonished her, telling her there was no better place than MIT to study what she was interested in. In the end, Lydia applied to MIT, and it was the only program that accepted her. "That taught me something," she says. "You won't get what you don't ask for."

David Baltimore

Villa-Komaroff calls MIT "graduate student heaven." She says, "I learned that hard work can be extremely fun." MIT was "not a soft and cuddly place." Lydia had to learn to ask questions and be assertive. She managed to convince two eminent scientists, David Baltimore and Harvey Lodish, to mentor her for a PhD thesis project that combined the study of viruses with the study of making proteins outside a cell. The two mentors had very different styles. Lodish had wild red hair and "looked about fourteen"; Baltimore was grave and more reserved. Sometimes their advice conflicted. But both men treated her as an equal.

Lydia published six papers during her doctoral program. Her thesis work detailed how the polio virus makes proteins. In 1975, she received her doctorate, one of the very first Latinas in the country to do so.

While she loved her graduate work, Villa-Komaroff remembers, she did suffer from a lack of role models with backgrounds that resembled hers. "I was almost done with graduate school," she says, "before I met scientists of color whom I could look to as mentors." In 1973, she helped found an organization called the Society for Advancement of Chicanos/Hispanics and Native Americans in Science (SACNAS). She calls SACNAS meetings "a magical experience." For once, she felt like part of a community of science where she was "not the only one."

After completing her PhD, Villa-Komaroff moved to the Harvard laboratory of Fotis Kafatos to work on splicing DNA into bacteria. But politics intervened. Activists in Harvard's home city of Cambridge opposed the idea of recombinant DNA. They feared that combining DNA from two organisms might create dangerous new creatures that could escape into the community. Students marched into city hall singing, "This Land Is Your Land." In July 1976, Cambridge suspended all recombinant DNA research in the city.

Recombinant DNA is a new DNA sequence created in the laboratory by bringing together and splicing DNA from different sources and often different species.

With one pathway closed to her, Villa-Komaroff accepted a position under Tom Maniatis at the Cold Spring Harbor Laboratory in New York. It turned out to be the most discouraging year of her career. She saw her husband only twice all year. And none of her experiments worked. She was trying to insert the genome (all the DNA) of the polyphemus silk moth into a plasmid, which

is a small circle of DNA found inside bacteria. At the time, neither she nor her boss knew that the silk moth DNA was far too long for the experiment to work. All Lydia knew was that her bacteria kept dying ...and dying. Discouraged, she thought of giving up science altogether. Maybe she would become a singer instead—except she had no training in singing. Now she advises students, "There will be a lot of times when there will be failure. Most experiments don't work." One of the most important traits of a researcher, she stresses, is persistence. At the time, she wrote the year off as a complete loss. However, skills she learned during that difficult year proved key to her later work.

Walter Gilbert

At the end of a year, Villa-Komaroff returned to Boston. Cambridge had loosened its restrictions, and a friend, Argiris Efstratiadis, suggested she join Walter Gilbert's lab to work on a new project. Arg had been a doctor and a Shakespearean actor in his native Greece. Now he was a graduate student. As for Wally Gilbert, Villa-Komaroff describes him as "a round, jolly genius." Gilbert ran an intense, egalitarian lab with a heady, informal atmosphere. Gilbert himself favored orange or purple turtlenecks, and one of his graduate students had dyed the boss's lab coat purple.

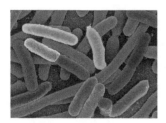

E. Coli Bacteria

The lab was trying to clone the gene for insulin, working to make millions of copies of the DNA that guided a cell to make insulin. Lydia's experience with enzymes made her a critical member of the team. Suddenly, all the group's experiments worked. They inserted the rat insulin gene into the DNA of bacteria. Miraculously, the *E. coli* bacteria translated the DNA instructions and successfully made insulin. Lydia was working alone in the lab one night when she saw the bacterial colonies growing. She ran to the lab of a friend named Bob Weinberg and told him, "I have the most wonderful news!"

"You're pregnant!" Bob guessed.

Lydia's friend and collaborator Arg Efstratiadis had a different reaction. When he heard the news, he shook his head of unruly brown curls and quoted a Greek saying. "Don't even tell the priest!" he warned her. After all, they were racing against two other groups working in California.

In only six months from the start of the project, Lydia's team published an important paper showing that their bacteria produced rat proinsulin that worked. Villa-Komaroff was first author, indicating that most of the work was hers.

The paper was a huge advance. It was the first time a mammalian hormone had been produced inside a bacterium. The team quickly filed a patent for their work, and Wally Gilbert founded a new company called Biogen to manufacture human insulin. He asked Villa-Komaroff to come work for the company, but she declined. "I had worked with two Nobel prizewinners," she says. "It was time for me to show I could stand on my own two feet." Instead, she accepted a position on the faculty of the new University of Massachusetts Medical School in Worcester. But she did join Biogen's scientific advisory board. Over the years, she learned a great deal about business from her association with one of the first biotechnology companies.

Model of
human insulin molecule

Molecular biology is the study of important molecules in the cell that are involved in reproduction and running the cell's activities, like DNA, RNA, and proteins.

Meanwhile, several companies raced to mass-produce the first human insulin grown in bacteria. The winner was a West Coast start-up company called Genentech, which produced the first recombinant human insulin in 1978. After passing through tests to show it was safe and effective, the new insulin came to market in 1982.

While Lydia worked in Worcester, her husband, Anthony, was building a department of academic general medicine at Harvard. In 1985, Lydia herself returned to Harvard for more research and less teaching. She collaborated with neurologists and other scientists to make molecular biology a useful tool, not just a separate field of its own. That meant collaborating with scientists from many different fields. For example, she worked with a neurologist from Children's Hospital to identify proteins that help develop vision in young mammals. She also showed that a molecule known as Gap-14 stimulated the axons, or signal-sending branches, of neurons to grow.

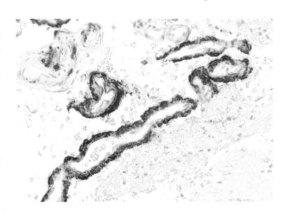

Beta amyloid plaques in brain

One of Villa-Komaroff's most important breakthroughs came in studying the molecule beta amyloid, which collects in the brain cells of people with Alzheimer's disease. Working with a student, Villa-Komaroff showed that beta amyloid damages brain cells. This finding encouraged others to study the protein and ways to stop it from piling up in cells.

Although working across fields was exciting and fruitful, funding all these different projects was becoming harder. Villa-Komaroff began to consider taking her broad interests and people skills (she calls them the "big sister syndrome") into administration, managing other people instead of doing her own research. In 1996, Villa-Komaroff left the laboratory to move to Chicago. There she became Northwestern University's vice president for research.

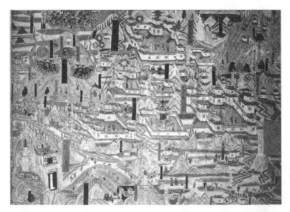

Mogao Cave painting, Dunhuang

At first, Villa-Komaroff felt uncomfortable when people asked why she was abandoning science. It took her about a year before she could assert with confidence that she would always be a scientist, even in new roles. Meanwhile, she helped recruit faculty and raise money for research projects as far from biology as mapping Buddhist caves in Dunhuang, China. She also took singing lessons at last and performed the part of Lady

Tiang in a Chicago performance of *The King and I.* She and Anthony spent every other weekend together, with a pact to do no work during the forty-eight hours they were together.

Seven years later, Villa-Komaroff returned to Cambridge as the vice president for research at the small and prestigious Whitehead Institute, which is affiliated with MIT. Both the chair of the board and the director of the institute were women. Villa-Komaroff joined the boards of biotech companies and the board of the American Association for the Advancement of Science (AAAS). In 2009, Wally Gilbert's son recruited her to a start-up company named Cytonome, which makes advanced cell sorters to help scientists in their research. As chief scientific officer and then head of the company, Villa-Komaroff built the company culture and raised money from investors.

Lydia Villa-Komaroff hated the idea of retiring until a friend reminded her that the Spanish word for retirement is *jubilación*—jubilation. Officially retired, Villa-Komaroff has embraced the cause of encouraging women and minorities in science. She brings data, examples, and ideas for how to change institutions to groups of her peers. At the same time, she continues to reach out to younger students. With no children of her own, she is especially proud of the young scientists she has mentored who have gone on to become professors, deans, division heads, and successful businesspeople. "I guess I am a mother," she reflects.

Lydia Villa-Komaroff's career has combined discovery as a scientist, leadership as an administrator, and work in private industry. She considers herself both a maker—especially a maker of important connections—and a barrier breaker. Her research has opened the door to new discoveries by others and to the creation of a whole new industry, biotechnology. Her constant message to young people is that studying science will empower them to make a difference in the world.

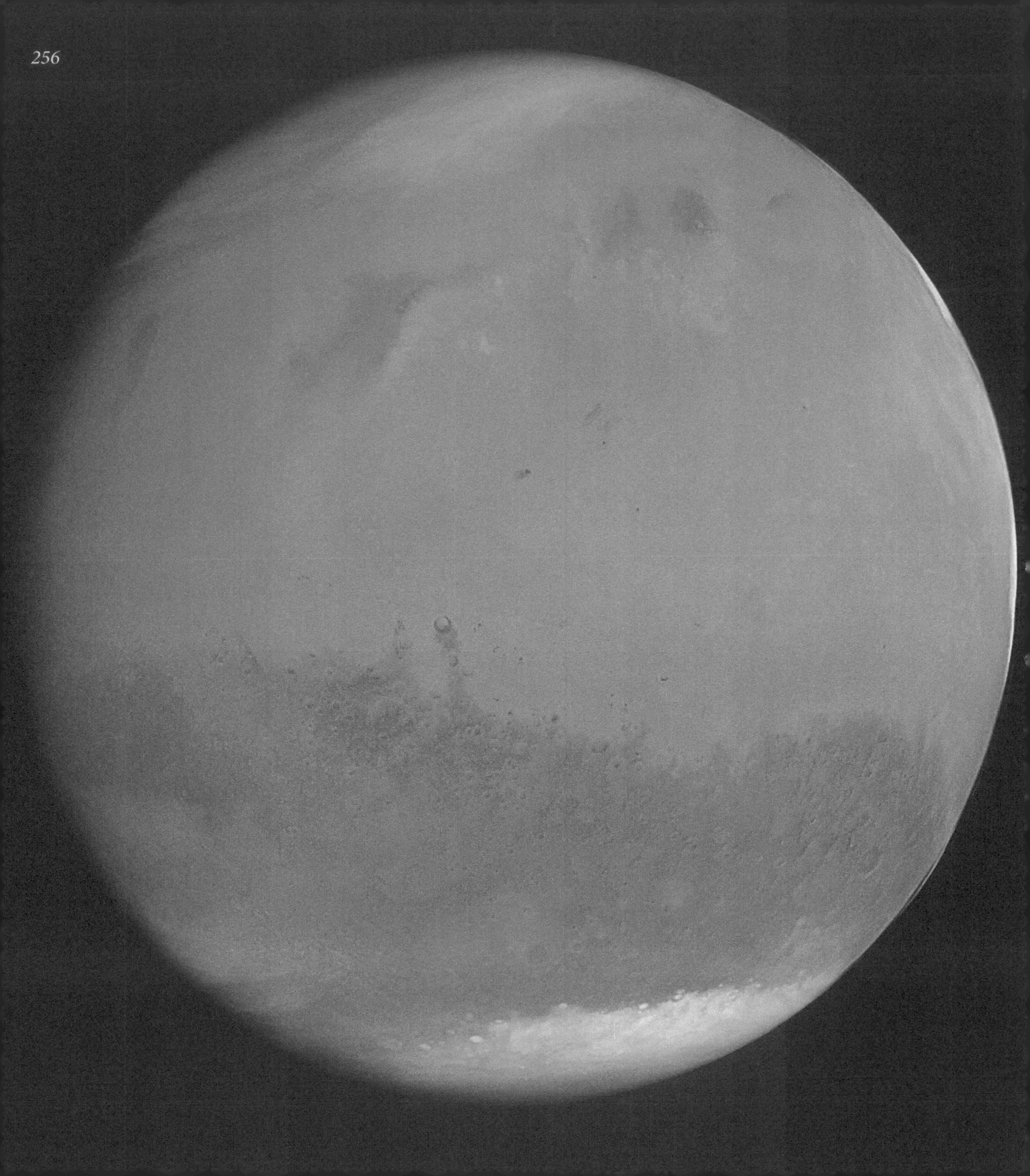

"*I would like to die on Mars. Just not on impact.*"
— Elon Musk, 2012

17. Interplanetary Dreams

Elon Musk
(b. 1971)

Of all the dreamers in this book, Elon Musk may be the wildest. He intends to save humankind. First, he hopes to preserve the earth; but if it's too late for that, he wants to make sure we can settle Mars—and soon.

Driven, brilliant, creative, often hard to get along with, Musk embodies many of the themes in this book. A brainy misfit as a kid, today he's a risk-taking billionaire who has brushed with bankruptcy. He's a hands-on engineer, a divorced father of five, a devoted brother, and an unbelievably demanding boss. He's crazily optimistic and very much a self-made man.

Elon Musk was born in South Africa on June 28, 1971. He was the oldest of three children. His father was an engineer, and his mother was a math and science enthusiast. Elon seemed odd to other children. Sometimes he got a blank look on his face and just tuned out. He loved to read, especially science fiction and encyclopedias. As a young teen, he got the idea that space travel would save humanity, and that he was the one who could make space travel happen.

Elon remembers his childhood as being no fun. South Africa under apartheid was an angry and often violent place. His parents divorced when he was around nine. Elon and his brother, Kimbal, lived with their father, an emotionally intense man who supplied them with books and even a computer, but, as Elon later told his biographer, somehow seemed to suck the joy out of a room. On occasion, he took his sons to work on a building site with him. At other times, Elon and Kimbal played Dungeons and Dragons, raced their dirt bikes, built rockets, and once tried to open a video arcade. Still, Musk says, "I did not have a good childhood…. It was like misery."

For one thing, Elon was a misfit at school, a nerd rather than an athlete. At age twelve, he wrote and published code for a computer game he called Blastar. But neither he nor Kimbal was a star on the rugby field. Other kids picked on them, especially on Elon, whose intensity and habit of spouting facts won him no friends. Once, late in middle school, a gang of bullies jumped him, threw him down the stairs, and then swarmed in, kicking. He blacked out and had to go to the hospital. Although the bullying went on for three or four years, Elon got no sympathy at home.

In the middle of high school, Elon transferred to a more academic, orderly institution. He didn't stand out; he did well in physics and computers, but nobody considered him one of the smartest students. He spent a lot of time thinking about clean energy, space travel, and how to get out of South Africa.

When he graduated at age seventeen, Elon tried a few months of college, but soon he dropped out. What he really wanted was to go to America. As a first step, he flew to Canada, where his mother had relatives—but where Elon had neither a job nor even a place to stay. For the next year, he found a series of odd jobs in

Apartheid, from the Afrikaans word for "apartness," was the name for South Africa's system of segregation that persisted under law from 1948 to the 1990s. It included strict economic and political oppression of all non-white people.

This sign at Durban Beach read: Under section 37 of the Durban Beach By-Laws, this bathing area is reserved for the sole use of members of the white race group.

far-flung places, working on a farm and cleaning a boiler room. By then, his mother, brother Kimbal, and sister Tosca had also moved to Canada. Elon enrolled at Queen's University in Kingston, Ontario, where Kimbal soon followed him. He dated, met his future first wife, Justine Wilson, competed for the best grades, and fixed up other students' computers to earn money.

After two years, Elon transferred on scholarship to the University of Pennsylvania. At last he was in the States. He studied physics and economics. With his friend Adeo Ressi, he rented a large house off-campus. On weekends, they converted the house into a nightclub, charging $5 admission to as many as 500 people. It paid the rent and more.

For two summers, Musk found an internship in Silicon Valley working for a video game company. After graduation, he and Kimbal moved west. Elon thought about getting a PhD at Stanford, but instead he decided to start his own company. He named it Global Link Information Network, later changed to Zip2. In those early days of the Internet (it was 1995), the idea was to sign up local businesses to be part of an Internet directory tied in to local maps.

"I'm nauseatingly pro-American. I would have come here from any country. The US is where great things are possible."
— Elon Musk, 2007

The brothers rented a small office. Elon did all the programming, while Kimbal was the salesman. Elon practically lived at the office, sleeping in a beanbag chair. When a venture capital firm invested $3 million, Elon became chief technology officer reporting to a boss. He didn't like losing control. In 1998, the company was sold, and Elon came away with $22 million at the age of twenty-seven. Still, he decided that in future he wanted to keep control of any company he founded.

Musk spent some of his Zip2 windfall on a luxury condo, a private plane, and a couple of Ferraris. But he invested most of his money in a new venture, an online bank he called X.com. It was a crazy idea. Who was going to trust the Internet to store and transfer their money? How could people be sure of money when they never actually held dollar bills in their hands? Elon made wild statements to the press about changing banking forever. A lot of people thought he was too fantastical—creative, driven, but also a master of hype who might not be able to deliver.

Soon, another start-up rented offices from X.com. Its name was PayPal, and its business plan competed directly with X.com's. At the offices on University Avenue in Palo Alto, both teams worked around the clock. The rooms smelled of sweat and leftover pizza.

Eventually, the two companies merged, with Musk as CEO. But the merger didn't go well. The teams argued about what technology to use. Programming glitches crashed the system. The company lost money at a rapid pace. Musk's style as a demanding know-it-all alienated some people both inside and outside the company. In January 2000, when Elon was on his honeymoon with Justine, company executives went to the board and demanded that he be thrown out as CEO. The original founders of PayPal came back to run the company.

The board's betrayal was a huge blow to Elon, but in the end he took it well. He continued to support the company, to serve on its board, and even to invest in it further. He helped guide PayPal through the dot-com bust, when many new Internet companies failed. In 2002, when eBay bought PayPal for $1.5 billion, Elon Musk, now thirty-one, walked away with about $180 million after taxes. Here was a sum he could invest in his dreams.

For Musk, those dreams were turning, as in his childhood, toward space. In 2001, at age thirty, he moved to Los Angeles to be nearer the heart of the space industry. He joined the Mars Society and began to think about a demonstration project to send an unmanned spaceship to start a garden under a dome on Mars. But soon his ambitions grew larger. NASA, Musk felt, was being too cautious. Its rockets were too expensive, and it wasn't working on interplanetary travel. America was losing its daring at a time when it should be sending humans to Mars.

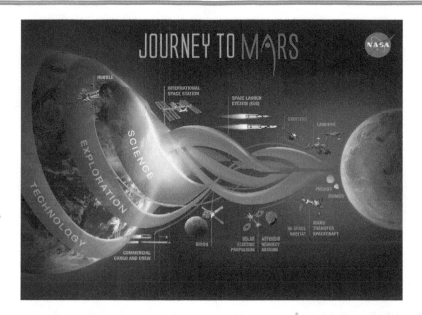

The first step, Musk thought, was to create low-cost, private rockets that could compete with NASA. Elon got together with friends and flew to Moscow to look into buying some old Russian missiles to convert into rockets. The Russians didn't take him seriously.

On the flight home from Russia, Musk convinced his discouraged partners that they should build their own rocket from scratch. He had spent the last six months learning everything he could about rockets. Musk showed his team a spreadsheet of what the costs would be.

In batches starting in June 2002, Musk put $100 million into his new rocket company, SpaceX. The company moved into a huge warehouse, where rocket scientists at computers worked just across from welders and builders. Musk announced that by early 2004, the company would launch its first satellite, and he got a contract from NASA to do so. Then he went on a spree to hire all the best engineers he could find. Like William Shockley so many years earlier, he began calling people up and recruiting them to work for him. He interviewed them all himself, trying to test their drive and intelligence.

SpaceX Grasshopper Test Vehicle launches in McGregor, TX

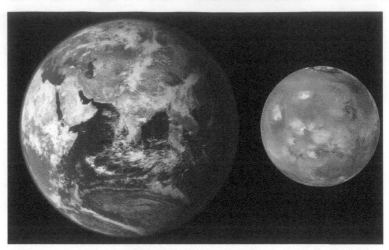

Mars-Earth comparison

SpaceX grew. The company bought a testing ground in Texas. Engineers spent ten days at a time there, testing two stages of engines for the Falcon I rocket. Everything took longer than Musk had promised. When it came time to think about launch tests, the company's plan to use the Vandenberg Air Force Base in Los Angeles fell through. So SpaceX moved launch operations to Kwajalein Island, one of the Marshall Islands near the equator in the Pacific Ocean. Engineers lived and worked there in rustic conditions for months at a time.

Finally, in March 2006, two years late, the Falcon I was ready for launch. It lifted off—and then, after twenty-five seconds, tumbled out of the sky. A vital nut had corroded in the island's salt air.

Re-building the rocket took a year. In March 2007, the new rocket lifted off. High in the sky, the first stage booster fell away, and the second-stage booster fired up. This time, the rocket flew for five minutes before it began to wobble. Then it exploded. Rocket fuel sloshing around the tank had left the engine exposed to the atmosphere, and when it sucked in air, the engine burst into flames. It was another disaster. SpaceX was burning through Musk's money, and now it had fallen more than three years behind schedule.

The third trial launch came in August 2008. This time the rocket broke apart even earlier, as the first stage gave way to the second.

After four years and three failures, SpaceX tottered on the verge of disaster. Musk's personal life was also going badly. He and his wife, Justine, had lost their infant son, Nevada, to Sudden Infant Death Syndrome (SIDS) in 2002. Elon wouldn't talk about it. In the marriage, his domineering personality sometimes took over. Justine told an interviewer from *Marie Claire*

The Time Machine poster, 1960

that shortly after their marriage, Elon told her, "I am the alpha in this relationship." In the five years after Nevada's death, he and Justine went on to have twins and then triplets, five boys in all. But perhaps due to the stress of Elon's life, the marriage fell apart. "If you were my employee, I'd fire you," he often told Justine. In June 2008, Musk filed for divorce. Two years later, he married an English actress named Talulah Riley. They have since divorced, remarried, and divorced again.

At the same time SpaceX was on the edge of blowing up, Musk also faced a crisis in his other great venture. Since high school, Musk had also been fascinated by the idea of electric cars. He hoped that electric cars could decrease the world's use of gasoline and help protect the earth's climate.

Amazing Science Fiction Stories, 1959

But electric cars were bulky, weak, and could not travel far before they needed to be recharged.

Then, in 2003, a former member of Stanford University's solar car team named J. B. Straubel approached Musk. Straubel wanted to put together 20,000 lithium ion batteries to make the motor of an electric car. Musk provided $10,000 in start-up funds, an investment that eventually led to much more.

Meanwhile, two Internet entrepreneurs named Martin Eberhard and Marc Tarpenning had started an electric car company

Nikola Tesla in front of the spiral coil of his high-voltage Tesla coil transformer

Asked whether he was the model for Tony Stark in *Ironman*, Musk replied, *"There are some important differences between me and Tony Stark, like I have five kids, so I spend more time going to Disneyland than parties."*

of their own. They named it Tesla, after the inventor of the electric motor, Thomas Edison's brilliant rival Nicola Tesla. Early in 2004, the two founders began to seek investors. One Friday, they flew down to Los Angeles to make a pitch to Elon Musk. By Monday, Musk had agreed to invest $6.5 million in the company. Musk became chairman of the board and eventually invested tens of millions more. He also got Straubel, the battery maker, to join the company.

In a building in San Carlos, California, Tesla produced its first car—one single black sports car called the Roadster—in January 2005. A red one came out a few months later, and Tesla promised to start selling cars to the public, at about $90,000 each, in 2006.

But as with the Falcon rocket, problems multiplied. When touched by fire, the packed batteries exploded with astonishing power. Luckily, no one was hurt. Soon six Tesla engineers were running an explosives research project behind the factory. In time, the team worked out how to arrange the batteries to stop fire from spreading.

By 2006, Tesla had a hundred employees, and California millionaires were writing $100,000 checks to buy two-seat Roadsters that could go from zero to sixty miles per hour in four seconds. The only problem was that the cars didn't exist yet. The company planned to deliver them in late 2007, but there were delays. Parts built abroad were unreliable, expensive, and slow to arrive. Musk re-analyzed production. It turned out each car was going to cost $200,000 to build—twice the sales price.

Musk flew back and forth between SpaceX in Los Angeles and Tesla near San Francisco. He replaced Tesla's CEO, twice. He told employees they would have to work day and night, sleeping under their desks, until the problems were overcome. He fired some people; others quit. By the beginning of 2008, there was still no car, and the company had run through $140 million. Musk couldn't support it forever, and with the nation entering the financial crisis, no eager investors stepped forward.

As 2008 wore on, Musk was running out of money as both his high-risk companies struggled with technical setbacks. Newspapers wrote of Musk being a big talker who couldn't deliver. A Web site known as The Truth About Cars started what it called a "Tesla Death Watch." Then, in September 2008, the fourth Falcon rocket launched with no disaster. Carrying a dummy payload weighing 300 pounds (NASA didn't want to risk losing any more real equipment), the Falcon successfully entered orbit. Just three months later, SpaceX received a contract from NASA for $1.6 billion for twelve trips to the International Space Station. The company was saved.

SpaceX finally looked as if it would survive, but Tesla was still teetering. Late in 2008, Musk stepped in personally as Tesla's fourth CEO. To save money, he laid off one-quarter of his workforce. He threw in his own remaining funds, begged investors for more time and money, and finally managed to patch together enough funding to pay his employees for a little longer. Altogether, by January 2009, investors had poured $187 million into the company. In return, Tesla had delivered a total of 147 cars.

Tesla finally began to do better during that year. Working under Musk's direction, its engineers and designers created the prototype of the model S, a sedan that would be able to carry seven people. In that year, two foreign car companies, Daimler and Toyota, invested in the company. Tesla also got a large loan from the government, which it paid off four years later. In 2012, the company went public. That same year, it began to ship Model S cars. Like Apple, Tesla had its own showrooms, and it sold cars with no high-pressure tactics. In 2015, *Consumer Reports* gave the Model S a rating of 100 out

"Frunk" - Tesla model S front trunk

A Tesla Supercharger station

A prototype Solar Roof Tile made by Tesla/Solar City

of 100, calling it "the best-performing car that *Consumer Reports* has ever tested."

Then Musk surprised the auto industry with another announcement: Tesla planned to build a network of electrical recharging stations across the country and eventually across the world. At these Supercharging stations, Tesla owners would be able to recharge their cars quickly and for free.

Elon Musk ran two companies, but he was also an important force in a third. In 2006, he had helped convince his cousins Peter and Lyndon Rive, who like him were entrepreneurs and recent immigrants from South Africa, to enter the solar energy market. To Musk, it just made sense: enough solar energy struck the earth every hour to power it for a year. If we were going to make progress against the fossil fuels heating the climate, using more solar power was a must. Elon invested $10 million in the new company, SolarCity, and became chairman of its board.

SolarCity's strategy was to buy and install solar panels. Homeowners and business owners leased the panels, making monthly payments. Since they didn't have to pay upfront, the buyers started saving money on their energy bills right away. Business boomed. By 2012, Solar City was the largest solar power installer in the country.

One of the problems with solar energy is that it doesn't work when the sun is not shining. SolarCity addressed this problem by buying storage batteries from Tesla to sell alongside its solar panel systems. SolarCity also installed solar power systems at Tesla's Supercharging stations to help the car company provide free energy to its customers.

The two companies grew closer. In 2016, Tesla bought Solar-City for $2.6 billion in stock. That same year, SolarCity introduced solar roof tiles in four styles, along with the Powerwall 2, which could store fourteen kilowatt-hours of power. That was enough to run most electrical appliances in a house during four days of no sun.

When in September 2017 Hurricane Maria stuck Puerto Rico with devastating winds that wiped out electricity on the island, Musk stepped in with an offer. Tesla/SolarCity, he said, could build a durable solar power system for the whole island. As a first step, Tesla provided solar panels for a children's hospital. Musk and the governor were still discussing next steps at the time of this writing. Meanwhile, Tesla won a contract to build South Australia's largest solar facility, big enough to power 30,000 homes. With characteristic bravado, Musk promised to complete the project in one hundred days or do it for free.

By 2017, Tesla's market value surpassed that of the huge Detroit-based auto companies. Although the Tesla 3 was behind schedule, the company delivered 100,000 cars that year. More important to Musk, Tesla had demonstrated that electric cars could be fast, beautiful, and even affordable. While the Roadster's final price was $109,000, the Model S sold for $57,000, and the Model 3 cost only $35,000. Moreover, Tesla was building a network of electrical charging stations that might eventually span the globe. Musk's vision is that Tesla will not only sell electric cars and become profitable, but that it will inspire competition from other car makers. Eventually, he hopes that electric cars take over entirely from gasoline-burning cars, thus reducing carbon emissions and helping to limit global warming.

As for SpaceX, by 2017 the company was regularly launching rockets to the International Space Station. SpaceX was even figuring out how to land its rockets back on Earth. (Previously, each rocket lasted for only one launch, as if you decided to throw away a jet plane after each trip.) Musk's idea was that the first stage of a rocket should be able to turn around and steer itself back to land on a drone ship in the ocean. Sticking the

In February 2018, SpaceX launched the Falcon Heavy, twice as powerful as any other functioning rocket at the time. As it launched, the rocket played David Bowie's "Space Oddity," and it carried Musk's own Tesla roadster into space. Two of the rocket's three booster stages re-landed successfully on a drone ship, while the third fell into the ocean a few hundred feet away. The Falcon Heavy will orbit around the sun a bit farther out than Mars.

SpaceX
Falcon Heavy

SpaceX Falcon 9

landing was hard, but by 2017, SpaceX had done it eight times. On March 30, 2017, a recycled Falcon 9 rocket launched for its second trip, delivered its load, and returned safely to Earth.

Despite these successes, Musk's companies have continued to experience high-visibility failures. Like other car companies, Tesla is developing self-driving cars. So far, two have crashed on the roads, and in one of these crashes the driver perished. And in January 2018, a SpaceX Falcon 9 rocket exploded in a fireball, destroying the satellite it was carrying. Company engineers analyze each failure, looking for ways to improve their creations.

SpaceX has signed up two customers for a personal trip around the moon in 2018—though observers suggest that the launch date may not come until 2020. For Musk, the birth of space tourism, like all SpaceX's strategies for making rocketry less expensive, is just one step toward a far nobler goal. "Creating the technology needed to establish life on Mars," he says, "is and always has been the fundamental goal of SpaceX."

Meanwhile, Musk continues to generate new ideas. One of his latest targets is traffic congestion. To solve it, he proposes building tunnels in which fast electric pods can speed customers to their destinations. For this idea to become workable, he says, the cost of building tunnels must come down to less than one-tenth of current costs. In 2016, Musk started The Boring Company to research and build tunnels. To promote the company, he has sold Boring Company hats and even zombie-apocalypse-fighting flamethrowers.

Elon Musk thinks and moves quickly. He spins off ideas, spectacular failures, and astounding successes one after the other. It's hard to imagine him pulling away from all his ventures to follow his deepest dream. Still, Musk insists that if he has his way, he'll land on Mars in his lifetime—and survive.

18. What About You?

Think of all the ways you are creative now. You're already an inventor! Maybe you dream up new rules to games, original recipes, fresh words to songs, unique dress designs, booby traps for your siblings, or different ways to decorate your room. Think back on your experience. All creative effort requires a mix of concentrating hard on something and letting your mind play freely. That's the same process inventors use.

I hope that reading this book has inspired you to dream of doing even more. Maybe you can imagine inventing the next product that will change the world, launch an industry, or just make life easier for lots of people. You're wondering if you, too, can be an inventor, a maker, a person who breaks barriers.

Consider the inventors and makers in this book. They are as diverse as America is—male and female; black, white, Asian, Native American, Latino; immigrants and native-born citizens. Many showed early signs of brilliance, but others had average school careers or were even considered slow. At least one was so scattered we might say today he had ADHD; another focused so intently on his work that some people found him antisocial. A few of these innovators zipped through school while others had little formal schooling and had to teach themselves.

One characteristic all of these makers shared was curiosity. They poked at things and took them apart, like Grace Hopper with her alarm clocks. They probed ideas in the same way. Alexander Graham Bell wondered why we couldn't send voices along wires. Elon Musk asks why a person can't zoom from Los Angeles to New York in an hour.

You can build your curiosity by taking time to wonder about the world. Step back from screens, go for a walk, look around and notice the way street cleaners work, the way coats are fastened, how roofs are made, how children learn to talk. Can you think of a way of doing these things better? Perhaps your dreams will venture even further than today's world, to cities underwater, farms on the moon, or viruses that cure blindness.

Some of the people in this book were risk-takers, eager to step into the unknown. Think of Madam C. J. Walker traveling to Denver with $1.50 in her pocket, An Wang starting a business with $600, or Elon Musk flying to Canada with no place to stay. Or think of Benjamin Franklin and Thomas Jefferson, both rebels who believed in the potential of free people to build a better nation. They were driven by the optimism Bob Noyce talked about—a willingness to leave safe harbors for new possibilities. Others, like Gertrude Elion or George Washington Carver, stayed for decades with one institution or business. A stable professional home allowed them the freedom to keep pursuing new ideas.

Along the way, these innovators found people to inspire, teach, encourage, or support them. They learned together, like Ben Franklin with his Junto; found the right mentors, like Gertrude Elion with George Hitchings; or relied on a supportive family member, like Alexander Graham Bell with his wife, Mabel.

The role models in this book were curious, optimistic, and often brave. They allowed themselves to become so fascinated by some question that they were driven to find out everything about it: how wheat grows, how DNA works in bacteria, how magnetrons produce heat, or how computers work inside—they had to know. Whatever the subject of their fascination, these innovators and makers got right down into the heart of the matter and learned all they could. Obsessed, they stayed up late at night scribbling notes or found themselves turning ideas over in their heads as they walked across a yard.

If you want to become an inventor, or even if you just want to increase the creativity in your own life, here's what the people in this book might suggest:

First, daydream. Recognize that your daydreams are worthwhile.

Second, build your curiosity. Wonder about something every day.

Third, take things apart. It may not be possible to make much sense of things if you take apart a computer, but have you truly figured out how a stapler works? A bicycle? A harmonica? A printer?

Fourth, make things, the way Robert Noyce and Lonnie Johnson did as boys. Draw them. Make models of paper or wood. Build simple circuits. Become familiar with different materials. How do they smell, feel, and work? Turn your drawings into models, and learn to think in three dimensions. Along the way, let your artistic side take over sometimes.

Fifth, don't be afraid to be a little different. If you're going to have new ideas, they're bound to seem strange to some of your friends. Stand up for yourself. Don't let someone talk you out of your interests, the way Lydia Villa-Komaroff almost let her chemistry professor convince her women couldn't be scientists.

Sixth, fall in love with something. Maybe it will be a cause, like Norman Borlaug's quest to end world hunger, Madam C. J. Walker's dedication to the welfare of black women, or Gertrude Elion's drive to cure cancer. Maybe it will be a dream, like Elon Musk's dream of visiting Mars. Let the dream grow inside you, and then set to work, watering it with experience and thought. One idea will lead to another. Assume that what you dream of can be done, and ask yourself what's getting in the way. Then learn all you can to break through that barrier. Challenge yourself to see beyond the obvious. Think about the puzzle, dream about it, work at it, set it aside for a moment, play at something else, and come back to your challenge with fresh eyes.

Then you will be the one to invent something new.

GLOSSARY

Abolitionist	A person working for the elimination, or abolition, of slavery.
Ballistics	The design of projectiles, bombs, etc., for best performance in flight.
Bushwhacker	In the Civil War, a guerilla fighter, usually a Confederate.
Cipher	A kind of code where one letter is substituted for another, or a message written in this kind of code.
Clone	An organism that is genetically identical to its "parent." To clone a gene is to make many copies of the same gene, which can then be analyzed.
Creditor	A person or company to whom money is owed.
Cutter	A light, fast boat used along the coast.
Common-law marriage	In a common-law marriage, a couple live together and consider themselves married without going through a legal ceremony.
Earnest money	Money given by one party to another, usually from a buyer to a seller, to seal a contract.
Electrolytes	Salts dissolved in the blood or other bodily fluids.
Elocution	The skill of speaking with clear pronunciation and expression.
Encephalitis	Inflammation of the brain, usually caused by infection.
Georgist	Follower of the 19th century economist Henry George, who believed that private ownership of land was the cause of inequality.
Germinate	For a seed or spore, to begin to send out shoots and grow.
Indentured servant	A person who is under contract to work without pay for another person for a specified length of time.
Knots	A measure of speed; nautical miles per hour. A nautical mile (2025 yards) is a bit longer than a mile on land.
Larynx	Voicebox; structure holding the vocal cords.
Leukemia	Cancer of the bone marrow, in which one kind of immature blood cell crowds out all the others, leading to infection and bleeding.
Monopoly	A single company having ownership or control of all the trade in a certain product or service.
Palate	Roof of the mouth, with a hard part in front and softer part in back.

Patent	A set of exclusive rights to manufacture a product for a certain amount of time, awarded by a government to an inventor.
Plasmid	In bacteria, a small ring of DNA that can be transferred to another bacterial cell during recombination.
Progeny	Offspring; the next generation.
Propagate	To spread, multiply, reproduce.
Puppet state	A nation that is free in theory, but whose government is actually kept in power by the military of an outside occupying power.
Recombinant DNA	DNA that includes segments or genes that come from somewhere else, including from another organism or species.
Sloop	A one-masted sailing boat or a small warship with two or three masts.
Stenography	The art of taking notes in shorthand.
Shorthand	A rapid method of writing by using strokes and symbols for sounds or common words.
Sudden Infant Death Syndrome (SIDS)	The unexplained death of a child less than one year old, usually while sleeping.
Tactile alphabet	Also known as finger spelling, a way of communicating with deaf or deaf-blind people by touching different parts of the hand that represent different letters.
Tariff	A duties or customs charge, similar to a tax, that a government imposes on imported or exported goods.
Trig function	Short for trigonometric function, a mathematical relationship between the sides and angles of a triangle.
Utopian	Aiming or trying for a government or society where everything is perfect; idealistic.
Valedictorian	The person in a high school graduating class with the best grades, often honored with the chance to give a speech at graduation.

BIBLIOGRAPHY

The kinds of sources a writer can find about creative people has changed a lot in three hundred years. For the most famous of the earliest inventors in this book, like Benjamin Franklin and Thomas Jefferson, there are excellent biographies, along with archives or collections of letters and documents. For the less famous, like slave inventors, records are sparse and incomplete—perhaps no more than a note in an abolitionist newspaper.

Newspaper articles and interviews provide source material for some of the nineteenth- and twentieth-century innovators in this book. But even these can be unreliable. For example, George Washington Carver claimed not to remember much of his childhood, and he cheerfully agreed with whatever others wanted to write about his early years, even when accounts differed.

Today, it is easy to find articles about historical figures on the Internet, often in blog posts written by history enthusiasts. Again, the researcher has to be careful. Bloggers often reproduce what they have read on other blogs, without necessarily verifying the information by checking different sources.

Some of the most recent innovators in this book have given interviews on television or recorded lectures that can be found online. The interview format may lead them to oversimplify some aspects of their work, but it very helpful to hear them describe their lives and ideas in their own words.

The trick in trying to create an accurate and balanced view of a person's life is to cross-check different sources, while carefully assessing each source's particular point of view. I have tried to do that in this book. In three cases, I have had the advantage of personal conversations with the subject of a chapter.

Here are the major sources I consulted.

Chapter 1. Lightning Tamer: Benjamin Franklin (1706–1790)

"Benjamin Franklin's Inventions." The Franklin Institute. https://www.fi.edu/benjamin-franklin/inventions.

Brands, H. W. *The First American: The Life and Times of Benjamin Franklin*. New York: Anchor Books, 2000.

Campbell, James. *Recovering Benjamin Franklin: An Exploration of a Life of Science and Service*. Chicago: Open Court, 1999.

Franklin, Benjamin. "A Plan of Conduct." In *The Writings of Benjamin Franklin, Volume I: Boston and London, 1722–1726*. http://www.historycarper.com/1726/01/01/a-plan-of-conduct/

———. *Autobiography of Benjamin Franklin*. New York: Macmillan Pocket Classics, 1913

Isaacson, Walter. *Benjamin Franklin: An American Life*. New York: Simon & Schuster, 2003.

Chapter 2. Patents and Promise: Thomas Jefferson (1743–1826)

Bedini, Silvio A. *Jefferson and Science*. Chapel Hill: The University of North Carolina Press, 2002.

Jefferson, Thomas, "Thomas Jefferson to Pierre Samuel Du Pont de Nemours, 24 April 1816," *Founders Online*, National Archives. http://founders.archives.gov/documents/Jefferson/03-09-02-0471.

———. "Thomas Jefferson to Roger Weightman, 24 June 1826," The Library of Congress, Thomas Jefferson. https://www.loc.gov/exhibits/jefferson/214.html.

———. "Thomas Jefferson to Robert Fulton, 17 March 1810," *Founders Online*, National Archives. http://founders.archives.gov/documents/Jefferson/03-02-02-0249.

———. *Notes on the State of Virginia*. With an introduction and notes by Frank C. Shuffleton. New York: Penguin Classics, 1999.

"Thomas Jefferson, a brief biography." Thomas Jefferson Foundation. https://www.monticello.org/site/jefferson/thomas-jefferson-brief-biography.

Chapter 3. Inventors Slave and Free: Benjamin Montgomery and Other Early African American Inventors (1791 – 1928)

Chamberlain, Gaius. "Benjamin Bradley." The Black Inventor Online Museum. http://blackinventor.com/benjamin-bradley/.

———. "Benjamin Montgomery." The Black Inventor Online Museum. http://blackinventor.com/benjamin-montgomery/.

———. "Elijah McCoy." The Black Inventor Online Museum. http://blackinventor.com/elijah-mccoy/.

———. "Granville Woods." The Black Inventor Online Museum. http://blackinventor.com/granville-woods/.

———. "Lewis Latimer." The Black Inventor Online Museum. http://blackinventor.com/benjamin-montgomery/.

———. "Thomas Jennings." The Black Inventor Online Museum. http://blackinventor.com/thomas-jennings/.

Fouché, Rayvon. *Black Inventors in the Age of Segregation: Granville T. Woods, Lewis H. Latimer, and Shelby J. Davidson.* Baltimore: Johns Hopkins University Press, 2005.

Greider, Katharine. "The Schoolteacher on the Streetcar." *The New York Times.* November 13, 2005.

Haber, Louis. *Black Pioneers of Science and Invention.* New York: Houghton Mifflin Harcourt Books for Young Readers, 1992.

Lienhard, John H. "No. 1076: Slave Inventors." Engines of Our Ingenuity. http://www.uh.edu/engines/epi1076.htm.

McMillen, Neil R. "The Life and Times of Isaiah T. Montgomery." Mississippi History Now. http://mshistorynow.mdah.state.ms.us/articles/55/isaiah-t-montgomery-1847-1924-part-I.

Sluby, Patricia Carter. *The Inventive Spirit of African Americans: Patented Ingenuity.* Westport, CT: Praeger Publishers, 2004.

Sullivan, Otha Richard. *African American Inventors (Black Stars).* New York: John C.Wiley & Sons, 2010.

Chapter 4. Scattered Genius: Alexander Graham Bell (1847–1922)

Bell, Alexander Graham. Alexander Graham Bell Family Papers. Library of Congress. https://www.loc.gov/collections/alexander-graham-bell-papers/about-this-collection/.

Bruce, Robert V. "Bell, Alexander Graham." American National Biography. http://www.anb.org/view/10.1093/anb/9780198606697.001.0001/anb-9780198606697-e-1300115.

Gray, Charlotte. *Reluctant Genius: Alexander Graham Bell and the Passion for Invention.* New York: Arcade Publishing, 2006.

Pasachoff, Naomi. *Alexander Graham Bell: Making Connections.* New York: Oxford University Press, 1996.

Rosenwald, Michael S. "Your iPhone's secret past: How cadaver ears and a talking dog led to the telephone." *The Washington Post,* November 3, 2107.

Shulman, Seth. *The Telephone Gambit: Chasing Alexander Graham Bell's Secret.* New York: W. W. Norton and Company, 2008.

Chapter 5. Hair-Care Millionaires: Annie Turnbo Malone and Madam C. J. Walker (1867 – 1957)

Bundles, A'Lelia. *On Her Own Ground; The Life and Times of Madam C. J. Walker.* Scribner, 2001.

Christie, Shelby Ivey. "10 Unknown Facts About Annie Malone: The First Black Female Millionaire in the US." *Atlanta Black Star,* July 16, 2015.

Damani, Seba. "Annie Malone: Madam C. J. Walker's Mentor." *SebaDamani* (blog), February 10,

2014. http://www.sebadamani.com/blog/annie-malone-madam-cj-walkers-mentor.

Malone, Annie T. *"Poro in Pictures": With a Short History of Its Development.* St. Louis, MO: Poro College, 1926. http://www.worldcat.org/title/poro-in-pictures-with-a-short-history-of-its-development/oclc/30941712?referer=di&ht=edition.

Peiss, Kathy. *Hope in a Jar: The Making of American Beauty Culture.* Philadelphia: University of Pennsylvania Press, 2007.

Quintana, Maria L. "Malone, Annie Turnbo (1869–1957). BlackPast.org. http://www.blackpast.org/aah/annie-turnbo-malone-1869-1957.

Trawick, Chajuana V. *Annie Malone and Poro College: Building an Empire of Beauty in St. Louis, Missouri, from 1915 to 1930.* Doctoral dissertation, University of Missouri, December 2011.

White, Claytee D. "Walker, A'Lelia (1885–1931). BlackPast.org. http://www.blackpast.org/aah/walker-alelia-1885-1931.

Chapter 6. A Feeling forPlants: George Washington Carver (c. 1862–1943)

Childers, James Saxon. "A Boy Who Was Traded for a Horse," *American Magazine*, Volume 114 (October 1932): 24–25.

"Struggle and Triumph: The Legacy of George Washington Carver." YouTube video, 28:18. Posted by George Washington Carver National Monument, July 20, 2016. https://www.youtube.com/watch?v=kDMkAXHR2g8. You can hear Carver's high speaking voice early in this film.

The George Washington Carver Biography. Modern Marvels documentary film, 45:07. Posted on YouTube by Television, August 2, 2015. https://www.youtube.com/watch?v=RQi-nTcS_Ns. Skips some important parts of Carver's life, but has outstanding photos and film footage.

Kremer, Gary R. (ed). *George Washington Carver in His Own Words*, Columbia, MO: University of Missouri Press, 2017.

McMurry, Linda O. *George Washington Carver: Scientist and Symbol.* New York: Oxford University Press, 1981.

"Struggle and Triumph: The Legacy of George Washington Carver." YouTube video, 28.18. Posted by George Washington Carver National Monument, July 20, 2016, https://www.youtube.com/watch?v=kDMkAXHR2g8. You can hear Carver's high speaking voice early in this film.

Vella, Christina. *George Washington Carver: A Life.* Baton Rouge: Louisiana State University Press, 2015.

Washington, Booker T. *Up from Slavery.* New York: Dover Publications, 1995.

Chapter 7. Feeding the World: Norman Borlaug (1914–2009)

Carter, Jimmy. Tribute to Dr. Normal Borlaug, July 12, 2010. The Carter Center. https://www.cartercenter.org/news/editorials_speeches/borlaug-tribute-saa2010.html.

De Gregori, Thomas R. "Green Myth vs. the Green Revolution. "Butterflies & Wheels. http://www.butterfliesandwheels.org/2004/green-myth-vs-the-green-revolution/.

———. "Recognizing a Giant of Our Time: A Tribute to Dr. Norman Borlaug." AgBioWorld. http://www.agbioworld.org/biotech-info/topics/borlaug/giant.html.

Dil, Anwar (ed). *Norman Borlaug on World Hunger*. San Diego: Bookservice International, 1997.

"Norman Borlaug: Man Who Saved a Billion Lives."University of Minnesota. https://borlaug.cfans.umn.edu/.

Paarlberg, Don, *Norman Borlaug: Hunger Fighter*. Foreign Economic Development Service, US Department of Agriculture, cooperating with the US Agency for International Development (PA 969). Washington, DC, US Government Printing Office, 1970.

Phillips, Ronald L. "Norman Ernest Borlaug, 1914–2009," Biographical Memoirs, National Academy of Sciences, 2013. http://www.nasonline.org/publications/biographical-memoirs/memoir-pdfs/borlaug-norman.pdf.

Vietmeyer, Noel. *Our Daily Bread: The Essential Norman Borlaug*. Lorton, VA: Bracing Books, 2011.

Woodward, Billy, Joel Shurkin, and Debra Gordon, "Norman Borlaug—Over 245 Million Lives Saved." In *Scientists Greater than Einstein*, 143–171, Fresno, CA: Quill Driver Books, 2009.

Chapter 8. Food, Glorious Food (pre-history to modern times)

Hamburgers

"History and Legends of Hamburgers." What's Cooking America. https://whatscookingamerica.net/History/HamburgerHistory.htm.

"The History of the Hamburger." Food History, The Kitchen Project. http://www.kitchenproject.com/history/Hamburger/.

Ketchup

Butler, Stephanie. "Ketchup: A Saucy History." History Stories, History, July 20, 2012. http://www.history.com/news/hungry-history/ketchup-a-saucy-history.

Wiggins, Jasmine. "How Was Ketchup Invented?" The Plate, National Geographic, April 21, 2014. http://theplate.nationalgeographic.com/2014/04/21/how-was-ketchup-invented/.

Popcorn

Avey, Tory. "Popcorn: A 'Pop' History." The History Kitchen, Public Broadcasting Service, October 29, 2013. http://www.pbs.org/food/the-history-kitchen/popcorn-history/.

Butler, Stephanie. "A History of Popcorn." History Stories. History, December 6, 2013.http://www.history.com/news/hungry-history/a-history-of-popcorn.

Fenlon, Wesley. The History of Popcorn at the Movies. Tested. October 4, 2018. http://tested.com/

art/movies/458433-history-popcorn-and-movies/.

"History." Cretors.com. https://www.cretors.com/page.asp?i=12.

"The History of Popcorn." Food History, The Kitchen Project. https://www.kitchenproject.com/history/popcorn.htm.

"Popcorn: Ingrained in U.S. Agricultural History." USDA National Agricultural Library. https://www.nal.usda.gov/exhibits/speccoll/exhibits/show/popcorn/.

Smith, Andrew F. *Popped Culture: A Social History of Popcorn in America*. Columbia, SC: University of South Carolina Press, 1999.

Smith, James. *An Account of the Remarkable Occurrences in the Life and Travels of Colonel James SmithDuring His Captivity with the Indians in the years* 1755, '56, '57, '58, & '59. Lexington, KY: John Bradford, 1799.

Wells, Jeff. "14 Classic Facts about Cracker Jack." Mental Floss, April 18, 2017. http://mentalfloss.com/article/77907/14-classic-facts-about-cracker-jack.

Potato Chips

Bellis, Mary. "Who Invented Potato Chips? ThoughtCo., November 1, 2017. https://www.thoughtco.com/history-of-potato-chips-1991777.

"Laura Scudder's Potato Chips Commercial (1950s)" YouTube video, 1:01. Posted by Throwback, May 15, 2011. https://www.youtube.com/watch?v=EYzbv8fDaAo.

"The Laura Scudders Pledge." YouTube video, duration 1:01 minutes. Posted by casey9961, April 20, 2009. https://www.youtube.com/watch?v=7hK52TfGw8I.

Mitchell, Dave. "The Story of Saratoga Chips and Their Mythical Makers." Chips, Crums and Specks of Saratoga County History (blog), June 18, 2013. http://chipscrumsandspecksofsaratogacountyhistory.com/2013/06/29/saratoga-potato-chip-stories-traditions-myths-and-legends/ (accessed December 11, 2017).

Chocolate Chip Cookies

Krake, Kate. "The Chocolate Chip Cookie Was Invented by Accident." Today I Found Out, Business Insider, March 16, 2013. http://www.businessinsider.com/the-chocolate-chip-cookie-was-invented-by-accident-2013-3.

Michaud, Jon. "Sweet Morsels: A History of the Chocolate-Chip Cookie." *The New Yorker*, December 19, 2013.

"Ruth Wakefield: Toll House Chocolate Chip Cookies" Lemelson–MIT Program. https://lemelson.mit.edu/resources/ruth-wakefield.

Waffles

"The History of Maple Syrup: From Early North American Days to the Present," Coombs Family Farms, December 1, 2013, https://www.coombsfamilyfarms.com/blog/the-history-of-maple-syrup-from-early-north-american-days-to-the-present/.

Swarthout, Mark "Cornelius Swarthout: Inventor of the Waffle Iron." Swarthout Family. http://www.swarthoutfamily.org/Famous/Waffle.htm. See pictures of waffle irons and patent application.

"Waffle History." The Nibble. http://www.thenibble.com/reviews/main/cereals/waffle-history.asp.

Ward, Alvin. "11 Golden Facts about Eggo Waffles." Food, Mental Floss, September 3, 2017. http://mentalfloss.com/article/68366/11-toasty-facts-about-eggo-waffles.

Wells, Jeff. "From Waffle Wafers to Belgian Breakfasts: A Brief History of Waffles." Mental Floss, August 24, 2016. http://mentalfloss.com/article/78997/wafel-wafers-belgian-breakfasts-brief-history-waffles.

The Microwave Oven

Freddoso, David. "Percy Spencer Cooked Up a Champion with the Microwave." Investor's Business Daily, December 2, 2015. https://www.investors.com/news/management/leaders-and-success/percy-spencer-wartime-engineer-inventor-microwave/.

"Microwave Oven." Southwest Museum of Engineering, Computation and Communication. http://www.smecc.org/microwave_oven.htm.

Ross, Rachel. "Who Invented the Microwave Oven?" Live Science, January 5, 2017. https://www.livescience.com/57405-who-invented-microwave-oven.html.

Tweedie, Steven. "How the Microwave Was Invented by a Radar Engineer Who Accidentally Cooked a Candy Bar in His Pocket." Business Insider, July 3, 2015. http://www.businessinsider.com/how-the-microwave-oven-was-invented-by-accident-2015-4.

Chapter 9. Blood of Life: Charles Drew (1904–1950)

"Charles Richard Drew, 'Father of the Blood Bank,'" American Chemical Society. https://www.acs.org/content/acs/en/education/whatischemistry/african-americans-in-sciences/charles-richard-drew.html.

"The Charles R. Drew Papers." Profiles in Science, US National Library of Medicine. https://profiles.nlm.nih.gov/ps/retrieve/Narrative/BG/p-nid/336.

Drew, Charles Richard. *Banked Blood: A Study in Blood Preservation*. Doctoral Dissertation College of Physicians and Surgeons, Columbia University, 1940.

Haber, Louis. *Black Pioneers of Science and Invention*, New York: Harcourt, 1970.

Kendrick, Douglas B. *Blood Program in World War II*. US Army Medical Department, Office of Medical History. history.amedd.army.mil/booksdocs/wwii/blood/.

Love, Spencie. One Blood: The Death and Resurrection of Charles R. Drew. Chapel Hill:

University of North Carolina Press, 1996.

Schraff, Anne E. *Dr. Charles Drew: Blood Bank Innovator*. New York: Enslow Publishers, 2003.

Yale, Elizabeth. "First Blood Transfusion: A History." JSTOR Daily Newsletter, April 22, 2015. https://daily.jstor.org/first-blood-transfusion/.

Chapter 10. To Conquer Canter, Leonard: Gertrude Elion (1918–1999)

Altman, Lawrence K. "Gertrude Elion, Drug Developer, Dies at 81." *The New York Times*, February 23, 1999.

Bouton, Katherine. "The Nobel Pair." *The New York Times Magazine*, January 29, 1989.

Church, Roy. *Burroughs Wellcome in the USA and the Wellcome Trust*. Lancaster, England: Carnegie Publishing, 2015.

"Gertrude B. Elion—Biographical." https://www.nobelprize.org/nobel_prizes/medicine/laureates/1988/elion-bio.html.

"Gertrude B. Elion, Winner, 1997 Lemelson–MIT Lifetime Achievement Award." YouTube video, 4:45, posted by Lemelson Foundation, February 28, 2009. https://www.youtube.com/watch?v=UY3DbLYbmE4.

Lesch, J. E. "Chemotherapy by Design." In *A Master of Science History: Essays in Honor of Charles Coulston Gillispie*, edited by Jed Z. Buchwald, 275–295. New York: Springer, 2012.

McGrayne, Sharon Bertsch. *Nobel Prize Women in Science: Their Lives, Struggles, and Momentous Discoveries*, Second Edition. Washington, DC: Joseph Henry Press, 2001.

Noyce, Pendred E. "Inventing Medicines." In *Magnificent Minds: 16 Pioneering Women of Science and Medicine*, 131–137. Boston: Tumblehome Learning, 2015.

"Science and the Written Word: Gertrude B. Elion." YouTube video, 27:29, from a CUNY TV interview, posted by cunytv75, March 7, 2016. https://www.youtube.com/watch?v=UMXxk7cx66k.

"Women of Valor: Jewish Heroes across Time." YouTube video, 11:41, posted by Jewish Women's Archive, March 18, 2013. https://www.youtube.com/watch?v=GgvgH4f-ZyA.

Chapter 11. Computer Whisperer: Grace Hopper (1906–1992)

Beyer, Kurt W. *Grace Hopper and the Invention of the Information Age*. Cambridge, MA: The MIT Press, 2012.

Computer History Museum. Oral History of Grace Hopper, interviewed by Angeline Pantages, Recorded December 1980.http://archive.computerhistory.org/resources/text/Oral_History/Hopper_Grace/102702026.05.01.pdf.

Grace Murray Hopper (1906–1992): A legacy of innovation and service." Yale News. https://news.yale.edu/2017/02/10/grace-murray-hopper-1906-1992-legacy-innovation-and-service.

"Grace Murray Hopper gives a general history of the computer, discusses working for the Navy on the COBOL programming language, and other topics." Arthur and Elizabeth Schlesinger Library on the History of Women in America. Schlesinger Library Luncheon Series audio collection, 102:00, December 14, 1983. http://oasis.lib.harvard.edu/oasis/deliver/deepLink?_collection=oasis&uniqueId=sch01242.

"Grace Hopper on David Letterman." 1986 interview on *The Late Show with David Letterman.* YouTube video, 9:59. posted by TheLazlo101, December 11, 2012. https://www.youtube.com/watch?v=1-vcErOPofQ.

Noyce, Pendred E. "Languages of the Admiral." In *Magnificent Minds: 16 Pioneering Women of Science and Medicine,* 109–116. Boston: Tumblehome Learning, 2015.

Chapter 12. Core Memories: An Wang (1920–1990)

Hevesi, Dennis. "An Wang, 70, Is Dead of Cancer: Inventor and Maker of Computers." *The New York Times,* March 25, 1990.

Historian. "An Wang: The Man Who Might Have Invented the Personal Computer," I Programmer, March 3, 2016. http://www.i-programmer.info/history/people/550-an-wang-wang-laboratories.html.

Kenney, Charles C. *Riding the Runaway Horse: The Rise and Decline of Wang Laboratories.* Boston: Little Brown, 1992.

Lee, J.A.N. "Computer Pioneers: An Wang." IEEE Computer Society. http://history.computer.org/pioneers/wang.html.

Wang, An, with Eugene Linden. *Lessons: An Autobiography.* Reading, MA: Addison-Wesley, 1986.

Chapter 13. The Chip That Changed the World: Robert Noyce (1927–1990)

Berlin, Leslie. *The Man Behind the Microchip: Robert Noyce and the Invention of Silicon Valley.* New York: Oxford University Press, 2006.

Hays, Constance L. "An Inventor of the Microchip, Robert N. Noyce, Dies at 62." *The New York Times,* June 4, 1990.

Hoff, Robert D. "Lessons from Sematech." *MIT Technology Review,* July 25, 2011. https://www.technologyreview.com/s/424786/lessons-from-sematech/.

Isaacson, Walter. *The Innovators: How a Group of Hackers, Geniuses, and Geeks Created the Digital Revolution.* New York: Simon & Schuster, 2014.

Kilby, Jack St. Clair. "Turning Potential into Realities: The Invention of the Integrated Circuit." Nobel Lecture, December 8, 2000. https://www.nobelprize.org/nobel_prizes/physics/laureates/2000/kilby-lecture.pdf.

Noyce, Robert. Multiple personal communications with author between 1955 and 1990.

Reid, T. R. *The Chip: How Two Americans Invented the Microchip and Launched a Revolution.* Revised Edition. New York: Random House, 2007.

Tedlow, Richard S. *Giants of Enterprise: Seven Business Innovators and the Empires They Built.* New York: HarperBusiness, 2003.

Wolfe, Tom. "The Tinkerings of Robert Noyce: How the Sun Rose on the Silicon Valley." *Esquire,* December 1983.

Chapter 14. Electronics Visionary: Gordon Moore (b. 1929)

Lécuyer, Christope, and David C. Brock. *Makers of the Microchip: A Documentary History of Fairchild Semiconductor.* Cambridge, MA: The MIT Press, 2010.

Moore, Gordon E. "The Accidental Entrepreneur." *Engineering and Science,* Summer 1994, pp. 23-30.

————. "Cramming More Components onto Integrated Circuits." Electronics 38, no. 8 (April 19, 1965): 114-117.

————. "Intel—Memories and the Microprocessor." In *The Power of Boldness: Ten Master Builders of American Industry Tell Their Success Stories* by Elkan Bout, et al. Washington, DC: Joseph Henry Press., 1996.

Moore, Gordon. Interview with author, April 29, 2017.

Schmitt, Laura. "An interview with Gordon Moore." *Ingenuity* 5:2(May 2000). http://archive.li/Acomo.

"Scientists You Must Know: Intel founder Gordon Moore." Chemical Heritage Foundation interview, July 14, 2013. Vimeo video, 16:38, posted by Science History Institute, 2014. https://vimeo.com/70293585.

Thackray, Arnold, Brock, David C., and Rachel Jones. "How Gordon Moore Made 'Moore's Law.'" *Wired,* April 16, 2015. https://www.wired.com/2015/04/how-gordon-moore-made-moores-law/.

————. Moore's Law: *The Life of Gordon Moore, Silicon Valley's Quiet Revolutionary.* New York:Basic Books: 2015.

Chapter 15. Fun and Games: Boards and Water Guns (1879-Present)
<u>Monopoly</u>

"Charles Darrow." Lemelson–MIT Program. https://lemelson.mit.edu/resources/charles-darrow.

Dodson, Edward J. "How Henry George's principles were corrupted into the game called *Monopoly.*" Henry George Institute.

http://www.henrygeorge.org/dodson_on_monopoly.htm.

Pilon, Mary. *The Monopolists: Obsession, Fury, and the Scandal Behind the World's Favorite Board Game.* New York:Bloomsbury US, 2015.

————. "Monopoly's Inventor: The Progressive Who Didn't Pass 'Go.'" *The New York Times,* February 13, 2015.

————. "The secret history of Monopoly: the capitalist board game's leftwing origins." *The Guardian,*

April 11, 2015.

Smith, Monica M. "The woman inventor behind 'Monopoly.'" Lemelson Center for the Study of Invention and Innovation, March 26, 2015. http://www.henrygeorge.org/dodson_on_monopoly.htm.

Scrabble

Burkeman, Oliver. "Spellbound." *The Guardian*, June 27, 2008. https://www.theguardian.com/lifeandstyle/2008/jun/28/healthandwellbeing.familyandrelationships.

"Discover the History Behind One of the World's Favorite Word Games!" Hasbro Gaming. https://scrabble.hasbro.com/en-us/history.

Kaye, Marvin. *Story of Monopoly, Silly Putty, Bingo Twister, Frisbee, Scrabble, Etcetera*. New York: Stein & Day, 1973.

Lambert, Bruce. "Alfred M. Butts, 93, Is Dead: Inventor of SCRABBLE." *The New York Times*, April 7, 1993.

Moore, Charlie. "Man of letters: Thai computer programmer is third best Scrabble player in the world despite speaking NO ENGLISH." Daily Mail.com., July 18 2016. http://www.dailymail.co.uk/news/article-3695715/Man-letters-Thai-computer-programmer-ranked-world-Scrabble-despite-speaking-NO-ENGLISH.html.

Read, Brock. "A Computer Program Wins Its First Scrabble Tournament." Wired Campus, The Chronicle of Higher Education, January 26, 2007. https://www.chronicle.com/blogs/wiredcampus/a-computer-program-wins-its-first-scrabble-tournament/2800

Thurman, Judith. "Spreading the Word: The New Scrabble Mania." *The New Yorker*, January 19, 2009.

Snowboarding

Burgeson, Gunnar E., Burgeson Harvey, and Vern C. Wicklund. Patent for an "improved sled." US Patent No. 2181391, filed March 7, 1938, and issued November 28, 1939.

"Burton Snowboards: Jake Carpenter." Transcript, National Public Radio, October 23, 2017. https://www.npr.org/templates/transcript/transcript.php?storyId=559034228.

"You should thank the man who built this board. His name is Sherman Poppen." Interview, Flakezine, November 10, 1994. http://www.flakezine.com/poppen.html.

Laskow, Sarah. "Snowboarding Was Almost Called 'Snurfing.'" The Atlantic, October 13, 2014. https://www.theatlantic.com/technology/archive/2014/10/snowboarding-was-almost called-snurfing/381308/.

MacArthur, Paul J. "Snowboarding: It's Older Than You Think." *Skiing History Magazine*, December 1, 2016.

Slotnick, Daniel E. "Tom Sims, Pioneer in Sport of Snowboarding, Dies at 61." *The New York Times*,

September 18, 2012.

van Dulken Steve. "Snowboarding Inventions." The Patent Search Blog, British Library, February 12, 2010. http://blogs.bl.uk/patentsblog/2010/02/snowboarding-inventions.html.

The Super Soaker

"Company Profile." Johnson Research and Development Company. http://www.johnsonrd.com/ie/co/coprofile.html.

Johnson Research and Development Company. "Animation of the JTEC" https://spectrum.ieee.org/static/jtec.

Jones, Willie D. "Super Soaker Inventor Invents New Thermoelectric Generator." IEEE Spectrum, Mar 1, 2008. https://spectrum.ieee.org/semiconductors/devices/super-soaker-inventor-invents-new-thermoelectric-generator.

Karlin, S. From squirts to hertz [Lonnie Johnson, inventor] IEEE *XPlore* http://ieeexplore.ieee.org/document/1015464/.

Kremer, William. "Lonnie Johnson: the father of the Super Soaker." *BBC NewsMagazine*, August 15, 2016.

Ryssdal, Kai. "The happy accident that changed squirt guns forever." *Marketplace*, July 8, 2014. https://www.marketplace.org/2014/07/08/business/brought-you/happy-accident-changed-squirt-guns-forever.

Chapter 16. DNA Wrangler: Lydia Villa-Komaroff (b. 1947)

"A Conversation with Lydia Villa-Komaroff 12-14-2002," Department of Biology and Howard Hughes Medical Institute. YouTube video, 52:52, posted by Conversations with Scientists, December 15, 2010. https://www.youtube.com/watch?v=tm58oRYxWgA.

Fekri, Farnia. "Lydia Villa-Komaroff Has Spent Four Decades Fighting for Diversity in Science." Motherboard, February 28, 2017. https://motherboard.vice.com/en_us/article/qkmded/lydia-villa-komaroff-sacnas-hoty.

Hall, Stephen S. *Invisible Frontiers: The Race to Synthesize a Human Gene.* New York: Atlantic Monthly Press, 1987.

"Lydia Villa-Komaroff (CytonomeST/SACNAS): How I Became a Scientist." YouTube video, 14:15, posted by iBiology Science Stories, September 26, 2011.https://www.youtube.com/watch?v=lE4Oya7Wgi8.

Villa-Komaroff, Lydia. Interview by author, October 11, 2017.

Villa-Komaroff, L, Efstratiadis, A, Broome, S, Lomedico, P, Tizard, R, Naber, SP, Chick, WL, and W. Gilbert. (Aug 1978). "A bacterial clone synthesizing proinsulin." *Proceedings of the National Academy of Sciences USA.* 75, No. 8 (August 1978): 3727–3731.

Weiler, Nicholas. "Lydia Villa-Komaroff Learned in the Lab 'What It Might Be Like to Fly.'" American Society for Cell Biology, July 30, 2014.http://www.ascb.org/ascb-post/lydia-villa-komaroff-learned-in-the-lab-what-it-might-be-like-to-fly/.

Chapter 17. Interplanetary Dreams: Elon Musk (b. 1971)

"The Boring Company: Frequently Asked Questions." https://www.boringcompany.com/faq/.

Heath, Chris. "How Elon Musk Plans on Reinventing the World (and Mars)." GQ, December 12, 2015.

"How Elon Musk does it: The Falcon Heavy's creator is trying to change more worlds than one." The Economist, February 10, 2018. https://www.economist.com/news/briefing/21736597-failure-most-definitely-option-falcon-heavys-creator-trying-change-more-worlds.

Musk, Justine. "'I Was a Starter Wife'": Inside America's Messiest Divorce." *Marie Claire*, September 10, 2010.

"Tesla's New Solar Roof Tiles Are Perfect for South Africa." October 29, 2016. MyBroadband. https://mybroadband.co.za/news/energy/185118-teslas-new-solar-roof-tiles-are-perfect-for-south-africa.html.

Vance, Ashlee. Elon Musk: *Tesla, Space X, and the Quest for a Fantastic Future.* New York: HarperCollins, 2017.

IMAGE CREDITS

End sheets: (modified) https://oceanservice.noaa.gov/facts/bfranklin.html. By Daderot [Public domain], from Wikimedia Commons.

Cover images: https://en.wikipedia.org/wiki/File:Improved_no2_Wagon.jpg, public domain. https://commons.wikimedia.org/wiki/File:Intel_C4004.jpg, By Thomas Nguyen [CC BY-SA 4.0], from Wikimedia Commons. Old telephone, http://l.rgbimg.com/cache1n8l73/users/j/ja/jazza/600/2djs3in.jpg. https://pixabay.com/en/wheat-ear-dry-harvest-autumn-865152/, CC0 Creative Commons. https://www.publicdomainpictures.net/en/view-image.php?image=42718&picture=dna, public domain.

p.12 Benjamin Franklin. https://upload.wikimedia.org/wikipedia/commons/8/87/Joseph_Siffrein_Duplessis_-_Benjamin_Franklin_-_Google_Art_Project.jpg

p.13 background. https://commons.wikimedia.org/wiki/File:Declaration_of_Independence_(1819),_by_John_Trumbull.jpg [Public domain], via Wikimedia Commons

p.13 Writing the Declaration of Independence. https://commons.wikimedia.org/wiki/File:Writing_the_Declaration_of_Independence_1776_cph.3g09904.jpg [Public domain], via Wikimedia Commons

p.14 First Latin School in Boston, MA. https://www.bls.org/apps/pages/index.jsp?uREC_ID=206116&type=d

p.14 Swim Paddle, modified from http://invention.si.edu/benjamin-franklin-s-inventions. A reproduction of swim paddles described in the writings of Benjamin Franklin, on display at the Benjamin Franklin Museum, photo by the author

p.15 Tallow Chandler. https://commons.wikimedia.org/wiki/File:Little_Jack_of_all_trades,_with_suitable_representations_(1814)_(14598475519).jpg By Internet Archive Book Images, via Wikimedia Commons

p.15 The New England Courant. https://commons.wikimedia.org/wiki/File:NewEnglandCourant_00001.jpg [Public domain], via Wikimedia Commons

p.16 https://commons.wikimedia.org/wiki/File:The_life_of_Benjamin_Franklin_(1848)_(14577770340).jpg By Internet Archive Book Images, via Wikimedia Commons

p.16 Deborah Franklin. https://commons.wikimedia.org/wiki/File:Deborah_ReadFranklin.jpg Attributed to Benjamin Wilson [Public domain], via Wikimedia Commons

p.18 Franklin Store. https://commons.wikimedia.org/wiki/File:Franklin_stove,_cross-sectional_diagram.jpg By en:cwkmail [Public domain], via Wikimedia Commons

p.19 Dissectible Leyden Jar. https://commons.wikimedia.org/wiki/File:Dissectible_Leyden_jar.png. By John Tyndall [Public domain], via Wikimedia Commons

p.20 Franklin Drawing Electricity from the Sky. https://commons.wikimedia.org/wiki/File:West_-_Benjamin_Franklin_Drawing_Electricity_from_the_Sky_(ca_1816).jpg [Public domain], via Wikimedia Commons

p.20 https://www.fi.edu/history-resources/franklins-lightning-rod. The Franklin Institute.

p.21 Glass Harmonica. https://commons.wikimedia.org/wiki/File:Unterlinden-Glass_harmonica_(3).jpg By Ji-Elle [CC BY-SA 3.0 (https://creativecommons.org/licenses/by-sa/3.0)], from Wikimedia Commons https://www.fi.edu/history-resources/franklins-glass-armonica

p.22-23 Alexander Agassiz, a preeminent oceanographer of the 19th century, attributed the first scientific basis for exploring the Gulf Stream to American statesman Benjamin Franklin. Franklin published this map of the Gulf Stream in 1769, 200 years before a submersible named after him drifted below the surface to study this river in the ocean. https://oceanservice.noaa.gov/facts/bfranklin.html. By Daderot [Public domain], from Wikimedia Commons

p.24 https://commons.wikimedia.org/wiki/File:Writing_the_Declaration_of_Independence_1776_cph.3g09904.jpg [Public domain], via Wikimedia Commons

p.26 Thomas Jefferson. https://commons.wikimedia.org/wiki/File:Thomas_Jefferson_Portrait.jpg Charles Willson Peale [Public domain], via Wikimedia Commons p.27, p 28 https://commons.wikimedia.org/wiki/File:Declaration_of_Independence_(1819),_by_John_Trumbull.jpg [Public domain], via Wikimedia Commons

p.28 Eston Hemings. https://alchetron.com/Eston-Hemings-1130644-W

p.28-29 https://commons.wikimedia.org/wiki/File:Notes_on_Virginia_-_Madisons_and_Amens_Caverns.jpg By Thomas Jefferson (?); A. Kollners lithography, Philadelphia [Public domain], via Wikimedia Commons

p.30 Comte de Buffon. https://commons.wikimedia.org/wiki/File:Buffon_1707-1788.jpg François-Hubert Drouais [Public domain], via Wikimedia Commons

p.30, p.34-35 Jefferson's Monticello. https://www.flickr.com/photos/tonythemisfit/2808122002.
Jefferson's Monticello (Pond Reflection) by Tony Fischer via Flickr, CC BY 2.0

p.31 Moldboard Plow. https://www.monticello.org/site/plantation-and-slavery/moldboard-plow (Thomas Jefferson Foundation)

p.32 Wheel Cipher. https://www.monticello.org/site/research-and-collections/wheel-cipher
Reproduction of Jefferson's Wheel Cipher (created by Ronald Kirby) disassembled (Thomas Jefferson Foundation)

p.33 US Patent Office. https://commons.wikimedia.org/wiki/File:United_States_Patent_Office_c1880.jpg
By US Patent Office [Public domain], via Wikimedia Commons

p.36 https://commons.wikimedia.org/wiki/File:Civil_war_trains.jpg By Mathew Brady, or his assistant [Public domain], via Wikimedia Commons

p.38 "City of Providence". https://commons.wikimedia.org/wiki/File:City.of.Providence.Anchor.Line.Steamboat.1909.Postcard.jpg By Absecon 49 [CC BY-SA 3.0 (https://creativecommons.org/licenses/by-sa/3.0)], from Wikimedia Commons

p.39 "Look Out". https://commons.wikimedia.org/wiki/File:%22Look_out%22_(Transport_Steamer)_on_Tennessee_River_-_NARA_-_5289791_restored.jpg Mathew Brady [Public domain], via Wikimedia Commons

p.40 Elizabeth Jennings. https://commons.wikimedia.org/wiki/File:Elizabeth_jennings_01.jpg By unknown; originally uploaded to en.wiki by Tonymartin on 31 May 2007 [Public domain], via Wikimedia Commons

p.40 First horsecar in Manchester, NH. https://commons.wikimedia.org/wiki/File:First_Horsecar_in_Manchester,_NH.jpg [Public domain], via Wikimedia Commons

p.41 Chester Arthur. https://commons.wikimedia.org/wiki/File:Chester_A_Arthur_1859.png By Rufus Anson [Public domain], via Wikimedia Commons

p.41 Cotton fields. https://www.publicdomainpictures.net/en/view-image.php?image=220751&picture=cotton-fields. CC0 Public Domain

p.42-43 https://commons.wikimedia.org/wiki/File:Riverboats_at_Memphis.jpg By Detroit Publishing Co. [Public domain], via Wikimedia Commons

p.44 an early house in Davis Ben. https://commons.wikimedia.org/wiki/File:Appletons%27_Davis_Jefferson_-_early_home_in_Mississippi.jpg By adapted from an earlier engraving in a book by the same publisher [Public domain], via Wikimedia Commons

p.44 "J.M. White". https://commons.wikimedia.org/wiki/File:J.M._White_(steamboat_1878).jpg By Samuel Ward Stanton (1870-1912) [Public domain], via Wikimedia Commons

p.45 "Alabama". https://commons.wikimedia.org/wiki/File:Samuel_Walters_-_Confederate_Raider_ALABAMA.jpg [Public domain], via Wikimedia Commons

p.46 Isaiah Montgomery House. https://commons.wikimedia.org/wiki/File:Isaiah_Thornton_Montgomery_House,_West_Main_Street,_Mound_Bayou_(Bolivar_County,_Mississippi).jpg By Unknown, Photographer [Public domain], via Wikimedia Commons

p.47 Mound Bayou Welcome Sign. http://www.wikiwand.com/en/Mound_Bayou,_Mississippi

p.47 Elijah McCoy. https://commons.wikimedia.org/wiki/File:Elijah_McCoy.jpg By Rights Held by: Ypsilanti Historical Society [CC BY-SA 4.0 (https://creativecommons.org/licenses/by-sa/4.0)], via Wikimedia Commons p.48 Patent for Sarah Goode's Cabinet Bed. https://commons.wikimedia.org/wiki/File:Sarahgoodebed.gif By Krhaydon [Public domain], from Wikimedia Commons

p.48 "Laundering" https://www.flickr.com/photos/internetarchivebookimages/14577507839/ Internet archive book images

p.49 L.H. Latimer. https://commons.wikimedia.org/wiki/File:Lewis_latimer.jpg [Public domain], via Wikimedia Commons

p.49 Bell's Telephone Patent Drawing. https://commons.wikimedia.org/wiki/File:TelephonePatentDrawingBell.jpg By Alexander Graham Bell [Public domain], via Wikimedia Commons

p.49 Granville T. Woods. https://commons.wikimedia.org/wiki/File:Granville_T_Woods_1903.png By Eddowes Brothers, photographers [Public domain], via Wikimedia Commons

p.52 Alexander Bell. https://commons.wikimedia.org/wiki/File:Alexander_Graham_Bell,_three-quarter_length_portrait,_standing,_facing_left_-_3c04275r.jpg [Public domain], via Wikimedia Commons

p.53 Notes about telephone experiment. https://www.loc.gov/resource/magbell.25300201/?sp=22 Notebook by Alexander Graham Bell, from 1875 to 1876.

p.54 Tactile alphabet. https://deafcomm.files.wordpress.com/2011/09/dma.png

p.56 How telegram works, illustrated by Chen-Hui Chang

p.58 Elisha Gray. https://commons.wikimedia.org/wiki/File:PSM_V14_D424_Elisha_Gray.jpg [Public domain], via Wikimedia Commons

p.61 An early model wall mounted telephone. https://commons.wikimedia.org/wiki/File:ChampaignCountyHistorical Museum_20080301_4271.jpg By Dori [CC BY-SA 3.0 us], from Wikimedia Commons

p.62 photophone. https://commons.wikimedia.org/wiki/File:Photophone_transmitter_4074931746_9f996df841_b.jpg [Public domain], via Wikimedia Commons

p.62 Bell and family. https://commons.wikimedia.org/wiki/File:Alexander_Graham_Bell_and_family.jpg By Not listed; part of the LOC's Gilbert H. Grosvenor Collection of Photographs of the Alexander Graham Bell Family. [Public domain], via Wikimedia Commons

p.63 Helen Keller and Alexander Bell. https://commons.wikimedia.org/wiki/File:PSM_V63_D084_Helen_keller_and_alexander_graham_bell.png [Public domain], via Wikimedia Commons

p.64 Bell tetrahedral antenna kite. https://commons.wikimedia.org/wiki/File:Alexander_Graham_Bell_facing_his_wife,_Mabel_Hubbard_Gardiner_Bell,_who_is_standing_in_a_tetrahedral_kite,_Baddeck,_Nova_Scotia.tif [Public domain], via Wikimedia Commons

p.65 Glenn Curtiss in His Bi-Plane July 4, 1908. https://commons.wikimedia.org/wiki/File:Glenn_Curtiss_in_His_Bi-Plane,_July_4,_1908.jpg By Alexander Graham Bell family (Christie's) [Public domain], via Wikimedia Commons

p.66 Bell and wife. https://commons.wikimedia.org/wiki/File:Alexander_Graham_Bell_in_Brantford,_Ontario,_Canada_-Alexander_with_his_wife_Mabel_Gardiner_Hubbard.JPG [Public domain], via Wikimedia Commons

p.68 https://commons.wikimedia.org/wiki/File:Madam_CJ_Walker_face_circa_1914.jpg By Scurlock Studio (Washington, D.C.) (photographers). [Public domain], via Wikimedia Commons. https://shsmo.org/historicmissourians/name/m/malone/ [The State Historical Society of Missouri, Manuscript Collection-St. Louis]

p.69 Annie Turnbo Malone, part of an oil portrait by Victor Harvey, c/o Missouri Historical Society. http://images.mohistory.org/image/5B4A8ACB-FA4F-1F0D-5448-D68B08259CA3//original.jpg https://shsmo.org/historicmissourians/name/m/malone/ [The State Historical Society of Missouri, Manuscript Collection-St. Louis]

p.70 Civil War contraband laborers repairing track. By Wikipedista:Ryj [Public domain], from Wikimedia Commons https://commons.wikimedia.org/wiki/File:The_Civil_War_through_the_camera_-_hundreds_of_vivid_photographs_actually_taken_in_Civil_War_times,_together_with_Elson%27s_new_history_(1912)_(14576384367).jpg

p.71 St. Louis World's Fair. https://commons.wikimedia.org/wiki/File:Bird%27s_eye_view,_World%27s_Fair,_St._Louis,_from_Robert_N._Dennis_collection_of_stereoscopic_views.jpg. New York Public Library [Public domain], via

Wikimedia Commons

p.71 A Street in St. Louis, ca. 1920. Missouri Historical Society. https://www.flickr.com/photos/mohistory/29240102770 public domain

p.72, p.73 Pages from the Poro College catalogue. National Museum of African American History & Culture.

p.75 Birthplace of Sarah Breedlove (Madam C. J. Walker) in Delta, Louisiana (CREDIT: Madam Walker Family Archives/A'Lelia Bundles)

p.78 Walker products. https://commons.wikimedia.org/wiki/File:Madam_C_J_Walker_items_Womens_Museum.jpg By Photo: User:FA2010 [Public domain], from Wikimedia Commons

p.80 Madam C. J. Walker circa 1915 (CREDIT: Madam Walker Family Archives/A'Lelia Bundles)

p.80 https://commons.wikimedia.org/wiki/File:MadameCJWalkerdrivingautomoblie.png [Public domain], via Wikimedia Commons

p.81 A'Lelia Walker circa 1926 (CREDIT: Madam Walker Family Archives/A'Lelia Bundles)

p.82 Madam Walker National Convention Badge (CREDIT: Madam Walker Family Archives/A'Lelia Bundles)

p.82 Villa Lewaro https://commons.wikimedia.org/wiki/File:Villa-lewaro_crop.jpg By Dmadeo; cropped by Beyond My Ken (talk) 19:28, 23 March 2011 (UTC) [CC BY-SA 4.0], from Wikimedia Commons

p.84 George Washington Carver. https://commons.wikimedia.org/wiki/File:George_Washington_Carver-crop.jpg By Arthur Rothstein (for U.S. Farm Security Administration) (Library of Congress[1]) [Public domain], via Wikimedia Commons

p.85 Digital photograph of an original oil portrait of George Washington Carver by artist Betsy Graves Reyneau, oil on canvas, 1942, Smithsonian National Portrait Gallery. https://www.flickr.com/photos/sgreeneptx/24251193559

p.86-87 https://commons.wikimedia.org/wiki/File:Gaillardia_in_Aspen_(91273).Jpg By Rhododendrites [CC BY-SA 4.0], from Wikimedia Commons

p.88 Liatris spicata. https://commons.wikimedia.org/wiki/File:Liatris_spicata_003.JPG By H. Zell [CC BY-SA 3.0], from Wikimedia Commons

p.89 Carver as artist. http://archive.tuskegee.edu/archive/bitstream/handle/123456789/759/Carver%20Collection042.jpg?sequence=1&isAllowed=y

p.90 Stinkhorn fungus in Alabama. https://commons.wikimedia.org/wiki/File:Stink_horn_fungus_in_Spanish_Fort,_AL_3.jpeg https://commons.wikimedia.org/wiki/File:Stink_horn_fungus_in_Spanish_Fort,_AL_4.jpeg By Timdwilliamson [CC BY-SA 4.0], from Wikimedia Commons

p.91 Booker T. Washington. https://commons.wikimedia.org/wiki/File:Booker_T_Washington_retouched_flattened-crop.jpg By Harris & Ewing (http://hdl.loc.gov/loc.pnp/hec.16114) [Public domain], via Wikimedia Commons

p.92 Children of African-American Sharecroppers, Little Rock, Arkansas by Ben Shahn, 1935. https://www.flickr.com/photos/pingnews/471960479 (pub domain)

p.92 Children of Cotton Pickers by Ben Shahn, 1935 (LOC) https://www.flickr.com/photos/pingnews/471949634/in/photostream/ (pub domain)

p.93 Motorized Jesup wagon. https://commons.wikimedia.org/wiki/File:20111110-OC-AMW-0024_-_Flickr_-_USDAgov.jpg By U.S. Department of Agriculture (20111110-OC-AMW-0024) [Public domain], via Wikimedia Commons

p.93 Tuskegee class in farm management, 1940. https://commons.wikimedia.org/wiki/File:Tuskegee_Institute_usda-photo.jpg [Public domain]

p.94 George Washington Carver, ca. 1902. https://commons.wikimedia.org/wiki/File:George_Washington_Carver,_ca._1902.jpg [Public domain], via Wikimedia Commons

p.96 Boll weevil. https://commons.wikimedia.org/wiki/File:Boll_weevil.jpg By Agricultural Research Service, United States Department of Agriculture. [Public domain], via Wikimedia Commons

p.96 Flower of a sweet potato plant. https://commons.wikimedia.org/wiki/File:Sweet_Potato_Flower_and_buds.jpg By Earth100 [CC BY-SA 3.0], from Wikimedia Commons p.96 Freshly dug sweet potato. https://en.wikipedia.org/wiki/Tuber#/media/File:Ipomoea_batatasL_ja01.jpg By miya [CC BY-SA 4.0], from Wikimedia Commons

p.97 Georgia peanut field. https://commons.wikimedia.org/wiki/File:Peanut_field,_Pelham.JPG By Michael Rivera [CC BY-SA 3.0], from Wikimedia Commons

p.98 Peanut harvest in Cameroon. https://commons.wikimedia.org/wiki/File:Harvest_of_peanuts.jpg By Fotso007 [CC BY-SA 4.0], from Wikimedia Commons

p.100 George Washington Carver Museum. https://commons.wikimedia.org/wiki/File:George_Washington_Carver_Museum.jpg By Jessamyn [CC BY-SA 3.0], from Wikimedia Commons

p.102 Dr. Norman Borlaug (modified) https://commons.wikimedia.org/wiki/File%3AElizabeth_Whelan_with_Dr._Norman_Borlaug.jpg By Cbwhelan [CC BY-SA 4.0], via Wikimedia Commons

p.103, p.111, Pieter Bruegel the Elder- The Harvesters. https://en.wikipedia.org/wiki/History_of_agriculture#/media/File:Pieter_Bruegel_the_Elder-_The_Harvesters_-_Google_Art_Project.jpg (public domain)

p.104 Borlaug as a young wrestler. https://commons.wikimedia.org/wiki/File:Wrestling_-_Norman_Borlaug.jpg By University of Minnesota Department of Plant Pathology from St. Paul, MN, USA [CC BY 2.0], via Wikimedia Commons

p.104 Sculpture of a food line during the Depression. https://www.flickr.com/photos/kevinwburkett/3415356132 By Kevin Burkett via Flickr, CC BY-SA 2.0

p. 105 Poster promoting the Civilian Conservation Corps made by the Illinois WPA Art Project Chicago. https://commons.wikimedia.org/wiki/File:CCC-poster-1935.jpg By Works Progress Administration, Federal Art Project; Albert M. Bender, designer [Public domain], via Wikimedia Commons

p.106 Wheat stem rust disease https://commons.wikimedia.org/wiki/File:Wheat_Stem_Rust_Disease_(05410063)_(9685492848).jpg By IAEA Imagebank [CC BY-SA 2.0], via Wikimedia Commons

p.106-107, p.107 Field of wheat, by Wonderlane via Flickr, CC BY 2.0 https://www.flickr.com/photos/wonderlane/3611109911

p.108 Crossing wheat. https://commons.wikimedia.org/wiki/File:CSIRO_ScienceImage_6851_Head_of_wheat_showing_flowering_parts.jpg CSIRO [CC BY 3.0], via Wikimedia Commons

p.109 Norman Borlaug in the field teaching a group of young trainees by International Maize and Wheat Improvement via Flickr. https://www.flickr.com/photos/cimmyt/4578622062/in/photostream/ CC BY-NC-SA 2.0

p.112, p.114-115 Field of wheat in Pakistan. https://commons.wikimedia.org/wiki/File:Wheat_crop_in_Rupal_valley_(northern_areas_of_Pakistan).JPG By Sajid ali raza [CC BY-SA 3.0], from Wikimedia Commons

p.113 The Borlaug Medallion. https://www.worldfoodprize.org/en/nominations/norman_borlaug_medallion/

p. 114 Sorghum. https://www.maxpixel.net/Cereals-Culture-Agriculture-Field-Sorghum-1621844 (public domain)

p. 114 Congressional Gold Medal. https://commons.wikimedia.org/wiki/File:2006_Norman_Borlaug_Congressional_Gold_Medal_front.jpg By United States Mint. Design: Obverse - Phebe Hemphill. Reverse - Don Everhart. [Public domain], via Wikimedia Commons

p.115 Norman Borlaug, https://www.flickr.com/photos/cimmyt/4578621620 by International Maize and Wheat Improvement via Flickr CC BY-NC-SA 2.0)

p.119, p.121 McDonald's drive-in, West Stadium Blvd., Ann Arbor - photo from advertisement in 1967 Omega. By Wystan via flickr //CC by 2.0

p.124 "Surprise Inside" label. https://www.flickr.com/photos/hermanturnip/3331692605/in/dateposted/ By Herman Turnip via flickr//CC BY 2.0

p.125 Crum's Place. https://en.wikipedia.org/wiki/File:Crum's_Place_marker.jpg#file. By Peter Flass. CC BY 4.0

p.125 Cornelius Vanderbilt. https://commons.wikimedia.org/wiki/File:Cornelius_Vanderbilt_Daguerrotype2.jpg By Produced by Mathew Brady's studio, restored by Michel Vuijlsteke [Public domain], via Wikimedia Commons

p.126 https://commons.wikimedia.org/wiki/File:Laurascudderlabel.tiff By Laura Scudder potato chip label [Public domain], via Wikimedia Commons

p.127 https://commons.wikimedia.org/wiki/File:WhitmanMA_TollHouseSign.jpg By Magicpiano [CC BY-SA 4.0], from Wikimedia Commons

p.129 Sap. https://www.flickr.com/photos/prairiegirl33/6869705840/in/dateposted/ by Tammy Friesen via flickr//CC BY-SA 2.0

p.130 Kellogg's Eggo Thick & Fluffy Cinnamon Brown Sugar Waffles. https://www.theimpulsivebuy.com/wordpress/2011/01/31/review-kelloggs-eggo-thick-fluffy-waffles-original-cinnamon-brown-sugar/ By theimpulsivebuy via flickr, CC BY-SA 2.0

p.131 Vintage Ad #1,418: Why Don't You Own a Raytheon Radarange. https://www.flickr.com/photos/jbcurio/5445409086 By Jamie via flickr//CC BY 2.0

p.132 https://commons.wikimedia.org/wiki/File:A_pair_of_waffles,_December_2007.jpg By @joefoodie (Flickr: Waffles) [CC BY 2.0], via Wikimedia Commons

p.134 Charles Drew. https://profiles.nlm.nih.gov/ps/access/BGBBCV_.jpg photo credit: National Library of Medicine (NLM)

p.135 Blitz aftermath. https://commons.wikimedia.org/wiki/File:Blitzaftermath.jpg By New York Times Paris Bureau Collection [Public domain], via Wikimedia Commons

p.136 Charles and siblings. https://profiles.nlm.nih.gov/ps/retrieve/ResourceMetadata/BGBBGL Courtesy of the Moorland-Spingarn Research Center. Public domain.

p.137 https://profiles.nlm.nih.gov/ps/retrieve/ResourceMetadata/BGBBFR. Courtesy of the Moorland-Spingarn Research Center.

p.139 Blood transfusion in 17th century. https://commons.wikimedia.org/wiki/File:Blood_transfusion,_17th_century._Wellcome_M0012957.jpg [CC BY 4.0], via Wikimedia Commons

p.142 Drew family. https://profiles.nlm.nih.gov/ps/retrieve/ResourceMetadata/BGBBGM Courtesy of the Moorland-Spingarn Research Center.

p.142 British Red Cross testing blood. https://www.flickr.com/photos/britishredcross/4398872986 By British Red Cross via Flickr CC BY 2.0

p.143 Blood donation poster, Scotland, 1944. https://commons.wikimedia.org/wiki/File:Poster_The_Scottish_National_Blood_Transfusion_Association.JPG (Public domain). Blood donation poster, American Red Cross. https://commons.wikimedia.org/wiki/File:%22Give_your_Blood_to_Save_a_Life%22_-_NARA_-_514403.jpg (Public domain). A Bloodmobile today http://www.931arw.afrc.af.mil/News/Article-Display/Article/677590/mcconnell-reservists-roll-up-sleeves-for-family/ U.S. Air Force photo by Tech. Sgt. Abigail Klein.

p.144 Charles Drew with medical residents at Freedmen's Hospital. https://profiles.nlm.nih.gov/ps/retrieve/ResourceMetadata/BGBBFJ Courtesy of the Moorland-Spingarn Research Center.

p.146 Charles Drew University logo. http://cdn.careersinpublichealth.net/uploads/school/logo/298/691px-CDU_Logo.JPG

p.148 Gertrude Elion. https://commons.wikimedia.org/wiki/File:Gertrude_Elion.jpg [CC BY 4.0], via Wikimedia Commons

p.149 Gertrude Elion oil painting by Sir Roy Calne. https://commons.wikimedia.org/wiki/File:Gertrude_Elion._Oil_painting_by_Sir_Roy_Calne,_1990._Wellcome_L0024105.jpg [CC BY 4.0], via Wikimedia Commons

p.150 Hunter College. https://commons.wikimedia.org/wiki/File:Thomas_Hunter_Hall_Hunter_College_CUNY_from_south.jpg By Beyond My Ken [CC BY-SA 4.0-3.0-2.5-2.0-1.0], from Wikimedia Commons

p.153 Henry Wellcome. https://commons.wikimedia.org/wiki/File:Henry_Wellcome_1890b.jpg [CC BY 4.0], via Wikimedia Commons

p.153 George Hitchings. https://commons.wikimedia.org/wiki/File:G._Hitchings._Wellcome_L0000749.jpg [CC BY 4.0], via Wikimedia Commons p.155 Children with leukemia receiving chemotherapy. https://commons.wikimedia.org/wiki/File:Pediatric_patients_receiving_chemotherapy.jpg By Bill Branson (Photographer) [Public domain], via Wikimedia Commons

p.156 Kidney transplantation. https://commons.wikimedia.org/wiki/File:Kidney_Transplant.png By BruceBlaus [CC BY-SA 4.0], from Wikimedia Commons

p.157 Foot with gout. https://commons.wikimedia.org/wiki/File:Gout_in_foot.jpg By https://www.flickr.com/photos/vagawi/ (https://www.flickr.com/photos/vagawi/3997775184) [CC BY 2.0], via Wikimedia Commons

p.157 Hitchings and Elion. https://commons.wikimedia.org/wiki/File:George_Hitchings_and_Gertrude_Elion_1948.jpg [CC BY 4.0], via Wikimedia Commons

p.158 Herpes lesions on the mouth. https://commons.wikimedia.org/wiki/File:Herpes_labialis_-_opryszczka_wargowa.jpg (Public domain)

p.158 The structure of Elion's medicines resembled a purine molecule. By Chen-hui Chang

p.160 AIDS poster. https://commons.wikimedia.org/wiki/File:A_large_insect_with_a_message_indicating_that_AIDS_is_not_Wellcome_L0052397.jpg (Public domain)

p.161 Hitchings and Elion. https://commons.wikimedia.org/wiki/File:George_Hitchings_and_Gertrude_Elion_1988.jpg [CC BY 4.0], via Wikimedia Commons

p.162 Hopper works on a manual tape punch computer, 1944. Image identifier SS2689982. New York Public Library/Science Source

p.164 https://www.flickr.com/photos/maaorg/5506849073 Courtesy of the Library of Congress CC BY-ND 2.0

p.165 https://commons.wikimedia.org/wiki/File:Commodore_Grace_M._Hopper,_USN_(covered).jpg By James S. Davis [Public domain], via Wikimedia Commons

p.166 Calhoun (now Hopper) college, Yale. https://commons.wikimedia.org/wiki/File:Calhoun_college.jpg By Namkota [CC BY-SA 4.0], from Wikimedia Commons

p.167 WAVES poster. https://commons.wikimedia.org/wiki/File:%22WISH_I_COULD_JOIN_TOO%22_WAVES_-_NARA_-_516164.jpg [Public domain], via Wikimedia Commons

p.168 https://commons.wikimedia.org/wiki/File:Harwell-dekatron-witch-10.jpg By Bad germ [CC BY-SA 3.0], from Wikimedia Commons. https://commons.wikimedia.org/wiki/File:PaperTapes-5and8Hole.jpg By TedColes [Public domain], from Wikimedia Commons

p.169 Harvard Mark I Computer. https://commons.wikimedia.org/wiki/File:Harvard_Mark_I_Computer_-_Right_Segment.JPG#file CC-BY-SA-3.0-migrated

p.169 Harvard Mark I Computer Team, 1944. Image identifier SS21318230. US AIR FORCE/Science Source

p.170 Flickr: Grace Hopper and UNIVAC https://commons.wikimedia.org/wiki/File:Grace_Hopper_and_UNIVAC.jpg By Unknown (Smithsonian Institution) [CC BY 2.0], via Wikimedia Commons

p.171 ENIAC (public domain) https://id.wikipedia.org/wiki/Berkas:Eniac.jpg. https://www.google.com/search?q=science+and+technology+(hardcover)&tbm=isch&tbs=simg:CAQSlwEJD4YBqr0dt3YaiwELEKjU2AQaBggUCAAIAwwLELCMpwgaYApeCAMSJrkQuhCcBJwNlwW4EJIEnQRqbMU2qC7JLeM5pS7-Iu8t4jnFOsY6GjBzhMIIQu3mcVPOQ5qahk_1U26T-5w0A-tYqjbTQJy7MKU4D0ykMSdQQw6wrNdSt4hMgBAwLEI6u_1ggaCgoICAESBM6GDbMM,isz:m&sa=X&ved=0ahUKEwic8Jm41LLaAhXQ-lQKHSCwAgwQ2A4IKCgC&biw=1872&bih=977#imgrc=fq7bMmeZLpLtIM:

p.172 Edmund Berkeley. "Photograph of Edmund C. Berkeley," Gallery, accessed June 15, 2018, http://gallery.lib.umn.edu/items/show/85.

p.173 COBOL punch card. https://commons.wikimedia.org/wiki/File:Punch-card-cobol.jpg By Rainer Gerhards, CC-BY-SA-3.0 via Wikimedia Commons

p.174 nuclear submarine public domain. https://commons.wikimedia.org/wiki/File:Delta-II_class_nuclear-powered_ballistic_missle_submarine_3.jpg

p.174, p.174-175 USS Hopper (ship named after Grace Hopper) public domain. https://en.wikipedia.org/wiki/USS_Hopper#/media/File:Flickr_-_Official_U.S._Navy_Imagery_-_USS_Hopper_leaves_Joint_Base_Pearl_Harbor-Hickam..

p.201 The Traitorous Eight. Courtesy of Intel.

p.203 https://upload.wikimedia.org/wikipedia/commons/8/82/Robert_Noyce_with_Motherboard_1959.png By Intel Free Press [CC BY-SA 2.0], via Wikimedia Commons

p.204 First commercial monolithic integrated circuit, Fairchild, 1961. By IEEE. https://www.flickr.com/photos/ieee125/2809342254

p.204 Jack Kilby. https://www.thefamouspeople.com/profiles/jack-kilby-6393.php By Editors, TheFamousPeople.com

p.205 Noyce family. Courtesy of the author.

p.206 Intel Building. Courtesy of Intel.

p.206 Noyce and Moore. Intel Free Press - https://www.flickr.com/photos/intelfreepress/8452088850/sizes/o/in/photostream/ (CC BY-SA 2.0)

p.207 Robert N. Noyce Building, Intel. https://www.flickr.com/photos/huangjiahui/4907798630 By JiahuiH via Flickr. (CC BY-SA 2.0)

p.207 Noyce and Moore. Courtesy of Moore Foundation.

p.208 Bob Noyce and Steve Jobs. Courtesy of Intel.

p.210 Intel Museum https://www.flickr.com/photos/ddebold/23712502139 By Don DeBold via Flickr (CC BY 2.0)

p.212 Moore with a silicon wafer. Photograph by Paul Sakuma, by permission of Moore Foundation.

p.213 https://commons.wikimedia.org/wiki/File:Pescadero_State_Beach_edit2.jpg By Brocken Inaglory [CC BY-SA 3.0], via Wikimedia Commons

p.213 Baby Moore. Courtesy of Moore Foundation.

p.214, p.215 Gordon Moore's grandfather, father, brother and Gordon as swimmer, p.216 Gordon Moore's wedding photo, Courtesy of Moore Foundation.

p.219 Moore and Noyce in front of FCI. Courtesy of Moore Foundation.

p.220 Moore on trail. Courtesy of Moore Foundation.

p.220 Moore fish. https://www.flickr.com/photos/jurvetson/368370/ By Steve Jurvetson by permission of Moore foundation.

p.222 Grinich, Moore, Noyce and Blank. Moore and Noyce reviewing papers. Courtesy of Moore Foundation.

p.223 Grove, Moore and Noyce. Courtesy of Moore Foundation.

p.223 https://commons.wikimedia.org/wiki/File:Cleanroom_suit.jpg. By Steve Jurvetson (https://www.flickr.com/photos/jurvetson/52583513/) [CC BY 2.0 (https://creativecommons.org/licenses/by/2.0)], via Wikimedia Commons

p.224 Intel CPU. https://commons.wikimedia.org/wiki/File:Intel_CPU_Core_i7_6700K_Skylake_perspective.jpg Eric Gaba, Wikimedia Commons user Sting [CC BY-SA 4.0], from Wikimedia Commons

p.226 Gordon and Betty Moore, by Susanna Frohman/San Jose Mercury News, by permission of Moore foundation.

p.228 Skateboarding. Photo via <a href="https://www.goodfreephotos.com/">Good Free Photos</a>

p.229 https://commons.wikimedia.org/wiki/File:BoardGamePatentMagie.png By Drawing for a Game Board, 01/05/1904. This is the printed patent drawing for a game board invented by Lizzie J. Magie [Public domain], via Wikimedia Commons

p.230 The Landlord's Game. https://commons.wikimedia.org/wiki/File:Landlords_Game_1906_image_courtesy_of_T_Forsyth_owner_of_the_registered_trademark_20151119.jpg By Thomas Forsyth [Public domain], via Wikimedia Commons

p.230 Henry George. https://commons.wikimedia.org/wiki/File:Henry_George_c1885_retouched.jpg [Public domain], via Wikimedia Commons

p.231 The Landlord's Game. https://commons.wikimedia.org/wiki/File:Landlords_Game_board_based_on_1924_patent.png By Lucius Kwok [CC BY 2.5], from Wikimedia Commons

p.231 Lizzie Maggie, https://en.wikipedia.org/wiki/Lizzie_Magie.

p.232 Charles Darrow. https://commons.wikimedia.org/wiki/File:Charlie_Darrow.png#/media/File:Charlie_Darrow.png BullsandBears - Own work. CC BY-SA 3.0

p.231 Brer Fox and Brer Rabbit game. https://landlordsgame.info/rules/bfnbr.html

p.233 Monopoly pieces. https://www.flickr.com/photos/izzie_whizzie/2325235254 by Elizabeth Ellis via Flickr CC BY-SA 2.0

p.234 Alfred M. Butts. Yvonne Hemsey/ Hulton Archive/Getty Images

p.234 Letter frequencies. https://commons.wikimedia.org/wiki/File:Alfred_Butts_letter_frequencies.JPG By w: Alfred Butts [Public domain], via Wikimedia Commons

p.234-235 Scrabble letters. https://pxhere.com/en/photo/537498 Creative Commons CC0, public domain.

p.236 Scrabble game using Quackle https://commons.wikimedia.org/wiki/File:Scrabble-example.png By Scrabbler94 [CC BY-SA 4.0], from Wikimedia Commons

p.237 Tom Sims' first board. http://www.simsnow.com/company/history, by permission of SIMS. Burgeson snowboard. https://images2.westword.com/imager/an-original-1939-sno-surf-rides-the-walls/u/745xauto/5114614/7423070.0.jpg

p.238 Snurfer patent diagram. https://commons.wikimedia.org/wiki/File:Snurfer_patent_3378274_diagram_excerpt.png. By Invented by Sherman R. Poppen, assigned to Brunswick Corporation uploaded by User:Lar [Public domain], via Wikimedia Commons. Snurfer ad. https://af62359ed6764b37dd8d-a09ab6654f67c1c7801ec2e0698b9db1.ssl.cf2.rackcdn.com/legacy_images/Northernexpress-01-02-2012/lib/13254504704f00c4e6aaeb9.png. Jake Burton & Donna Carpenter.

p.239 Tom Sims freestyle. ttps://tinyurl.com/yb6ycs9g By Bud Fawcett.

p.239 Snowboarding. https://commons.wikimedia.org/wiki/File:Snowboarding.jpg By Ripley119 [CC BY-SA 3.0], from Wikimedia Commons

p.240 Lonnie Johnson. https://www.flickr.com/photos/tedxpeachtree/37884595976 By TEDxPeachtree Team via Flickr. CC BY-SA 2.0

p.240 Scene from "Lost in Space". https://commons.wikimedia.org/wiki/File:Wally_Cox_Lost_in_Space_1966.JPG By CBS Television [Public domain], via Wikimedia Commons

p.242 Super Soaker. https://www.flickr.com/photos/barretthall/3542735720 By popofatticus. CC BY 2.0

p.243 Super Soaker HydroBlitz. NBC/NBCUniversal/Getty Images.

p.246, p247 Lydia Villa-Komaroff and p.248 Lydia and family. Courtesy of Lydia Villa-Komaroff.

p.247 Child with diabetes before and after insulin treatment. https://commons.wikimedia.org/wiki/File:Cases_before_and_after_insulin_treatment_Wellcome_L0031615.jpg CC BY 4.0, via Wikimedia Commons

p.249 Lydia and brother Richard as kids. Courtesy of Lydia Villa-Komaroff.

p.249 black-and-white rat. https://commons.wikimedia.org/wiki/File:Fancy_rat_blaze.jpg CC BY-SA 2.0], via Wikimedia Commons

p.250 Anthony Komaroff. https://commons.wikimedia.org/wiki/File:Tony_Komaroff.jpg By Dashlogan [CC BY-SA 3.0], from Wikimedia Commons

p.250 David Baltimore. https://commons.wikimedia.org/wiki/File:David_Baltimore_NIH.jpg [Public domain], via Wikimedia Commons

p.251 SACNAS logos. Courtesy of SACNAS.

p.251 DNA. https://www.publicdomainpictures.net/en/view-image.php?image=42718&picture=dna Public domain.

p.252 Wally Gilbert. https://commons.wikimedia.org/wiki/File:Walter_Gilbert_HD2008_portrait.JPG Science History Institute [CC BY-SA 3.0], via Wikimedia Commons

p.252 Bacteria E. Coli. By Mattosaurus [Public domain], from Wikimedia Commons

p.253 Model of human insulin molecule https://es.m.wikipedia.org/wiki/Archivo:Human-insulin-hexamer-3D-ribbons.png By Benjah-bmm27, Public domain, via Wikipedia.

p.254 Beta amyloid plaques in brain. https://commons.wikimedia.org/wiki/File:Cerebral_amyloid_angiopathy_-2b-_amyloid_beta_-_very_high_mag.jpg By Nephron [CC BY-SA 3.0], from Wikimedia Commons

p.254 Mogao Cave Painting. https://commons.wikimedia.org/wiki/File:Mogao_Cave_61,_painting_of_Mount_Wutai_monasteries.jpg By Chinese artist(s) from the 10th century [Public domain], via Wikimedia Commons

p.256 OSIRIS Mars true color. https://commons.wikimedia.org/wiki/File:OSIRIS_Mars_true_color.jpg By ESA - European Space Agency & Max-Planck Institute for Solar System Research for OSIRIS Team [CC BY-SA 3.0-igo], via Wikimedia Commons

p.258 Elon Musk. https://commons.wikimedia.org/wiki/File:Elon_Musk_2015.jpg By Steve Jurvetson [CC BY 2.0], via Wikimedia Commons

p.259 Elon Musk stands inside a rocket awaiting assembly. https://commons.wikimedia.org/wiki/File:Elon_Musk_BFR.jpg By SpaceX [CC0], via Wikimedia Commons

p.260 Durban Sign. https://commons.wikimedia.org/wiki/File:DurbanSign1989.jpg By Guinnog [CC-BY-SA-3.0], via Wikimedia Commons

p.263 Journal to Mars. https://commons.wikimedia.org/wiki/File:NASA-JourneyToMars-ScienceExplorationTechnology-20141202.jpg By NASA [Public domain], via Wikimedia Commons

p.263 SpaceX test vehicle launch. http://www.spacex.com/gallery/2013-0

p.264 Mars Earth Comparison. https://commons.wikimedia.org/wiki/File:Mars_Earth_Comparison_2.jpg By NASA/JPL/MSSS & User:DrLee [Public domain], via Wikimedia Commons

p.265 https://commons.wikimedia.org/wiki/File:Poster_for_the_1960_film_The_Time_Machine.jpg [Public domain], via Wikimedia Commons https://commons.wikimedia.org/wiki/File:Amazing_science_fiction_stories_195910.jpg By Ziff-Davis Publishing / Leo Summers [Public domain], via Wikimedia Commons

p.266 Nicola Tesla. https://commons.wikimedia.org/wiki/File:Teslathinker.jpg [Public domain], via Wikimedia Commons

p.267 Tesla model S front trunk. https://commons.wikimedia.org/wiki/File:Tesla_Model_S_SAO_2016_9502.jpg By Mariordo (Mario Roberto Durán Ortiz) [CC BY-SA 4.0], from Wikimedia Commons

p.268 Tesla Supercharger station. https://commons.wikimedia.org/wiki/File:Charging_Tesla_Model_S_01.jpg By Jeff Cooper [CC BY 2.0], via Wikimedia Commons

p.268 Tesla SolarCity solar roof tile. https://commons.wikimedia.org/wiki/File:Tesla_Solar_City_Roof_Tile.jpg By Bnc319 [CC BY-SA 4.0], from Wikimedia Commons

p.269 Falcon Heavy. https://commons.wikimedia.org/wiki/File:Falcon_Heavy_cropped.jpg By SpaceX [CC0 or CC0], via Wikimedia Commons

p.270 Falcon 9. http://www.spacex.com/falcon9

p.271 https://www.publicdomainpictures.net/en/view-image.php?image=42718&picture=dna, public domain. (Modified)

INDEX

Pendred (Penny) Noyce is a doctor, science education advocate, and author of 12 books of fiction and nonfiction for young people. Three of her books have won Outstanding Science Trade Book awards from the National Science Teachers Association and Children's Book Council.

Pendred Noyce's NSTA-CBC (National Science Teacher Association - Children's Book Council) Outstanding Science Trade Book K-12 Award-winning titles:

Inspiring lives of 33 pioneering women of science and medicine over four centuries.

MAGNIFICENT MINDS
978-0-9897924-7-9 (hardcover)
978-1-943431-25-0 (paperback)

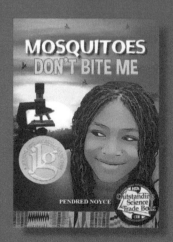

MOSQUITOES DON'T BITE ME
978-1-943431-30-4 (hardcover)
978-1-943431-37-3 (paperback)

An unusual trait takes Nala Simiyu on an African adventure and into danger.

REMARKABLE MINDS
978-0-9907829-0-2 (hardcover)
978-1-943431-13-7 (paperback)